WOMEN'S ANGER

WOMEN'S ANGER

Clinical and Developmental Perspectives

Deborah L. Cox, Ph.D.
Southwest Missouri State University

Sally D. Stabb, Ph.D.
Texas Woman's University

Karin H. Bruckner, M.A., L.P.C.
Independent Practice

USA	Publishing Office:	BRUNNER/MAZEL *A member of the Taylor & Francis Group* 325 Chestnut Street Philadelphia, PA 19106 Tel: (215) 625-8900 Fax: (215) 625-2940
	Distribution Center:	BRUNNER/MAZEL *A member of the Taylor & Francis Group* 47 Runway Road, Suite G Levittown, PA 19057-4700 Tel: (215) 269-0400 Fax: (215) 269-0363
UK		BRUNNER/MAZEL *A member of the Taylor & Francis Group* 1 Gunpowder Square London EC4A 3DE Tel: +44 171 583 0490 Fax: +44 171 583 0581

WOMEN'S ANGER: Clinical and Developmental Perspectives

1 2 3 4 5 6 7 8 9 0

Printed by Braun-Brumfield, Ann Arbor, MI, 1999.
Cover design by Curt Tow. Cover image created by Lorin Bruckner and adapted by Curt Tow.

A CIP catalog record for this book is available from the British Library.

⊗ The paper in this publication meets the requirements of the ANSI Standard Z39.48-1984 (Permanence of Paper).

Library of Congress Cataloging-in-Publication Data

Cox, Deborah L.
    Women's anger : clinical and developmental perspectives /
Deborah L. Cox, Sally D. Stabb, Karin H. Bruckner.
        p.   cm.
    Includes bibliographical references and index.
    ISBN 0-87630-945-7 (case : alk. paper)
    ISBN 0-87630-946-5 (pbk. : alk. paper)
    1. Anger. 2. Women—Psychology. I. Stabb, Sally D. II. Bruckner, Karin H.
III. Title.
    BF575.A5 C68 1999
    152.4'7'082—dc21
                                                    99-29693
                                                        CIP

ISBN 0-87630-945-7 (case)
ISBN 0-87630-946-5 (paper)

Not a million voices together joined
Nor thine own, murmuring alone forever
Can stir in me what one burning draught
Of that potion, so strong and good, doth raise!
It brings a mighty wave to press within my veins,
Which, raging forward, soon comes to crest
And in its crashing climax releases
A phoenix new and brilliant, free to soar—
Naught else but soul then lives within!
                                        —Anonymous

*To the Texas Woman's University
community of scholars, teachers, practitioners, and friends
which brought the three of us together
and which continues to support the professional
and personal growth
of not only ourselves
but of all the women and girls it touches.*

CONTENTS

PREFACE

I feel there is something unexplored about women
that only a woman can explore.
—Georgia O'Keefe

The central purpose of this book is to bring together a wide variety of sources of information about women's and girls' anger in a unique format that is developmental, clinical, and feminist in nature. To our knowledge, basic theory, research, and clinical insights have not been integrated previously in this way. Although the book begins with a solid grounding in theory and empirical work, it ultimately focuses on practical therapeutic issues regarding women and girls, as well as the lived experience of anger for women and girls. The work grows out of our own desire to understand what happens to girls' anger as they mature, and the role of socialization and culture in shaping the expression and experience of anger over the lifespan. Our own research, clinical work, theorizing, and personal experience all have played a part in this endeavor.

The book is intended for use by professional mental health practitioners (psychologists, counselors, marriage and family therapists, social workers) and academics in related areas such as counseling, clinical and social psychology, gender and women's studies, family studies, education, and perhaps sociology. The book also will be of interest to graduate students in these fields as they prepare for their professional careers.

The scope of the book moves from theory and research into clinical issues, and incorporates the experiences of women and girls throughout, via verbatim text of focus groups and excerpts from clinical cases. The introduction provides a first look at the major themes of the book, highlighting the role of anger in the process of self-definition, as well as the anger-diversion processes which often impede self-development. We feel a great deal of concern about anger's place in society as its potential for clarifying relationships gets lost in its frightening reputation. Because of our interest in the ways anger is regarded, especially compared with other emotions, we review the theoretical and empirical bases for contemporary theories of emotion. Current models of emotion are presented, along with the views of emotion derived from theories of psychotherapy and from developmental psychology. Because broad theories of emotion try to account for all major types of emotion (fear, sadness, happiness, and so forth), we must distill them to see what they have to say about anger.

Because of our specific interest in the place anger occupies in women's lives, we attempt to trace the dominant cultural attitudes and influences on women's and girls' anger from a life-span developmental perspective. The experience and expression of anger is constantly being shaped by both the subtle and blatant forces of socialization, shifting over time as little girls grow through puberty, become young women, and mature through their middle and elder years. Further, this work integrates academic and therapeutic perspectives on women's anger, reflecting the authors' multiple roles as researchers, therapists, and teachers. We bring these two (often separate) worlds together to look at a number of topics, including the relationship of anger to the clinical symptom clusters of depression/anxiety, somatization, and consumption and the ways that anger is suppressed, internalized, segmented, and externalized. Because the measurement of anger is important not only clinically but also socially, we take some time to delve into issues in the assessment of anger, along with current, accepted models for treatment in the world of psychotherapy.

In creating this work, we talk with real women about their anger socialization. Themes that emerge from our qualitative focus groups and clinical interviews with women and girls serve as a framework to showcase what a diverse collection of women and girls have to say about their anger in their own words. Our aim is to provide rich and human descriptions that bring life to both the commonalities and the uniqueness in girls' and women's anger experiences. Developmental and feminist analyses of themes link comments to the broader focus of the book. Additionally, the life-span process of how women negotiate, understand, and experience anger is related to self-identity development models. Ultimately, we attempt to draw our work together with some recommendations and future directions for theory, research, practice, and sociopolitical action.

We hope that our combined focus on life-span development, clinical application, and feminist interpretations of women's and girls' anger represents a fresh look at the role of this much maligned emotion. Anger is a fundamental message that something needs attention in our interpersonal contexts, and how women and girls learn to feel, think, and behave around this crucial emotion deserves our exploration. Socialization and culture play key roles in shaping the unhealthy ways in which feminine anger is negotiated; thus it is our hope that a feminist and developmental approach to these issues ultimately will improve the everyday emotional lives of women and girls, through self-awareness, therapy, and social change.

ACKNOWLEDGMENTS

I would like to thank the following people for their contributions to this work and to my continued personal and professional growth. First and foremost, thanks must go to my spouse and dedicated collaborator, Dr. Joe Hulgus, for his rich companionship and constant championing of my life's work. Thanks goes to the rest of my family as well, for their untiring love and confidence. A number of other friends and professionals also deserve my appreciation at this time, including Dr. Maryanne Watson, for her inspiration about the healing benefits of assertive anger expression, and Dr. Sally St. Clair, for her wisdom and guidance of my developing personal imagery, a gift that enables me to move forward in this and other projects. Heartfelt thanks also goes to Dr. Larry Campbell for helping me to pry open so many locked corridors in my consciousness and to speak with the purity of knowing.

Others to whom I owe thanks for their contributions to this book include Dr. Asra Haque-Kahn, Avra Johnson, and the many personnel of the Dallas Public Schools who helped to expedite my data collection process. Among this group are Dr. Myrtle Walker, Dr. David Tacher, Vivian Taylor, and Donna Bearden. Appreciation goes to Drs. Roberta Nutt, Linda Rubin, and Ronald Palomares of Texas Woman's University for their support of this work. Thanks also goes to the many women clients with whom I have had the opportunity to work and whose words and stories inform this volume. Each in her own special way becomes a part of my history, a part of my continued passion for the work of feminist psychology, and part of my heart.

Finally, much gratitude goes to my coauthors, without whom this book would not have been possible. To my dear friends Sally and Karin, thank you for your openness to this unfolding process and for sharing this vision with me.

Deborah L. Cox, Ph.D.

There are a number of people I wish to thank for their immense help and support in this project. For me, the writing of this book was punctuated by a debilitating medical crisis in my life, and the work is now somehow tied in my psyche to this event. We were more than halfway through the manuscript when I was diagnosed with Meneire's disease, a disturbance of the vestibular system of the inner ear, resulting in episodes of extreme dizziness, nausea, and loud ringing in the ears. For the better part of a year, I was unable to drive, and only periodically able to read, work at my computer, teach classes, and walk without holding onto the walls or someone's arm.

Therefore, I wish to express my deepest gratitude to those people who waited with me until I was well enough to work again, and who took care of me emotionally and physically during this time. First of all, my parents and my partner Martin, who got me through the worst of my vertigo episodes and helped me manage life on a day-in, day-out, and middle-of-the-night basis. Your love and patience is deeper than I ever imagined, and your faith in my ability to recover and regain my life has been so important.

I also wish to thank my colleagues at work, who allowed me to modify my schedule and picked up the slack I left. In particular, Drs. Linda Rubin, Roberta Nutt, and Michael Gottleib, good friends as well as coworkers, were ongoing supports. Drs. Bud Littlefield, Ron Palomares, and Dinah Graham, who drove me for two semesters on the 80-mile round-trip commute we all share, were invaluable—Bud especially, who along with his wonderful wife Janie and his optimistic daughter Jamie (who also has Meneire's disease), took me into his home when I was extremely sick and temporarily alone. I also thank the doctoral students who shared in driving duties, Dave Popple, Dave Rose, and Jann Synoground, and all the students who were so understanding. My good friends, from many times and places in my life, were also important, especially those who contacted me often (Alison Mack) and sometimes came to stay with me (Greta Brinkman).

Last but not at all least, I wish to acknowledge the people that were most closely involved in the book project itself; my two coauthors, Deborah and Karin, who were patient, helpful, flexible, and caring throughout the many delays I brought upon us all. Thanks for hanging in there with me! Finally, I wish to thank Bernadette Capelle of Brunner/Mazel, who has remained steadfast and enthusiastic in her support of this book through the modifications of our timeline that my illness provoked.

As my health returned, I was able to work on this book more and more. It is perhaps no coincidence that the manuscript was completed as the last remnants of dizziness were leaving me and as I regained many aspects of my former life. There were many times during my illness when

I was angry—angry at the loss of my independence, my fun, my socializing, my professional abilities, angry at the injustice of how arbitrary this illness seems to be, sometimes angry at people trying to cheer me up. I believe the anger was a necessary part of coping with the illness, and it has enriched my experiential understanding of this complex emotion. Without the people mentioned above, this book—emerging as it did with the coming and going of this bout of Meneire's disease—would not have been possible for me.

Sally D. Stabb, Ph.D.

I would like to gratefully acknowledge the work of Dr. Maryanne Watson and Dr. Art Arauzo, who inspired my fascination with anger as a therapeutic issue. Their insistence upon the relevance and importance of clear anger expression sometimes took me places I did not want to go but so needed to be. I am thankful for their courage and insight, and their willingness to share both. I would also like to thank my mentor and friend, Janet Beeler, for showing me what a woman's competence can look like, and for being willing to say, "Yes, you can!" as many times as it takes. Perhaps this book is a sign I am starting to agree!

Both Lynn Mikel Brown and Dana Jack gave time, talents, and perspective to this project. I am grateful for their willingness to dialogue and their detailed and honest appraisal of our work. Also, for the past several years I have enjoyed the support of two women who have been instrumental in my personal and professional development, Beverly Bonnheim and Dr. Nancy Amos. Both not only have been outstanding role models as therapists but also have touched my life in ways that have left deep and wonderful imprints, and I want to thank them for their generous sharing of themselves.

I would like to recognize the tremendous gifts my clients have given me in sharing their thoughts, their emotions, and their lives. They have taught me more about anger than I could learn from any book, and I am grateful for the priviledge of witnessing their work and their journeys.

I cannot begin to acknowledge here my gratitude to my parents who gave me a great, enduring love for learning that has so enriched my life and carried me to this point. To my father, Harry Hoglander, and to my mother, Joan Gilman, thank you for showing me how and why we find ways to give something back and to truly make a difference.

Most importantly, I wish to thank my children, Lorin, Benjamin, and Gailynn, who have so generously and patiently made a space for my work in our family. Your flexibility and unselfishness have made it possible to do what I needed to do to accomplish this goal, and your insistence that our lives must certainly go on as usual has kept me grounded in reality.

Thank you for this, and for so much more—you continue to amaze and delight me!

Lastly, to Sally and Deborah, my respect for you both has only increased throughout this process. I will always be grateful for the opportunities this project has given me; to find a voice, to use it, and to learn to appreciate the worth of my message for myself and others as well. Thank you for valuing what I have been able to bring to this work, and for sharing with me your own powerful words.

Karin H. Bruckner, M.A., L.P.C.

Introduction:
The Paradox of Anger

Liberation means the power to transcend obstacles.
The obstacles are educational, religious, racial, and cultural patterns.
These have to be confronted,
and there is no political solution which serves them all.
The real tyrants are guilt, taboos, educational inheritance—
these are our enemies.

Practical problems are often solved by psychological liberation.
The imagination, the skills, the intelligence, are freed to discover solutions.
Undirected, blind anger and hostility are not effective weapons.
They have to be converted into lucid action.

–Anais Nin

A White, middle-class, 17-year-old girl takes a scalpel and carefully cuts a 1-inch incision on her arm, lining it up with four similar gashes, one made on each of four days previously. Her bedroom door is open just a crack. A 34-year-old White, working class woman takes a bag of rotting garbage and in a rage, slams it through a large window of her would-be boyfriend's kitchen while he is away from home. Decaying chicken bones and lettuce, junk mail, coffee grounds, and tissues lay scattered in the broken glass, strewn across the shiny, white linoleum. A 60-year-old African American grandmother marches into a principal's office, demanding fair treatment for her 13-year-old grandson. A 9-year-old rural farm girl wrestles a school mate to the ground outside the school, hitting her and pinning her arms behind her head. Two minutes later she is sitting in class demure, polite, clothes in place. A 14-year-old Hispanic girl, facing the insults of two visiting same-age male cousins, turns away from them, lowers her eyes, and walks away in silence. All of these women and girls are angry.

In some of these cases, anger serves as a fundamental mechanism by which the self is defined. In others, anger is diverted, and an opportunity for self-growth gives way to constraining and gendered social imperatives. That anger can both promote the clarity of self-defintion and lead to dysfunction through deviation forms the first of several themes of this book.

Each of these women and girls experiences this anger differently, acts on it differently, expects and receives different outcomes in her interpersonal context as a result of her emotion and behavior. Some experience their anger as liberating—as clarifying and as a vehicle for creating instrumental self-definition. These girls and women know the authority of their own voices and internal standards—and use their anger as a means for gaining self-knowledge as well as an impetus for constructive action. Some, however, experience their anger as alien, as vulgar and useless, as dangerous or sinful, as oppressive, and as in opposition to their true selves. These women and girls tend to look for ways of simplifying, containing, explaining away, holding at bay—or avoiding altogether—the familiarity of their own anger. In fact, some manage such an artful avoidance of the embrace of their angry selves as to forget—to lose access to that way of knowing the world and themselves.

Yet all of these women and girls share at least a somewhat common biology, as well as a somewhat common and life-long exposure to dominant cultural attitudes and messages about women and anger. What unites them and what differentiates them? What complex roles do cognitions about anger, the affective experience of anger, and the actual behavioral manifestations of anger play in these women's and girls' lives? An everpresent ambivalence or conflict and an ongoing negotiation of internal and external dynamics seem to charcterterize these issues, and such questions and observations form the starting points for this book.

This work also grows out of both personal experience and the professional research and clinical therapy work of the coauthors. Thus, it carries with it an acknowledged feminist value position. In particular, we hope this book will be used by practitioners, teachers, students, researchers, or anyone wanting to understand women's anger in context. We seek to pull together a diverse literature that spans biological, psychological, and social-contextual influences on women's anger in a format that is both concise and accessible to readers. Our feminist perspective is evident in our desire to convey the complex nature of the anger experience for women as an internal phenomenon, as well as in its relationship with interpersonal interactions and the broader social environment. This value position becomes clear in our recommendations for both "personal and political" change and empowerment.

To our knowledge, a life-span developmental perspective that incorporates the theoretical, research, and clinical literatures on girls, adolescents, and adult women has yet to be used as an organizing framework to focus on women's anger. We believe this developmental foundation, in combination with our clinical feminist perspective, provides a unique lens through which to view and understand women and anger. The initial chapters of the book serve to lay the theoretical and empirical groundwork for an understanding of the biopsychosocial nature of women's and girls' anger. Anger issues in therapy are discussed next, with emphasis on both instrumental and destructive aspects of anger. The relationship of anger to various presenting problems is noted, and therapeutic strategies, debates, and outcomes are explored. This is followed by qualitative examples that highlight the book's earlier points and bring vivid images of anger in a diversity of women's and girls' lives to the reader's attention. These descriptive narratives provide a richness of detail, context, and subtlety that give life to the more academic research foundation already presented. In fact, case examples and pieces of qualitative interviews are used throughout the book to reflect the ways in which we see women's anger lived in actual experience. The book concludes with an integrative discussion that explicitly weaves together the content covered using developmental, clinical, and feminist frameworks as unifying devices.

☐ The Paradox of Anger: Defining and Diverting Self

Another central point in this dialogue has to do with the ways in which some girls and women must detour their direct, honest relationship with anger in favor of some less authentic experience or expression. These compromises to genuine, spontaneous affect become ingrained in ways of knowing—cloudy lenses through which to view self and the world at large. Unfortunately, the detours and compromises also become unconscious defining principles themselves—containers into which many women must contort, bend, and compress their experience to fit and be stored indefinitely. This work aims to explain how this occurs, with existing theory as

well as by proposing new models to incorporate elements of anger socialization not articulated by existing frameworks.

A survey of the theoretical, empirical, and clinical literature illuminates complex and often contradictory perspectives on anger, mirroring
the different values and worldviews of various authors. In the crudest of
terms, some see anger expression as largely adaptive; others see it as largely
destructive, with the social prohibitions around anger expression as necessary. We believe that these contradictions need to be, and can be, integrated. The contradictions can be seen as a coin; one side revealing positive benefits in defining the self through social interaction, the other side
reflecting the diversion of anger into negative processes and behaviors.
The paradox is that these processes can coexist together in the same person and often are even evident within a single social interactional episode.
Although we hold that constructive anger expression is often underused
and that legitimate anger is often diverted into problematic pathways, it is
important to note that we cannot promote a simplistic promotion of anger
expression nor an all-out condemnation of anger diversion without regard
to contextual factors.

A number of psychotherapy theories support a parallel conclusion
about anger's role in self-definition. For example, humanistic and existential theories (Rogers, 1959) see emotion as a valued aspect of experience,
with motivating properties. Emotions provide important information about
the self in relation to the environment and direct our awareness to what is
personally relevant in order to mobilize the self for action (Greenberg &
Safran, 1989). In particular, anger involves evaluative judgments about
past and present situations and concerns about the future and intentions
for action (Solomon, 1976).

From a Bowenian family systems point of view, the constructive
use of anger reflects attainment of differentiation of self, a state of known
separateness from or distinctiveness relative to one's family or partner,
and so forth (Papero, 1990). Recent research in family psychology also has
emphasized the concept of metaemotion, which is how parents think about
and feel about their own and their childrens' emotions (Gottman, Katz, &
Hooven, 1996). Encouraging the constructive expression, acceptance, and
understanding of emotions such as anger has been shown
to positively impact a child's mental health or development in a variety of
ways.

Some models illustrate processes that can explain anger's role in either self-definition or the diversion of self, depending on which direction
is encouraged in a particular social exchange. These models emphasize the
largely enculturated nature of emotional expression and experience
(Kitayama & Markus, 1994), as well as the role of appraisal processes
(Ellsworth, 1994; Frijda, Kuipers, & ter Schure, 1989; Smith, Haynes,

Lazarus, & Pope, 1993) or integrated, script-like feeling-perception plans (Schweder, 1994).

Similarly, behavioral theories of emotion posit that individuals learn emotional responses in relation to environmental contingencies (Skinner, 1953), while acknowledging that emotions stem, at least in part, from innate propensities and dispositions (Rachman, 1978). Women's and girls' anger expression or supression in these perspectives would be modeled, rewarded, and/or punished.

What is particularly interesting about these behavioral, appraisal, and cultural models is that although they could be used to examine anger-related processes of both defining and diverting the self, that is, clarifying one's position and felt needs in the moment versus bypassing them, they have in fact been mainly used to illuminate the latter. For example, in tracing the dominant cultural attitudes and influences on women's and girls' anger from a life-span developmental perspective, we see a tension gradually emerging between "what is" relative to emotion and "what should or must be" according to society's demands. Socialization forces differ at various ages, and therefore the experience and expression of anger shifts over time as toddlers grow into early childhood, as young girls make the transition into adolescence, as adolescent girls mature into women, and as women negotiate the multiple roles and challenges of early, middle, and later adulthood (the anger experiences of elderly women are barely beginning to be explored).

Bypassing authentic anger also may be recognized as problematic from the perspectives of some psychoanalytic and experiential family therapies, which conceptualize dysfunction as stemming from the suppression of emotion. Misdirected anger in some family-systems perspectives could be conceptualized as the rerouting of the emotion into dysfunctional interpersonal triangles, coalitions, boundary difficulties, or chaotic dynamics (Nichols & Schwartz, 1995).

A third major point embedded in this work involves the myriad of clinical and subclinical sets of symptoms that, in one way or another, become tied to anger in the empirical literature. Research in the clinical domain often supports the idea that the diversion of anger—usually examined as "suppression"—is harmful. In general, clinical studies suggest that women internalize or suppress (a word that is variously defined) their anger at higher rates than men, and this has a variety of somatic and psychological consequences (Droppelman, Thomas, & Wilt, 1995). Both suppressed and vented anger have been shown to correlate with unhealthy physiological reactions in various populations, many of which are detailed elsewhere in this book.

Yet, despite recent evidence that anger expression has positive physical and mental health consequences for women (e.g., Faber & Burns, 1996;

Mikulincer, 1998), overt anger in women continues to be generally seen as unattractive, unfeminine, and alienating to vital relationships (Bernardez-Bonesatti, 1978; Lerner, 1985). It is likely that many therapists do not choose to assess anger expression, do not view a lack of anger expression as problematic, and do not conceptualize it as a fundamental process in identity development. Although anger expression is encouraged in a few therapies (e.g., Chandler, 1993), many clients and therapists alike continue to be ambivalent about this course of action. Women clients often report that they cannot get angry, or if they do, they fear they will be overwhelmed by anger and will be unable to stop their raging, or to keep it from destroying themselves or everyone around them. For example, we often hear women in therapy say, "I'll explode" or "I'll go crazy" or "I'd burst into flames" when first challenged to examine the consequences of anger expression. Feminist therapists and those who work with trauma survivors encourage anger expression as a healing mechanism in working through abuse issues, however the outcome data on these interventions is in its infancy. Double messages to women abound in the self-help literature, much of which continues to provide ways to suppress anger, or, if giving advice regarding healthy expression of anger, still sends an underlying message that anger is negative to begin with (Tavris, 1989). These issues provide a context in which to make anger a focal point in women's therapy.

At the other end of the spectrum, there exists the reality that some women have serious problems in controlling their anger and may become aggressive to others, psychologically disorganized, or harmful to themselves as a result of their rage. We offer a new and alternative view of diagnostic categories that focuses on the individual woman's struggle to maintain self in the face of society's more problematic injunctions, rather than viewing symptoms as reflective of characterological dysfunction of the woman herself. We suggest that the symptoms experienced by women engaged in this struggle in their own socialization are organized into clusters that underlie traditional psychiatric diagnoses and that these symptom clusters can be traced back to an anger-diversive process. Even distress at everyday, subclinical levels often signals the use of a degree of bypassing wherein a woman chooses avoidance over self-definition.

Self-definitional aspects of anger as well as anger-diversion processes are evident in the everyday experiences of women and girls. For example, themes of anger suppression, somatization, gender-role expectations, relationships with boys, and self-definition all become evident in the following portrait, from an in-school focus-group interview with one fifth-grader done by one of the authors, who worked with the girls at this particular school for the period of a year.

Clementine, as she chooses to be named for our interview, is an African American girl in the fifth grade at a public Montessori Academy located in one of the poorest sections of a metropolitan area. She is a middle child of eight but lives only with her grandmother and great-grandmother at this time, a situation that seems to both afford her the energy and devotion of two elders as well as keep her isolated from the rest of her immediate family. Her mother's financial burden in raising eight children makes it necessary for her to live with these matriarchs, but the arrangement also protects Clementine from the violent behavior of her older brothers, a phenomenon she alludes to only briefly in our group interview before changing the subject or looking down at her lap. Given each of these elements, it's difficult to determine Clemetine's feelings about her living arrangement and one could suspect she experiences a collage of clashing emotions including ambivalence, sadness, anger, and relief.

At the age of 12 years, Clemetine stands about 5 feet, 5 inches, considerably taller than any of her male or female peers, and slouches considerably as if to obscure her stature. Even prior to our interview, I (Deborah) had become very familiar with this fifth grader by virtue of her often-distressed countenance, as she tends to be in the hallway crying angry tears about some offense by a classmate or an injury sustained in gym class. Clementine has difficulty expressing her feelings in words, but appears to experience almost daily wounding, either physically through her own accidents or emotionally at the hands of her teacher or her peers. She manifests identical external responses to both, namely, tears and a very angry-looking scowl, as she detaches herself from the epicenter of class activity to a remote area of the room or leaves the classroom altogether to sit alone in the hall.

At these times, Clemetine looks as if she wishes for some kind of solace or verbal exchange. However, her female peers report that when Clementine becomes "upset," she withdraws from friends, spurning their attempts to talk with her about her sources of frustration. Nevertheless, she does understand her own frustrated attempts to support a friend who is angry and who appears to withdraw in a similar fashion: "I get mad . . . I hate it when she ignores me."

Our group conversation takes place at a large table in an enclosed area of the school, usually reserved for teachers and parents. Clementine and I, along with two of her friends from the fifth grade, meet during the school day over tortilla chips and queso. We discuss the issue of anger, both in girls as well as in boys, reflecting on the reactions of significant people to this emotion and its display. Clementine lists the anger elicitors in her life including, "people dying in my family and fights with my friends—or when somebody's sick in the hospital like my grandma."

If feeling angry at home, Clementine says she goes into her room to "lock my door, turn on my stereo real high—up as loud as I can and like to get into trouble again . . . because it's like testing your parents like—my teacher told me about that—cause when I get mad at my grandmother, that's what I'll do, turn the radio up real loud. Then she like 'turn the radio down' like that and I act like I don't hear and then when I fall asleep I turn the radio down."

The interview continues:

DC: So you kinda test her when you're angry—kinda like you want a re-action from her and then when you get the reaction—how do you feel?

C: A little better [laughs]. In a way I do, because she don't really hit you or nothin', she don't—she'll scream at you so you'll feel a little bit better [laughs].

DC: Why does that make you feel better?

C: 'Cause when she screams it makes me laugh.

About another girl in Clementine's class, she reports noticing the following angry behavior and gives her own personal response as well.

C: Now when Latisha's angry—she's a girl in our class, she cries alot—so we never know why—it kind of makes you feel funny.

DC: Funny? Funny how?

C: Like I feel sorry for her. Sometimes she just makes me cry. I don't know why, but . . .

Her peers report that she throws away her lunch when she becomes angry, and then refuses to eat for the rest of the day. Clementine herself reports that her grandmother tries to coax her to eat at these times, and that she sometimes manages to avoid food for several days in a row. She reports feeling as if she will vomit should she ingest food when she's angry.

Clementine's avoidance of spontaneous, clear, direct expression of anger appears in her self-punishment, her avoidance of food and friends and conversation when she is angry, and looks similar to that experienced by many grown women. Although she acknowledges being angry often, she somaticizes via gastrointestinal expression of her anger and uses indirect means to communicate displeasure with her grandmother. All these examples have to do with Clemetine's minimization and distortion of—or avoidance of—her anger.

However, one of the most salient themes in Clementine's anger portrait is the way in which she minimizes her grandmother's anger. This 12-year-old speaks of her caretaker's frustration as if she is very amused at the sound of it—almost as she tries to incite this feeling in the older woman, only to then turn it against her in a passive show of indifference. The point serves to illustrate the final major thrust of the present work, a point residing subtly between the lines of description regarding anger socialization in women. Not so easily recognized or described are the insidious internal processes by which larger social imperatives *become* vehicles for intrapsychic training, the *how* in the mixture of broad cultural rules and up-close emotional development in the girl and the woman.

Clementine helps us illustrate how and why we are pushing the envelope on this subject of anger socialization by showing a bit of what is available to our inspection when we step up very close to the picture and look carefully, deliberately for clues as to how girls internalize social anger messages and how these come to be a part of a dilemma in the self-development process. If we stand close to paintings, such as Clementine's, we see the detailed brush strokes, the vehicles for light and color, that turn macrolevel social order into microlevel experience. Clementine shows us how a feeling she cannot readily embrace or give voice to in herself changes from an instrument for self-clarification to a weapon of self-destruction. Clemetine laughs at the situation she has particpated in setting up around her grandmother, as if to mock the woman's anger—a feeling she has learned to mock and destest in herself.

It is this further two-edgedness of women's anger experience that compels us to continue our visitation of this socialization process, so well articulated by other authors (e.g., Brown, 1998; Miller & Surrey, 1990). We wish to come in closer for a between-the-lines and brush-strokes look at this paradoxical phenomenon. The very psychological element that offers a woman such power for self-definition, defense, and clarity, the feeling that reveals an injustice in the social-contextual sphere of her existence so often becomes the feeling that, through countless subtle transformations, costs her self-esteem, self-credibility, and intellectual potency. Just as the stealthful intruder quietly picks up a weapon in the unsuspecting resident's home and uses it to do harm to an individual, so the anger-socialization forces insidiously deface a woman's instrument of self-protection and train her in using it against herself.

We acknowledge the many recent descriptions of girls' and women's resistance in the face of anger socialization (e.g., Brown, 1998; Way, 1995) and wish to encourage continued exploration of such resiliency and out-spokenness. Our work here offers not a contradiction of those stories but a different and new level of interpretation of the anger socialization process. What remains here to be described is the microlevel incorporation of the many double-binding, self-negating cultural anger mythologies that continue to exist in many societies.

Additionally, processes of self-definition have received increasing attention in recent years, with classic models of ethnic-minority identity development (Cross, 1971; Sue & Sue, 1990), gay and lesbian identity development (Cass, 1979), White identity development (Helms, 1990), and feminist identity development (Downing & Roush, 1985) all gaining prominence and generating an ever-growing body of research. We posit that important anger currents run through and link all of these models; that the diversion of anger may be characteristic of the earliest stages of these models, and that the self-definitional aspects of anger have a place in the more tumultuous middle stages. In this way, anger becomes a crucial common thread in our understanding of *self* development, across such boundaries as ethnicity, gender, and sexual orientation.

Although the diversion of anger and anger's role in self-definition are major themes woven throughout this book, we consider the book to be a work in progress, a snapshot not only of current models and research but of each author's development and of each woman and girl who is quoted. These are but the latest pages; as the years go by, we could add more pictures, more stories. As one Latin American woman with whom we spoke and listened so aptly describes this phenomenon: "I'm different than my mom and my daughters are going to be . . . very different from me. So it keeps changing."

2

CHAPTER

Anger in Emotion Theory

Alas, that wisdom is so large,
And truth so manifold!
—Emily Dickinson

This chapter serves to situate the rest of our discussion of women's anger within the context of certain current theories of emotion. The rationale for including such background reflects our awareness of the complexity of emotion in general, and our desire to use current models to understand women's anger in particular. At first glance, it is easy to assume that we all know what emotions are and can start with that a priori knowledge and go forward with an exploration of women's anger. However, upon closer examination, the construct of emotion has been remarkably elusive, hotly debated, and fraught with methodological difficulties in its study. The debates surrounding the nature of emotion and the research upon which current models of emotion are based serve to inform, as well as limit, our conceptualizations of women's anger. In particular, it is noteworthy that we find in the literature no feminist theories of emotion per se. Many feminist writers and researchers present reviews of relevant research (e.g., Crawford, Kippax, Onyx, Gault, & Benton, 1992) or discuss specific aspects of emotion, such as the socialization of expression of emotions or feelings about self, but a unified feminist theory of emotion has yet to emerge.

Talking to women about anger, we receive a variety of definitions, often confusing the "pure" emotion state with some form of acting out (e.g., violent or rejecting behavior toward another). For instance, one of our graduate students calls upon her own definition of anger but realizes it has been tainted by years of family interaction, expectations, and patterns of emotion-avoidance in general.

> Anger, to me, is something violent . . . or, or bad somehow. It's a wrong thing, something to avoid because there's so much danger tied up in it. I mean, when I think of anger, I remember my ex-husband's violent temper outbursts, or my grandmother's cold shoulder tactics . . . she would just reject you. So, I have a really hard time thinking about anger in general without associating it with these things. It's . . . yeah, it's so tied to having bad things happen. You just don't want to go there.

Definition of anger resides at the heart of this exploration and provides an opportunity for us to view the complexities and contradictions inherent in much nonconscious anger socialization. Given the major emphases of this work, as outlined in Chapter 1, we pull selectively from the vast collection of available models to illustrate our overarching premise that emotion and anger are neither singly pre- or postcognitive, neither wholly health-promoting or -compromising, but mutually, holographically embedded (e.g., Morones & Mikawa, 1992), continuously influencing each other and shaping experience. Further, we aim to illustrate how social and biological forces coalesce in the experience of anger to render it double-edged in its power to motivate, liberate, and clarify, as well as to socialize or be turned against self. In this way, defining anger depends upon many contextual influences. Taking stock of its usefulness or effects forces us to listen to the perceptions of the one who is feeling it.

With these goals in mind, this chapter gives a brief overview of a number of important topics, including current interactional theories of emotion, the development of emotion, and emotion as viewed by theories of psychotherapy. In the last part of the chapter, specific applications of these general theories to women's anger are highlighted, with the intention of illuminating what appears unique about anger versus other emotions and what appears unique about women's anger in particular.

☐ Current Interactional Theories of Emotion: Caveats and Concerns

The study of emotion is highly challenging, and numerous debates exist in the current literature. The most up-to-date theories of emotion all acknowledge the phenomenon as a complex one, usually with interrelated cultural, social, subjective, and physiological components (Averill, 1994, 1997; Ekman & Davidson, 1994; Kitayama & Markus, 1994; Plutchik, 1997; Russell, 1997). Different researchers and theorists have chosen foci that may emphasize one or two aspects in detail, but all seem to at least acknowledge the others' contributions at this point. Despite this, such fundamental issues as the definition of emotion remain controversial, and methods continue to be inherently imperfect. Only in the domain of the function of emotion do we see a great deal of consistency. Thus, this topic is addressed first.

- What is the function of emotion in general, and how does that inform our understanding of women's anger?

Current theorists appear to be unanimous in the opinion that emotions serve an adaptive function. For example, Ekman (1994, p. 15) states, "Emotions evolved for their adaptive value in dealing with fundamental life tasks." Panksepp (1994, p. 20) declares, "The general function of emotions also seems obvious if one assumes they provide coherent and ingrained ways of coping with major challenges to the welfare of an organism." Scherer (1994, p. 27) notes that emotions function "in response to the evaluation of an external or internal stimulus event that is relevant to central concerns of the organism." In Schweder's (1994, p. 33) perspective, emotions, "are experienced as a perception of some self-relevant condition of the world and as a plan of action for the protection of dignity, honor, and self-esteem." Kitayama and Markus (1994, pp. 1–2) note that the components of emotion function as "processes by which individuals try to accomplish, collectively and personally, a form of adaptation and adjustment to their own immediate sociocultural, semiotic environment." Plutchik (1997, p. 19) views emotions as "basic adaptive patterns . . . in the service of individual and genetic survival. Emotional behaviors act as signals of intentions of future action that function to influence the interpersonal relations of the interacting individuals." He also comments, "Emotions are not disruptive, maladaptive states, but rather act to stabilize the internal state of the organism" (p. 20). Averill (1994, p. 12) writes, "basic emotions presumably are those that fulfill vital functions . . . an emotion may be vital to the survival of the species (biological criteria), the society (social criteria), or the self (psychological criteria)."

Consensus about anger's adaptive nature clearly develops from these quotes. In fact, newer approaches each contribute to an idea widening in acceptance, namely, that instead of rendering us less rational or competent, our feelings organize our thought processes, our communication, and our social interactions to help us effect change (Thompson, 1991). Emotions help us live and engage more effectively.

Finding agreement becomes much more challenging if other aspects of emotion are examined. In fact, the very definition of an emotion, and, by extension, anger, stirs controversy. The definitional question goes to the heart of historical debates in models of emotions, and to understand anger from all sides, we must look into the immense and long-lived imbroglio of emotion conceptualizations in general. The major players in these debates, broadly speaking, are theorists who believe physiology and evolution explain emotion best; and social-constructionist approaches that posit that emotion is best understood as interpersonally and culturally created. The latter camp may include cognitive theorists, who believe emotions are largely determined by how we think. This split between pre- and post-cognitive elements in defining emotion relfects the age-old nature-versus-nurture controversy. Rather than attempt to precisely answer the definition question, we present a small taste of the debate, an argument that consistently upturns the following questions in various forms.

- Are there "basic emotions"—some set number of agreed-upon and consistently recognizable and experienced (across age, culture, gender, and other aspects of diversity) emotions?

Physiological advocates generally say yes. However, debate still exists about whether or not there is one kind of generic arousal, two primary states of positive and negative physiology (that become more specifically defined or refined through appraisal, cultural rules, and so forth), or whether there exist physiological patterns specific to several (usually six or seven) "basic" emotions. For example, Izard's (1993) theory of discrete emotions posits the basic emotions of joy, sadness, anger, fear, disgust, and shame. Each emotion is thought to have "distinct functions in the way it organizes perception, cognition, and actions" (p. 631).

The dimensional approach sees emotion as occuring on two dimensions. One is arousal (high versus low) and the other is valence (positive versus negative). Others argue that emotions are variable or that they have fuzzy boundaries and blend into one another (circumplex models) or at best can be put into broad families or classes.

Cultural and social-constructionist approaches say there are as many emotions as each cultural group would define—based on language, world view, somatic experience, and so forth. The words for or concepts of specific emotions may not even make sense in some other cultures. For example, the Ifaluk of Micronesia do not have a word for what in English we call *anger* (Wierzbicka, 1994). Likewise, the Ifaluk have a concept called *song* for which there are no English words; "song" is an emotion that is manifested by pouting or refusing to eat in order to make another person feel guilty for some wrongdoing. Usually the person demonstrating "song" is of higher status than the person who has acted incorrectly, and thus it serves to teach differences between right and wrong.

- Is physiological arousal necessary to define an emotion? Do different emotions have discrete, consistently identifiable, physiological patterns (across age, culture, gender, and other aspects of diversity)?

Levenson (1992) says this question has been difficult to tackle for many reasons. Emotions are short-lived, occur in complex contexts along with other psychological processes such as attention, appraisal, and social interaction, and must be measured against an ongoing stream of other autonomic nervous system (ANS) functioning. Izard (1993) believes that emotion is at least partially defined by physiological responses. In his theory of differential emotions, specific feelings each have a unique set of neural processes, which, regardless of whether or not they actually are expressed, always lead to a unique conscious experience. The subjective experience of emotion may or may not be articulated, but it is always felt. Izard states, "Thus emotion has three levels or aspects—neural, expressive, and experiential—and the term 'emotion' refers to all three components operating as an integral system" (p. 633).

- What are the differences between mood, personality, reflexes, and physiological arousal?

Again, what exactly is anger? Can we say that someone, particularly, some woman, is just an angry person? If so, based upon what—her own report, her affective display, or her interactions with others? In most definitions, emotion is a very short-term phenomenon—moments, minutes, rarely longer. There is some debate about whether or not certain experiences that may be sustained over time, such as hope, for example, are "true" emotions. Usually, if an emotional experience persists over hours or days, it is then termed a *mood*. If moods become chronic or integrated into a person's everyday way of being in the world over months or years, we choose to call them *personality*. As stated previously, some theorists see physiological arousal as a necessary prerequisite for emotion to occur. Some see physiological arousal as a concomitant response for many, but not all, kinds of emotion. Reflexes (for example a startle response) are usually distinguished from emotion but also may be considered a primitive version of emotion or a precursor of emotion.

So, can we assume some people just have angry personalities? To what are we really referring if we do? Are we talking about more anger than most people experience, or just old anger that has never been fully assimilated into the person's whole character—anger that lives at the surface, easily identifiable to others, that has not been fully received or dealt with by its bearer? These questions remain unanswered in the empirical and theoretical emotion literature but offer starting points for continued exploration and dialogue. Because anger tends to be conceptualized as an informant to action or reassessment, perhaps it should be regarded as a brief experience if it is managed effectively or instrumentally. Perhaps "living with anger" for longer periods of time indicates either the perceptual experience of being chronically abused or insulted or the experience of managing one's anger in such a way that it never becomes fully resolved.

- How is anger experienced in its various forms and what place does subjective experience have in defining anger (across age, culture, gender, and other aspects of diversity)?

This question is particularly challenging. A number of theorists talk about differences in somaticizing versus emotionalizing, or the degree to which emotions, in general, are experienced bodily rather than verbalized. Obviously, all data here must be tied to self-reports of subjective, internal states. Studies depend on participants' awareness of their emotion states as well as the personal, relational, and cultural meanings those people assign to their emotions. Thus, these self-reports are by definition language- and culture-bound. This also raises the issue of whether or not some emotions are unconscious, and if so, how do we perceive them? If unconscious, are they "real?" Who decides? If my therapist says I am angry, but I have no conscious awareness of this emotion, who is right? We may never be able to answer these questions to the satisfaction of all concerned.

We can, however, refine the prototype for anger with comparison to closely related emotions such as hate and jealousy. Typified by warm or hot and tense sensations, anger often involves an urge to express feelings to a partner in a hostile manner or to physically hurt the other, and actual behaviors that involve criticizing, complaining, yelling, and throwing things

(Fitness & Fletcher, 1993). Again, anger is described as short-lived in comparison to other related emotions, such as jealousy (which involves third parties), the prototypical anger scenario being a two-party phenomenon. Hate also falls under anger as a subcategory but is distinguished from anger by a sense of helplessness or decreased control, more negative self-cognitions, and more behaviors that involve withdrawal and acting cold (even if people have the desire to verbally or physically act out). It appears that people feel hate if it is not safe for them to feel anger, or, in other words, if they perceive themselves to be powerless to act on their anger. Perhaps hate is a form of anger experience that requires suppressing and transforming action-oriented feeling into a smoldering internal discontent.

• Is there a necessary conscious (or unconscious) cognitive component to anger?

    This question raises some debate among theorists. Izard (1993) does not include thinking as a part of the experience of emotion. However, he notes that "emotion experience is cue-producing, and, as such, it normally recruits the cognitive system" (p. 633). So when we feel, our thoughts at some point become aroused and fill in meaning. Izard does posit that cognitions also may activate emotions, because the neural processes that underlie emotion can be triggered by brain activity involved in thinking. So, we can reexperience anger upon being reminded of an event that took place yesterday, or 5 years ago. Some disagree with the specific idea that we can have an emotional experience of which we are unconscious, for example, Lewis (1993), who argues that emotional experience always must include attention and conscious self-awareness. This notion opposes the idea that we can feel anger without really knowing why or being able to articulate its source. In Lewis's framework, there always exists some level of cognizance about the anger we experience.
    In this book, we rely more heavily on the ideas coming from social-constructionist approaches, as well as from interactional theories of emotion. Namely, our models for anger socialization and diversion of anger experience rest upon assumptions such as those of Izard (1993) and others who allow room for an embeddedness of cognition and emotion.

• Is it necessary to know and understand the interpersonal, social, and cultural context of a situation in order to define an emotion?

    Social constructionists essentially say yes. In Heise and O'Brien's (1993, p. 491) review of these models, emotion is defined as "intelligent conduct, contrived according to cultural rules so as to effect desired interpersonal outcomes." Also from a social-constructionist perspective, Saarni (1993, p. 493) writes that "emotions, beliefs (i.e., representations), and relationships are inextricably intertwined" and that emotions arise in a context of cultural intersubjectivity. There are both "strong" and "weak" versions of social constructionism. The strong version holds that all human emotions are language- and belief-based social products. The weaker (and more popular) view is that even though there is some limited range of "naturally occuring" basic emotional response, what interests social constructionists is to what extent emotions are socially constructed, the processes whereby this construction occurs, and the determination of what social ends are served by emotions (Oatley, 1993).

Methodological Issues

"Method" makes itself very apparent if we attempt to define emotion in research. The study of anger, and emotion in general, requires a definition, yet each time a researcher defines emotion, she or he imposes an encultured and language-bound construct on the participants in that study (regardless of quantitative or qualitative method). This problem is particularly acute in cross-cultural research on emotion, which paradoxically holds great promise for clarifying the definitional debates mentioned earlier.

Even if a researcher is working with culturally similar participants, who have generally shared meanings for words, the study of emotion is slippery. Much of the data required depends upon self-report and is thus subject to idiosyncratic expression and interpretation. Both feeling states and cognitive appraisals are internal events, so researchers must rely on individuals' subjective reports of these phenomena. Additionally, some aspects of emotional experience or expression may be nonconscious or out of awareness because of the fact that they are embedded in cultural assumptions that are so pervasive as to be unrecognizable to an individual. To take a relatively trivial example, an American woman at work may become angry if she has no choice in the decor of her own office, but she may not be able to articulate the fact that her anger is situated in the individualist values of the United States and the ideological foundations by which each person is entitled to "inalienable" rights to life, liberty, and the pursuit of happiness.

If a researcher chooses to study a behavioral aspect of emotion, more "objective" measures may be obtained, such as those found in the detailed coding systems developed to study facial expression of emotion. Still, these methods rely on underlying assumptions that participants share meanings of words in the experimental protocols, such as asking, "show me an angry face" or, in judging photographs, "How does this person feel?" Likewise, it is problematic to assume that overt behavior always accurately reflects an internal state. Aggressive behavior need not be accompanied by anger; a friendly smile may belie an underlying feeling of sadness, resentment, or boredom. Given that children quickly learn the display rules of emotion in their particular cultures, the problem of inner experience versus outer expression seems an ongoing one.

Likewise, in attempts to study the physiological nature of emotion, protocols that involve taking physiological measures during or after the induction of fear, anger, and so forth assume that such inductions have been successful and accurate in producing the desired emotion. Yet many question if watching a scary movie induces the same reaction as an actual scary event, for example. In other studies, correlational data may indicate relationships between emotions (e.g., hostility) and physiological measures, but causal conclusions cannot be drawn from such work. Cacioppo, Klein, Berntson, and Hatfield (1993) note that measures of ANS activity used in emotion research, such as heart rate and skin temperature, may miss important aspects of physiological response that are not as readily observable or measurable—not to mention phenomenological feelings and meanings.

Finally, if researchers adopt a model in which the external social-cultural context or situation is seen as a crucial variable in determining emotion, then that environment must be accurately measured or assessed as well. This is a daunting task, and taxonomies of situations are far less available in the psychological literature than taxonomies of internal attributes (personality, etc.). In studying gender differences in emotion, the situation becomes even more complicated. As Brody (1985) notes, gender-role stereotypes may influence raters' or observers' measures of emotionality. These stereotypes also underlie the conceptualization of measures (see Chapter 4) and definitions of what is normative and are related to social-desirability biases. As we discuss elsewhere in this book, the instruments used to measure anger and other emotion also define it and shape the ways in which it is described and experienced as well.

☐ Underlying Components of Anger in Emotion Theory

Current integrative theories of emotion cannot be understood adequately without the appropriate background information. Because integrative theories synthesize aspects from many areas of inquiry, these component areas deserve our attention. Six major areas are briefly mentioned here for their utility in our discussion of anger: ethology and sociobiology, physiology, cognitive appraisal, socialization and culture, individual differences, and phenomenology.

Ethology and Sociobiology

Ethology is the observational study of animal or human behaviors as they occur in the field, unmodified by experimental settings, tasks, procedures, and so forth. For example, Eibl-Eibesfeldt (1980) documents numerous cross-cultural observations of unstaged human behavior supporting the position that the expressive patterns that control and regulate human behavior are found cross-culturally. These patterns are universally consistent in their expression and in the ways that they act as basic social signals. Although children often express these patterns nonverbally, as language usage develops, both verbal and nonverbal modes are used to express emotional patterns.

From the sociobiological perspective, Gray (1982) and other writers (Izard, 1991; Tomkins, 1963) suggest that emotions are the products of evolution, and that primary emotions serve biologically adaptive functions. These notions, based on Darwin's evolutionary theory, view emotional responses as reflective of survival needs, promoting survival-related problem solving. A typical definition of emotion from the sociobiological point of view is found in Weinrich (1980, p. 133):

> An emotion is the result of a conscious or unconscious decision-making process; it results from an external event changing what is adaptive for the individual to do. It is the internal motivator that creates a readiness to change behavior to increase adaptation. An emotion can be discharged by an act that would (if successful) bring the external world more into line with what would be adaptive for the individual.

There is basic agreement among theorists in this tradition that the structure for certain primary core emotions is wired into the human organism. Plutchik (1980) cites support for the following criteria in establishing the innateness of emotional response: that emotional expressions appear in similar forms in many other species, that they appear in the same form in infants as in adults, that they appear across cultures, and that they are shown in identical ways in sighted individuals as well as those born blind.

For example, a recent study by Galati, Scherer, and Ricci-Bitti (1997) reviewed literature on the facial expression of emotion in blind individuals. Their summary indicates that blind persons are able to display basic emotions such as fear, anger, joy, and sadness. Furthermore, these expressions seem to be clearer and more "readable" by others if they are produced spontaneously, than if they are produced voluntarily (i.e., when told, "Show me an angry face"). This suggests that feelings like anger produce some spontaneous visual display or other set of behaviors in human affect and that this automatic, untrained show informs its audience about something experienced, an update that is very important to the overall situation, both for sender and receiver. This notion becomes important in our look at women's anger because it supports our contention that overt displays of feeling serve a purpose that is at its core well intentioned and helpful. The urge to scowl or shout or speak in a firm tone seems to arise from this primary hard wiring, which, therefore, seems innately tied to persons' adaptively coping with social or other demands.

To continue with this theme, Smith and Lazarus (1990) elaborate on Tomkins's (1962, 1963) idea that sensory motor reflexes, physiological drives, and emotions are fundamental resources that allow all animals to adapt, but that advanced species have evolved toward less dependence on innate reflexes or drives and greater dependence on emotions to let them know about their environments. Startle, pain, and pleasure may best be thought of as innate reflexes rather than emotions, according to Lazarus, Averill, and Opton (1970). These reflexes may in fact be thought of as potential "preemotion" states (Lazarus, 1991), as they play a critical role in the development of the motivational structure on which emotion and appraisal depend. According to Lazarus, emotions constitute an adaptation process distinct from reflexes, as they make possible a greater variability and flexibility of response. In essence, they facilitate the organism's ability to learn from experience.

In the best of all circumstances, for a woman, this learning process possibly includes the acquisition of self-protection skills, such as detecting the potential to abuse in a partner or discriminating instances in which her credibility is being undermined. To learn from experience here means the possibility of taking matters into her own hands, of acting in her own best interest, whether fleeing or fighting back, offending or assuaging, or joining together or clarifying her individuality.

Physiology

In a similar way, the physiology of emotion forms a backdrop for this discussion of women's anger, broadly emcompassing three overlapping domains: brain structure and lateralization; ANS functions (both sympathetic and parasympathetic systems); and neurotransmitters, neuro-peptides, and hormonal influences. Each is considered in turn, although the reader should be aware that there are complex interactions among all these systems. Developmental changes in physiology also are briefly reviewed. The adverse physiological effects of suppressed emotion (e.g., repressed hostility, etc.) are reviewed in Chapter 4's discussion of clinical issues.

Brain structures that have been identified as critical to the experi-ence of emotion include the amygdala, the hippocampus, and the neocor-tex. Melnechuk (1988) offers a metaphorical conceptualization of the neuroanatomic basis of emotion, describing a two-way gate system oper-ating between the two primary brain regions thought to be central in emo-tional response, namely the frontal cortex and the hypothalamus. The fron-tal cortex provides intentional, cognitive, and imaginative functions; the hypothalamus provides body-state information and appears to be funda-mental in both the subjective experience of strong, basic emotions and in evoking behaviors associated with emotion via the endocrine system and the ANS. Linking these two main components is the amygdala, which also receives sensory information. Pribram (1980) argues that the stability and transitions in and out of emotional states involve the three processes of arousal, activation, and effort. Arousal is regulated by the amygdala, acti-vation by the basal ganglia, and both arousal and effort by the hippocam-pus and the pituitary-adrenal cortical system.

The hypothalamic-pituitary-adrenocortical system regulates the pro-duction of cortisol (Stansbury & Gunnar, 1994), which is the hormone responsible for circadian patterns of sleep and wakefulness and also plays a role in stress and emotional response. Most likely, when a stressor is noticed, levels of cortisol-releasing hormone, vasopressin, and adrenocor-ticotropic hormones appear, which begin to influence central nervous sys-tem functioning in the first 5 to 10 minutes. During this time, additional appraisal activities continue, and if this evaluation leads to a conclusion that the situation is still a threat, cortisol levels begin to rise. This process leads to a sense of increased energy and concentration, attention to the environment, and the facilitation of avoidance behaviors. States of negative affect, especially sadness, are associated with elevations in cortisol. Further, the hypothalamic-pituitary-adreno-cortical stress response also seems to be influenced by our cognitive appraisal processes (e.g., the perceived controllability of a situation).

Dawson (1994) writes about her study of the relationships between emotion and brain lateralization in infants using electroencephalographic techniques to monitor brain activity, finding the type of emotional expres-sion to be associated with asymmetries in frontal electroencephalo-graphic activity. On the other hand, intensity or degree of reactivity of emotion appears related to a generalized activation of both right and left frontal regions. The left frontal region shows a specialization for the expression of happiness and interest; activation of the right frontal region is associated with the emotions of fear, disgust, and distress. The generalized activation of both lobes, found with higher intensity of emotion, seems to reflect the diffuse influence of subcortical structures on the cortex, which may serve to increase readiness to receive and respond to important external events.

Similarly, both Fox (1994) and Davidson (1993) suggest that left frontal activation is associated with active approach, positive affect, exploration, and sociability, and inhibition of left frontal activity is related to depression and lack of positive affect. Right frontal activation is associated with withdrawal or negative affect—fear or anxiety in particular. Right frontal inhibition is related to impulsivity and hyperactivity. Porges, Doussard-Roosevelt, and Maiti (1994) also summarize previous research on lateralization. Their conclusions are that the right hemisphere is associated with expression and interpretation of emotion, regulation of attention, and primary control of emotion. Damage to the right hemisphere shows lack of emotional expression in speech. Negative emotions are associated with the right hemisphere, and there is also strong support for fight versus flight behaviors being associated with the right hemisphere. Although the left hemisphere is associated with positive emotion and interest, Porges, Doussard-Roosevelt, and Maiti believe the research evidence to be less conclusive here.

A recent study by Harmon-Jones and Allen (1998) is particularly interesting as it focuses on lateralization specific to anger. Anger traditionally has been thought of as a "negative" emotion, and most of the brain lateralization research (as noted here) associates negative emotion with the right hemisphere and withdrawal. However, Harmon-Jones and Allen suggest that anger is an approach emotion, in keeping with evolutionary-adaptive perspectives that anger motivates behavior to cope with a blocked goal or a perceived social injustice and provides an individual with energy, determination, and vigor to counteract fear and to mobilize for action. Experimental results using topographic brain mapping of anterior alpha activity find electroencephalographic asymmetry in support of their hypothesis. These researchers build a strong case for separating affect valence (positive versus negative) and motivational direction (approach versus withdrawal). Clearly, not all "negative" emotions induce withdrawal and right-hemisphere activation. At least one "negative" emotion, anger, induces approach and left-hemisphere activation. This appears to be a significant refinement over previous work that confounded affect valence with motivational direction—and becomes significant, again, if we consider the desire to act upon anger in the moment. The idea of anger's approach motivation highlights its potential helpfulness in promoting one to act on one's own behalf in certain situations.

Another argument for the primacy of spontaneous anger response involves a look at ANS function. The ANS regulates homeostatic functions and is composed of two subsystems, the sympathetic nervous system (SNS) and parasympathetic nervous system (PNS). Both of these subsystems originate in the brainstem and regulate a variety of organs. The SNS is associated with increased metabolic output and the PNS with growth and restorative processes. The two subsystems usually work in contrasting ways to each other (e.g., SNS dilates pupils, PNS constricts them), although some processes require both systems. Although historically ANS functions have been used as indices of emotion, Campos, Mumme, Kermoian, and Campos (1994) note that in more current thinking, ANS patterns function as social signals, as well as internal reactions to the environment. What is important to our discussion is that these standard assessments of emotion are given new, relational importance. For example, blushing, flushing and pallor, dry mouth and sweaty brows, pupillary dilation and cold hands, and patterns of respiration convey powerful messages to the perceiver.

The somatic anger processes described here seem to be mediated by neurotransmitters, neuropeptides, or hormones (e.g., Panksepp, 1994; Pribram, 1980). Certain neuropeptides govern the activation and inhibition of specific emotions, whereas others play subsidiary roles, such as modulating the intensity or duration of an emotional response. Generally, though, they promote wide-ranging autonomic changes in both the brain and viscera, providing communication between central and peripheral emotion processes. For example, arginine vasopressin most likely mediates arousal, expectancy, and urges to dominate or persist. Panksepp links this neuropeptide to heightened irritability and anger. Another neuropeptide, adreno-corticotropic hormone is released by the anterior pituitary and also seems to vary with negative affect. In contrast, endorphins most likely promote serenity and satisfaction and possibly quell separation distress, and reduce anger or aggressive impulses.

Although deep considerations of the physiological models of anger fall outside the major foci of this discussion, used as a backdrop these major research trends cast illumination on the automatic, internal anger response. Anger in this light appears more licit, more explainable, easier to accept in its crudest and most unconstrained forms. To consider an automatic visceral process accompanying the phenomenological experience of anger is to acknowledge a side to the emotion that departs from controllability, that speaks to its innateness and its rightful place in human experience.

Cognitive Appraisal

The question "How do we become angry?" includes related questions, such as, "What kinds of things make us angry?" "Under what circumstances do we become angry?" "How do our thought processes mediate that emotional upsurge?" and "Why do certain situations anger some but not all of us—and to such varying degrees?" Appraisal is generally construed as our mental "sizing up" of a situation to determine its significance to our immediate stake in things and has been used to answer some of these questions in theory. Historically, the James-Lange theory of emotion (James, 1890) and Schacter and Singer's (1962) two-factor model both distinguish between physiological arousal and cognitive appraisal. They each view emotion, and again by extension anger, as a third type of experience: a product of the interaction between the two. Thus, these very early models set the stage for current thinking regarding the role of appraisal in emotion and the mysterious relationship between thought and feeling.

In Dodge's (1991) model of social information processing, he outlines a basically cognitive framework determined by the processes of encoding, interpretation, response search, response evaluation, and enactment. His theory casts emotion as both goal direction and the experience of feelings. However, unlike Lewis's (1993) position, Dodge argues that (a) all cognition is emotional, in the sense that all processing occurs with some level of arousal and energy; (b) the goal directing aspect of emotion drives attentional processes; and (c) our phenomenological experience of emotion can alter interpretation and vice-versa. In other words, as we reflect upon what we want to change or obtain, we attend to those things affectively and cognitively. We both think and feel about them simultaneously. Thus, Dodge sees cognition and emotion as integrated with each other but gives prominence to cognitive information processing as the basis for emotion.

Stein, Trabasso, and Liwag (1993) present a cognitive appraisal model of emotion that is knowledge-based and situated, by which the authors mean that it explores the content of emotions, as well as conditions that elicit emotion, and plans or actions carried out in response to emotional reactions. Stein and colleagues assume that people have the ability to act intentionally and are goal-directed. People assess and monitor the status of their goals, particularly those with a high degree of salience or meaning to them. In this model, we have an emotion if our preestablished schemas about those goals do not match new information we receive. This mismatch triggers both a cognitive evaluation process and ANS arousal, which together constitute emotion.

Taking a cross-cultural perspective on appraisal, Ellsworth (1994) proposes that cultural differences in reported emotion can be explained by variation in how people appraise situations across cultures. She identifies a series of basic appraisal dimensions: attention/novelty (a change in the environment), valence/pleasantness (is the change positive or negative?), agency/control (can I do anything about it?), and norm/self compatiblity (have I lived up to or fallen short of some standard of my community or myself?). Different cultures encourage different interpretations of social situations along these dimensions, which most likely result in different emotions. This idea echoes in the work of Frijda and Mesquita (1994), who also see appraisal as a key element in their model of emotion. Appraisal involves conscious or unconscious cognitive evaluations. Primary appraisal involves judging an event as positive or negative, now or in the future. Secondary appraisal involves taking stock of further details of the event that have some relevance to our coping with it, such as the event's cause, outcome, or controllability. Similar to Ellsworth, Frijda and Mesquita see the dimensions of appraisal as cross-culturally consistent but cite strong evidence that one culture may emphasize some dimensions more than others. For example, people in individualistic cultures may see controllability as a more important dimension than people in collectivist countries. Thus, they may feel stronger negative affect in situations that are appraised as uncontrollable.

Socialization and Culture

Culture and appraisal join together powerfully if we consider the process of emotion socialization. Rosaldo (1984) contends "feelings are not substances to be discovered in our blood but social practices organized by stories that we both enact and tell. They are structured by our forms of understanding" (p. 143). Not only does the experience of an emotion rely on a person's internalized knowledge of the social situation (Frijda, Kuipers, & ter Schure, 1989), but experiencing the emotion plays a pivotal role in changing that social situation. Feelings do this by allowing the new construal of the situation and by instigating the person engaging in some action. Thus, a cyclical relationship develops between what is felt, done, and subsequently experienced.

In keeping with the more popular version of social contructionism noted previously, theorists in this tradition usually posit a neurological substrate for emotional response that is wired into the organism and includes specific configurations of expressive motor behaviors corresponding to primary emotions (fear, anger, sadness, surprise, disgust, joy). However, constructivist thinkers do not limit their formulations of human emotion to this biological substrate or the primary emotions involved. Rather, the view holds that this basic neurological template becomes further elaborated in the human being into subtle blends of emotional experience (love, pride, envy, humility, and so forth). In this way, we respond to the environment immediately and reflexively, making perceptual-motor appraisals related to our biological and psychological survival. This constant appraisal process increases in sophistication as we mature and develop emotional memory networks consisting of many, many images of things in our environments, combined with the accompanying physiological responses, our affective and motor responses, and the conceptual appraisals we make of these images and events.

If we attend to or generate information that matches one of the components of our network, other associated components likely become activated. An emotion prototype or network, as Lang (1983) terms it, automatically activates if we attend to stimuli matching sufficient coded information in our prototype. The experience of emotion thus reflects the activation of a cognitive-affective network. Emotional experience in the constructionist approach becomes complicated by ongoing learning and assessment. We may then modify not only how we show emotion but also how we experience feelings. Further, an emotion prototype could involve expectations for outcomes in an emotion-eliciting situation, including interpersonal ones. Constructionists propose that these shaped emotional and interpersonal experiences actually alter the social context in which they emerge. To illustrate this complex phenomenon using anger, we gradually come to experience intricately blended forms of this emotion over time as it becomes associated with power, shame, yearning, or satisfaction. Our metaemotional experiences become rich mosaics of learning wherein anger automatically evokes such concomitant states as disgust with self, fear of detection and reprisal by another, or, conversely, a sense of urgency in communication to the target—depending upon the kinds of situations we experience and appraisals we make over time.

In speaking of the effects of socialization on emotion, literally hundreds of studies could be cited giving specific examples of how family, friends, neighbors, teachers, coworkers, the media, and our various in-groups and out-groups shape our expressions and experiences of emotion. Many of these receive consideration as we progress through our discussion. The processes involved are largely learned (consciously or unconsciously); we observe, model, get rewarded and punished, develop patterns of appraisal and attribution, and so forth.

Moving from social constructionism to a still broader perspective, the reasons for considering emotion in cross-cultural study encompass at least four different goals (Schweder, 1993), each of which can help frame extant research in anger-socialization terms. First, determining the generic shape of the meaning system that defines an experience as emotional facilitates our understanding of what constitutes anger. Second, exploring which particular emotional meanings are constructed in different ethnic groups and regions of the world contributes to our theorizing about which aspects of emotion are most subject to cultural training, and thus most likely to appear in some socialized form. Third, in determining the extent to which the experience of various states are "emotionalized" versus "somaticized," and in which ethnic groups or regions of the world this happens, we develop a further refined perspective on the ways in which emotion socialization takes place, and the forms in which it manifests. Finally, further elaborating upon emotionalized and somaticized meanings in various groups advances our specific knowledge about the vehicles transporting this kind of information to individuals, shaping the meanings they make of everyday encounters with feeling. Herein, we learn about which emotions are appropriate for which circumstances, and how they are to be controlled and modified (Oatley, 1993).

White, Western, Male Bias

Much of the current research and theorizing on emotions is thought to be limited by a largely White, male, and American/European bias. The nature and effects of this bias are now moderately well articulated. For example, dialogue such as that by Miller and Surrey (1990) provides strong argument for studying women's anger using qualitative designs and settings. Although studying gender differences in experimental or naturalistic designs helps to clarify some emotion-related issues, taking soundings from deep within a woman's lived experience furnishes much more in the way of texture and meaning. This format allows individual women to give voice to their own detailed and contextualized experiences, using the language that best fits their articulation of them. This language then can be used to reformulate existing theory for purposes of creating instrumentation that fits with diverse women's experiences.

Concepts such as "happy" or "angry" are not universal but seem to be cultural artifacts of Anglo culture reflected in, and continually fortified by, the English language (Weirzbicka, 1994). The set of labels available for describing emotion in any given language reflects a culture's unique outlook on people's feelings. These culturally specific labels also reflect a group's notions of connection between feelings, thought, morals, and social interaction. Weirzbicka gives a detailed analysis of cultural differences in how language is used to describe feelings and sensations. For example, American ideals regarding emotional expression in general are summarized beautifully. She concisely encapsulates the Anglo American perspective, which encourages people "to feel something good all the time, to be aware of what they feel at any given moment, to be able to analyze and verbalize their feelings, to control their feelings and thus to prevent themselves from feeling something bad for a long time, to think before saying something to someone when the thing one wants to say could cause the addressee to feel something bad, to separate the expression of one's opinions from any expression of feelings, to behave as though one felt something good all of the time (or most of the time) and so on" (p. 190). This dominant script for social behavior affects men, women, boys, and girls from both majority and minority groups in the United States. To the degree that such a narrative is internalized and important to the self, it serves as a standard against which a person's emotional reactions and expressions are evaluated—for self or others.

For the moment, note the discrepancy between knowing what one feels all the time and always feeling something positive. We could speculate that this double-bind situation sets the stage for many, if not most, individuals' hostage status in relation to unreasonable emotional standards—and the coupling of this with a requirement to notice, but also to alter, what feelings are there. For women, this emerges as a constant tension between the self-awareness so central to feminine emotional development and self-denial. What there is to be realized often disrupts internal self-portrayals, resulting in a kind of split-off experience.

Labouvie-Vief, Orwoll, and Manion (1995) provide an insightful analysis of the historical Western narratives of mind and gender, noting that traditional rationalistic theories of mind not only seperate body (including emotion and passion) and mind but see mind as split between the objective or rational and the subjective or psychological. These dualities have taken on gendered aspects, with male development associated with "the heroic journey of . . . rise, victory, and ascent to height, mind, and spirit" and feminine development associated with "defeat, passivity, surrender, and descent to organismic depths" (p. 239). The authors argue that these Western narrative structures have fundamentally influenced models (theory, research paradigms) of development as well as shaped core experiences for individuals. They also note that recent trends to challenge these traditional views may be leading to a more integrated, balanced perspective in which developmental maturity could be defined by restructuring dualities to reintegrate parts of the self that were, in a sense, abandoned.

Similarly, Sabini and Schulkin (1994) remind us that we need not choose between biological and social-constructionist realities in conceptualizing emotion. In other words, emotion can be both socially constructed and grounded in nature. Their fundamental point is that the cause of humans evolving in their emotional expression have to do with carrying out practical, social interactions that promote survival. Therefore, it is practical to assume that anger, in all its varied and elusive forms, serves some important roles in these social interactions and that we could predict problematic outcomes associated with the previously mentioned cultural push-pull around its full acknowledgment. Perhaps too, this tension around anger contributes something meaningful to the surrounding social process, however subversive its effects.

Notably, we find very limited research specific to emotional development, experience, or expression in African American, Hispanic, or other ethnic minority populations within the United States. The points raised by Barbarin (1993) in his review of the emotional and social development of African American children are a rare exception. He contrasts the extensive evidence of high rates of emotional disturbance in African American children with the dearth of information regarding what would constitute positive emotional development within this ethnic group. Barbarin clearly implicates the devastating convergence of economic disadvantage, limited access to support services, and social oppression within the interlocking systems of family, schools, and community in the etiology of these problems. He also cites recent research that supports the incorporation of an Afro-cultural identity in African American children as a key factor in their positive emotional adjustment.

In one other recent example, Gross and John (1998) find that within their five facets of emotional expressivity, differences between White American and Asian American participants emerge in three domains. Asian Americans report more masking of their feelings, weaker emotional impulses, and less expressive confidence than do Whites. The authors hypothesize that these differences reflect socialized aspects of emotional experience and expression.

Cultural Rules for Expressing and Experiencing Emotions

If the focus of emotion study shifts to broader cultural dimensions (e.g., individualistic versus collectivist cultures) or to the cross-cultural study of emotion (between countries or nation-states, rather than within one country), much more information becomes available. In general, culture impacts emotions by determining not only how they are expressed but often how they are felt as well (McConatha, Lightner, & Deaner, 1994; Sommers, 1984). As one example, in Sommers' work, the four cultures she studies (Americans, Greeks, West Indians, and Chinese) agree that hate, terror, and rage are the most negative and potentially destructive emotions but vary in their attitudes towards spontaneous expression of these and many other emotions.

Emotions seem to play different roles in peoples' lives, depending upon their cultural heritage and world view. Triandis (1994) summarizes a large body of work regarding emotion in individualist and collectivist cultures. He speculates that in collectivist cultures there is more emphasis on emotions that are attached to group membership, group-linked success, or other-focus [heightened attunement to needs and feelings of others] such as empathy or a sense of indebtedness. Positive emotions are felt if people cooperate and promote group nurturance and order. In contrast, people in individualistic countries more likely focus on self-related emotions, such as anger and happiness. People in individualist cultures more likely feel good about being alone and feel positive emotions if in a position that highlights them as unique. Therefore, we could expect that anger, in collectivist cultures, is experienced if group norms are violated or group goals are blocked. Individualistic cultures more likely see anger coming from a wider variety of circumstances and experienced as more self defining. Women in the United States who have an autonomy-centered world view likely experience anger differently from women who hold a more collectivist world view, regardless of where they live. Among individualist nations, emotions better predict life satisfaction than do norms (others' collective views of what is desirable); norms and emotions predict life satisfaction equally in collectivist cultures (Suh, Diener, Oishi, & Triandis, 1998). Thus, Suh and colleagues note an important point: The meanings attached to feeling states can vary cross-culturally. Though the eliciting circumstances are the same, culture may dictate how, and to what extent, emotions affect a person's life.

Individual Differences

Although culture and biology may provide broad-based understandings of emotion, it is still true that each person remains a unique individual, and variations in the experience of and expression of emotion occur because of individual differences in personality, temperament, attachment, and experiences. Some recent research efforts have been directed at understanding the relationship of such individual difference variables to affect. For example, Gross and John (1997) studied individual differences in emotional expressivity. These authors note that such individual differences may arise from the variation in individuals' day-to-day experiences or immediate situations ("inputs" to their "emotion programs"), from unique appraisals, from personality traits, or from temperamental differences in the activation of emotional thresholds. Subsequent expressions of emotion may be modulated to conform to cultural display rules or for personal reasons.

In follow-up work, Gross and John (1998) integrate current findings to reveal a hierarchical map of individual differences in emotional expressivity. Five facets of expressivity were found: (a) expressive confidence, (b) masking, (c) positive expressivity, (d) negative expressivity, and (e) impulse intensity. People high in expressive confidence show positive self-esteem and less depression and are described by these authors as "resilient undercontrollers." Those high in masking make habitual attempts to cover their true feelings and also show higher levels of neuroticism, lower agreeableness, and lower conscientiousness. These people tend to think that expressing negative emotion is socially unacceptable but also tend to view themselves more negatively as well as more depressed. People who show higher levels of positive expressivity also tend to be more extraverted and seem to spontaneously express positive emotions. Conversely, those higher in negative expressivity seem to spontaneously express negative emotion but also are aware and concerned about how this makes others think of them. Finally, emotional expressivity refers to the potency of a person's emotional impulses and shows positive relationships with agreeableness and private self-consciousness in this sample. All of these facets reflect differences that occur among individuals, highlighting the complexity of emotional development across individuals and groups.

Schimmack and Diener (1997) identify affect intensity as an individual difference variable. People high in affect intensity experience both positive and negative emotions more strongly than persons low in affect intensity. Also, people who rate goals and outcomes as more personally salient tend to experience more intense affect. The stronger they feel it, the more important it likely is to them. This point is important to a discussion of women's anger in its suggestion that although certain levels or intensities of anger become pathologized, we could speculate about those "out of control," or "out of proportion," anger experiences as reflective of the (albeit perceived) critical nature of events involved in their production. Rather than being diagnostic, the experience of chronic or "unreasonable" anger flares could signal the weight of the occurrence for a person. Further, people who repress seem to consciously experience less negative affect than those who do not. Schimmack and Hartmann (1997), in studying the influence of individual differences in repressive coping style on the availability and accessibility of emotion memories, find that repressors estimate the frequency of unpleasant emotions to be smaller than do other groups. They conclude that a repressive coping style influences mainly the experience of emotions, rather than the accessibility of emotional memories.

In a related vein, King (1998) finds that some individuals are ambivalent over emotional expression, meaning that they feel conflicted about whether or not to express their emotions. They may regret expressing emotion after the fact or regret inhibiting the display of emotion. Individuals high in emotional ambivalence also report confusion in reading the emotions of others and may even infer the opposite emotions of those conveyed by simple emotional scenes and facial displays. So it may be conjectured that disturbances in clear expression of felt experience have some linkage with blocked ability to decode emotional material coming from others.

Self-monitoring, or guarding and continuously analyzing one's emotional expression, becomes involved in this process of responding to emotional cues. Graziano and Bryant (1998) find differences in high and low self-monitoring individuals in their use of internal versus external cues for making attributions about their own emotions. High self-monitoring individuals rely more on situational cues to guide their evaluations of their emotions; low self-monitoring individuals rely more on their own immediate, internal reactions. Again, there seems to be a link between the ability to use spontaneous feeling material as it occurs and a kind of clarity about one's feelings. Clarity and ownership of felt experience propagates clarity in reading others' affective displays and in expressing one's own.

Phenomenological Experience

Little is available in the way of research or theory on our phenomenological experience of emotion. Paradoxically, a great deal of what is written about emotion is based on people's reports of their own feeling experiences. Writings on emotion and culture come close to illuminating people's experience of emotion, for example, by bringing to light the different ways in which language is used to express emotion and in discussions about the degree of somaticization experienced in relation to emotion. Physiological studies of emotion tap into the body's degree and types of arousal, establish relationships between hormones, neurotransmitters, and emotional responses, and tell us what areas of the brain are activated by different emotions. Cognitive theories help us to understand the role of such constructs as schemas and appraisal in emotional processes. Humanistic and existential theories of psychotherapy claim that emotions are to be valued as an integral aspect of human experience. Yet none of these perspectives depict the individual's subjective experience of emotion nor allow for knowing what another feels, or even knowing what one feels oneself, or just actually feeling.

Perhaps the closest we come to grasping the human anger experience in emotion research is through qualitative interviewing, listening to people tell the stories of their own emotional lives, furnishing the richness of personal meaning to the events called "feelings." The closest we approach phenomenology of feeling in this book is when women share with us, in their own words, their emotional experiences and, at times, inner feelings (through journal excerpts, for example). Even this dialogue, however, remains one step removed from the ongoing experiential stream of emotional response for an individual. Words, although allowing for meaning exchange at some levels, leave much in the way of meaning essence behind. Pure physiological measures also fail to capture the cultural, social, and individual meanings that make emotion more than just a visceral response. Averill (1997) suggests that much art, music, and poetry can be viewed as attempts to put emotional experiences into verbal or other symbolic forms. However, we leave this section with the conclusion that an individual's phenomenological experience of emotion is fundamentally unknowable to another person, and, at best, can be expressed imperfectly only by that individual to another, or even perhaps to herself or himself.

☐ Three Major Integrative Models of Emotion

Having discussed numerous components of emotion, we turn now to three theories that have synthesized some, most, or all of these components into an integrated whole. These models reflect the work of some of the current major theorists in the field of emotion.

Lazarus

Lazarus' (1991) theory of emotion includes relational, motivational and cognitive elements, combining several issues discussed thus far. Emotions always involve person-environment relationships that present potential harms or benefits to the individual, and thus, in our view, an opportunity for self-definition. We experience motivation as acute emotions or "moods," which are reactions to the status of goals in everyday encounters. So, feeling happens in response to the possibility that we will lose or gain something meaningful and gives rise to the urge to self-define by fighting for a certain meaningful outcome.

"Cognitive" in this model refers to knowledge and appraisal of what is happening in a person's adaptational encounters. Lazarus (1991) discusses emotion in terms of its divergence from innate reflexes. He suggests that higher-order species evolve toward less dependence upon reflexive, physiological activities, even though these processes underlie the development of emotion (e.g., startle response). Human emotion intertwines with complex social structures and meanings, making our evaluation of these meanings adaptive. By extension, to know, to perceive one's needs accurately, to discern a difference between what is going on in the socioemotional field and what is wanted or needed, and to feel appropriately frustrated or angry with the circumstances constitute adjustment.

A set of core assumptions forms the basis of Lazarus' (1991) theory. These core assumptions are vitally important in our study of anger and have much to say about how we experience and cope with anger. First, each emotion involves its own innate action tendency (Frijda, Kuipers, & ter Schure, 1989). In anger, the action tendency is "attack," but attack can be inhibited or transformed into something else entirely (e.g., emotional numbing and withdrawal). The snuffing out or reshaping of the anger attack response occurs if we perceive that we cannot effect change in our immediate circumstance or we see ourselves as powerless in some other way.

Second, according to this model, each emotion has its own pattern of physiological changes, such as increased heart rate, blood pressure, and periperal blood flow in anger (Levenson, 1988, 1992). A good deal of accumulated evidence now shows that at least where very strong, basic emotions such as fear and anger are concerned, specific ANS patterns for discrete emotions can be identified. In his extensive review of ANS differences among emotions, Levenson (1992) cites (in addition to his own results) 10 studies that support heart-rate acceleration during anger, 20 studies that support heart rate acceleration during fear, four studies supporting heart rate acceleration during sadness, and five studies showing heart rate deceleration during disgust. Additionally, in distinguishing between fear and anger, 15 studies show a differential pattern between these two emotions, with fear linked to lower diastolic blood pressure, cooler surface temperatures, greater vasoconstriction, and lesser blood flow in the periphery than anger. These patterns of response fit with an interpretation that anger is closely associated with an action tendency to "fight," while fear is associated with an action tendency to "flight."

Third, the action tendency in each emotional experience provokes a psychophysiological response pattern to prepare the organism to act upon the person-environment relationship for purposes of creating change. In other words, without some kind of appraisal, no emotion occurs. Further, without the appraisal of a personal stake in a situation, no emotion occurs. Taking stock of these individual concerns happens via primary appraisal, a relatively straightforward concept encompassing our ongoing (possibly unconscious) assessment of what is going on around us and how our needs and wants figure into those happenings. The more complicated secondary appraisal concerns what resources and options one has available for coping and also has to do with the assignment of "blame" or "credit" in a situation, whether directed at self or others.

Secondary appraisal includes an internal assessment of one's coping potential and future expectations in the situation. Interdependence exists among attribution, knowledge, and appraisal. That is, each piece of one's knowledge (overt or covert) about a particular scenario feeds into the next piece by offering meaning; "Who's right?" "Who's wrong?" "What do I need here?" Whether blame or credit becomes directed internally or externally influences one's experience of anger, guilt, shame, or pride. As mentioned previously, attributions and future expectations have impact on the way one handles the feeling (whether or not one experiences some degree of influence or control and whether or not one expects things to get better or worse). Expecting that one cannot change an unhappy situation can foster a decrease in one's ability to cope (Lazarus, 1991). The model suggests that the behavioral flow between cognition and emotion goes both ways, so not only does thinking influence how we feel, but how we feel influences how we think about situations, that is, our appraisals. Lazarus' theory allows room for the notion that emotions may begin as physiological reflexive responses in infancy and constantly grow in complexity, sophistication, and breadth of possibilities for evoking stimuli as the individual matures. In other words, perhaps the emotion and cognition flow goes back and forth throughout a person's emotional development. So, according to this conceptualization, it is fair to speculate that we somehow alter our anger experiences in light of the likelihood that we can actually have an instrumental impact on things. If we perceive that we cannot act in our own best interests, we may stop experiencing the sharp, clear signals of anger and instead experience our anger as redirected, muffled, or disowned. Lazarus also suggests that cognition continues into the response state. So, instead of the usual separation between thinking and feeling, cognition and emotion may represent points along a continuum, versus discreet psychological entities. This notion runs parallel to the idea of altered anger experience and opens the door to our consideration of socialized anger, as it suggests that the ways in which we "manage" anger have transformational properties.

Mayer, Salovey, Gomberg-Kaufman, and Blainey (1991) include "management-related processes" in their definition of mood to highlight a similar idea, that is, that what we do to the feeling in our attempts at coping with it make up the gestalt of our overall emotional state—suggesting it would be difficult to know the difference between "what I feel" and "what I'm supposed to feel—or at least what I let others know that I feel."

At some point, for some people, it becomes virtually impossible to tease those apart. Coping, in Lazarus' (1991) view, makes up the psychological analogue of action tendencies, a rather complex, deliberate, and planful set of behaviors that follow emotion. Coping not only follows emotion, it shapes subsequent emotion, a direction of effect that Lazarus says has been underemphasized in traditional coping theory. Such a notion of coping appears to be a recursive process based on an individual's ability to self-reference, acquiring insight about one's internal and external behavior and how they are received by others.

Problem-focused coping likely entails a plan of action for changing the person-environment relationship in some way, according to Lazarus' (1991) model. On the other hand, emotion-focused coping attempts to alter the contents of one's mind through avoidance, denial, or distancing and could be called "cognitive coping." Again, Lazarus emphasizes that the driver of such coping is appraisal, as emotion is a reaction to meaning. His theory makes room for consideration of humans' responses to their own emotions, or metaemotion, a phenomenon we speculate to be central to anger socialization. The more we experience our own adverse reactions to our anger responses (i.e., shame, guilt, or hopelessness), the more seasoned our future anger becomes. The patina that forms in and around our memories of being angry and having either instrumental, positive outcomes or defeating, disempowering ones causes a particular look and feel to evolve along the internal surfaces and crevices of our anger, transforming the ways in which we experience it.

Markus and Kitayama

Markus and Kitayama (1994), in the summary chapter of their book on emotion and culture, present an integrated model for understanding the cultural shaping of emotion (see Figure 1). The model may be considered integrative because it synthesizes cultural, sociopsychological, and individual subjective and behavioral aspects of emotion and also acknowledges physiological processes.

The model complements our present discussion as it casts clarifying light, by extension, on the cultures in which anger socialization emerges, metamorphosizing individuals' experience and use of anger for self-definition and empowerment, or for self-reproach and social control. The dotted lines in the figure are meant to reflect Markus and Kitayama's (1994) view that the boundaries between self and society, between inner and outer, are blurred. The components of the models show interdependence, being "telescoped" within each other as well as related through the pro-

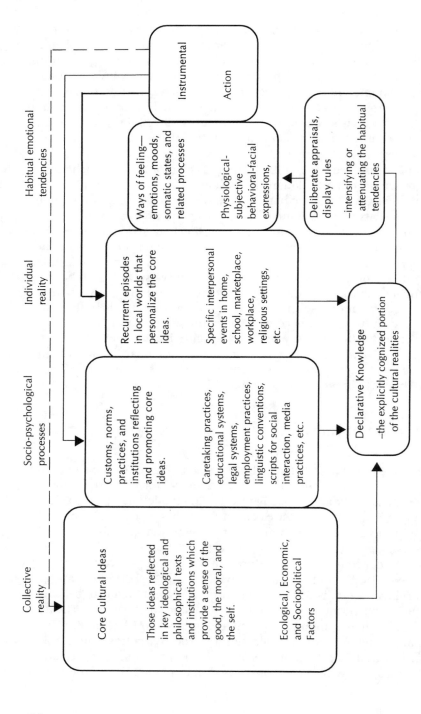

FIGURE 1. The cultural shaping of emotion. Adapted with permission of the American Psychological Association. Copyright 1994, from Markus, H. R., and Kitayama, S., "The Cultural Shaping of Emotion: A Conceptual Framework" (p. 342) in S. Kitayama and H. R. Markus (Eds.), *Emotion and Culture: Empirical Studies of Mutual Influence.*

cesses indicated by the solid and dotted arrows. The shading on the figure indicates individuals' potential effects on both their immediate social reality and on the realities of their cultural group (upper half, white); the bottom half (gray) refers to self and collective knowledges that become encoded in memory and may or may not be available for conscious evaluation.

Each of the four major components of the model is described here. First, core cultural ideas influence collective realities by constraining and supporting particular, culture-specific sets of everyday ways of thinking, acting, and feeling. These are the aspects of life, such as definitions of identity, what is good, and what is right, that are developed over time in a particular cultural group. This core collective reality is shaped by broad historical, economic, sociopolitical, and ecological factors. Core cultural ideas are often so pervasive as to be taken for granted or "invisible"; that is, many or even most people in a particular culture may not be able to articulate these underlying assumptions, even though they are affected by them. For instance, in Western European cultures, ideology concerning parents' authority to dictate their children's emotional and affective displays lingers below the surface of conscious awareness for many people, much of the time. Some members of a society may have the cultural expertise to identify and understand these deeply embedded aspects of their own culture, but each individual in the culture need not be consciously aware of these elements. In the United States, many people feel it is their personal right to pursue the livelihood and lifestyle of their choice, without having any explicit knowledge of the Declaration of Independence or the Bill of Rights (outside, perhaps, of knowing these documents exist). Such ideas lurk collectively in the unconscious life of a group of people, quietly affecting their relationships with one another, their choices and lifestyles, and their emotional awarenesses.

Second, social-psychological processes include language customs, practices of socialization or training, implied "scripts" that dictate how we are to behave in most situations, and educational, religious, and media customs. These develop out of core collective ideas, transmit them, and shape the social settings in which individual realities (the third component) take place. These social-pyschological processes, although existing independently of any one person's actions, thoughts, or feelings, are "made possible and real by each participating individual's social behavior" (p. 341). For example, each time a woman looks down at the sidewalk, allowing an approaching man to study her without the responsibility that comes with being observed, she unconsciously participates in the place setting embedded in such a situation. Herein, the two parties involved reflexively reinforce their own adherence to the tacit agreement that men will gaze directly at women if they so wish, and women will protect themselves from

the power differentials embedded in such situations by moving their attentions elsewhere. A silent agreement, or social contract, is signed.

The customs and norms that constitute sociopsychological processes
are transmitted through diverse mechanisms, including caretaking and
schooling practices, social scripts for behavior, and language. In each language, there are lexical constructions and specific emotion vocabularies
that reflect core collective ideas. Different cultures use different words to
identify, constrain, highlight, or elaborate emotions as construed in that
culture. For example, Wierzbicka (1994, p. 148) cites recent work by
Bugenhagen (1990) on emotion words in the Austronesian language
Mangap-Mbula, in which "images involving liver are used for talking about
all kinds of feelings." If angry, the liver fights (*kete-(i)malmal*). If very angry, the liver is hot (*kete-(i)bayou*). If uncontrollably angry, the liver swirls
(*kete-(i)beleu*). In some subgroups of U.S. culture, getting "too big for one's
britches" or needing to be "taken down a notch" signify assertiveness that
brings with it too much empowerment to be tolerated by the immediate
social encirclement.

The third component, that of individual realities, or one's "local
world," include the usually familiar and repetitive specific, interpersonal
events that occur in one's home, school, workplace, community, and so
forth. For example, American parents may routinely ask their children,
"Did you have fun in school today?" reinforcing the desirablility of positive emotion in U.S. culture. Markus and Kitayama (1994) see individual
realities as personalizing the core ideas embedded in the first and second
components of the model. Variables such as gender, age, religion, ethnic
group, generation, and region of the country, as well as overarching cultural values and practices, all affect personal realities. The social conventions of one's immediate interpersonal settings thus strongly influence
emotional appraisal and expressive processes. Knowing we are expected
to enjoy ourselves and experience happiness at holidays or in social situations helps to hold in place our expectation that others enjoy themselves
too, and vice-versa.

Finally, a person's habitual emotional tendencies include the feelings and somatic experiences reflecting all of that person's physiological
responses and ongoing appraisals of happenings in the environment. We
get to observe these tendencies in facial expressions and gestures (e.g.,
grimacing, holding a blank stare), the most individualized expressions of
core cultural ideas. No two people have exactly the same emotional response to an event. According to Markus and Kitayama (1994), we develop a unique emotional experience (and thus our outward demonstration of it, however subtle to the outside observer) based upon our histories
of "emotional conditioning," or the cumulative impact of our attempts to
make meaning of what we feel, think, or want and how these fit into core

cultural ideas of which we are a part. We continuously participate in a conditioning process by experiencing and making sense of experience and responding to cultural cues, which at some point become indistinguishable from our own spontaneous reaction. Thus, the authors of this model see emotion as fully embedded in, not just influenced by, cultural institutions, ideas, and practices.

Averill

Averill's (1997) integrative model of emotion has five levels (see Figure 2) and corresponds with Markus and Kitayama's (1994) model in that it attends to the influence of sociocultural rules and mores on emotional experience. The levels interrelate, as indicated by the arrows on the graph. Although this serves as an excellent conceptual and organizational tool for understanding the various components of emotion, it should be noted that the levels and components interact in a dynamic, reciprocal way, allowing the individual to construct emotional meanings in an ongoing fashion. For example, Averill recognizes that one may act in a certain way as expected by social roles (level III) regardless of one's emotional state at the moment (level IV).

Level I, biological and social potentials, contains the genetic endowment of the species (reproductive capacities, attachment, and so forth) as well as social systems of behavior that reflect institutionalized patterns of socialization (customs, symbols). Level II, fundamental capacities and predispositions, includes temperament, broadly defined personality traits, emotional intelligence, and emotional creativity.

Level III can be thought of as comprising both social roles and specific psychological abilities. Social rules for emotion are included here, which govern what constitutes a particular emotion, as well as when and how that emotion is to be exhibited. Emotion roles are likewise a part of level III, these include privileges (special social circumstances or behaviors that are allowed in specific emotional states, such as when a person can yell in anger) and restrictions (social rules about what one cannot do related to specific emotional states, such as when one cannot yell in anger). Level III also includes obligations (things one must do related to certain emotions or risk strong social sanctions, such as when one must apologize) and entry requirements (who—as determined by gender, developmental level, class, occupation, or some other socially constructed variable) is allowed to express or act on specific emotional states. An entry requirement for expressing anger materializes in the level of intensity that an attorney or police officer is granted in arguing a case, apprehending a suspect, or facilitating some just outcome.

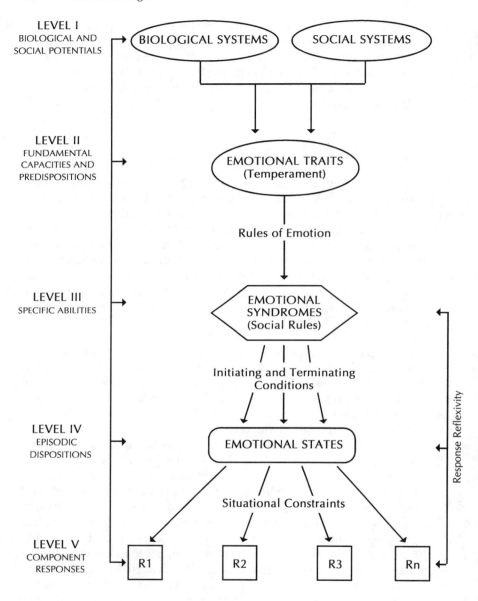

FIGURE 2. Averill's framework for the analysis of emotional behavior. Reprinted with the permissioin of Academic Press. Copyright 1997, from J. R. Averill, "The Emotions" (p. 522) in R. Hogan, J. Johnson, and S. Briggs (Eds.), *Handbook of Personality Psychology*.

Level IV, episodic dispositions, reflects a current emotional state, including cognitive elements such as attention, perception, language, and problem solving, as well as physiological arousal. Averill sees level V, component responses, as the most concrete of the five stages. These are aspects of emotion that are readily observable to others or often can be reported via self-observation. There are six component responses: cognitive appraisals, peripheral physiological changes, expressive reactions (e.g., what I am doing with my hands and voice), verbal behaviors, instrumental acts (what I am doing to change things), and feelings. Looking at anger through Averill's theoretical lens, it seems that people would most readily recount level V emotion, the most readily available aspects of the anger experience. In this way, emotion that resides on levels II, III, or IV may be easier to deny, distort, or ignore and may in fact be beyond many people's immediate awarenesses. Therefore, we could expect that if the most immediate or accessible sensation is a scripted or externally imposed social rule- or privilege-based expression of anger, its origin and point of distortion could be sealed from conscious awareness. To illustrate, the woman who expresses contempt for the kind of "in-your-face" self-expressions of anger she sees in radical feminists most likely does so at level V, safely away from the overt, recognizable concealment action of many sociocultural rules that feed her loathing for these images. She realizes only her distaste for other women who openly display outrage and demand that injustices be corrected. What she cannot clearly see are the ways in which these images become distasteful to her. Brown (1998) speaks of *ventriloquation*, a way of verbalizing, using other people's voices and words, in a nonconscious way, regarding conventional femininity. This ventriloquation, demonstrated by groups of girls with whom she engages in lengthy qualitative study, seems to emanate from larger social prescriptives for the girls' behavior. We can regard women's level V self- and other-referencing in much the same way as emotional policing moves from larger cultural expectations to microlevel recitations about the appropriateness of anger expression.

☐ Emotion as Viewed by Developmental Psychology

In Durkin's (1995) exceptional book on developmental social psychology, he notes that in general, traditional developmental theory may be criticized for its narrow focus on infancy, childhood, and adolescence (to the exclusion of adulthood), as well as an over-reliance on cognitive models. For example, he notes that emotions "remained peripheral" (p. 20) to

Piagetian theory, as well as to the work of many more contemporary cognitive developmentalists. Thus, if the early developmental psychology literature is examined, what emerges is a variety of research findings on the expression of emotion and on the recognition of emotion, but little linkage with formalized developmental theory.

This is changing, however, and can be seen most clearly in current models of attachment and of emotional regulation. Biological, social-learning, and cognitive-developmental theories all contribute to integrating the research findings. Biological models account for the cross-cultural consistency seen in infant emotional expression, as well as forming the basis for attachment. Social-learning theories (reinforcement, punishment, and modeling) help to describe the processes by which the socialized rules of emotional expression and response are acquired and maintained. Cognitive-developmental models further assist in our conceptualization by linking patterns of emotional expression, experience, and understanding with the emerging cognitive skills of infants, children, and adolescents. Abilities to differentiate self from other, to take another's perspective, or to reason hypothetically are clearly associated with changes in emotional understandings over time. As Thompson (1991, p. 270) succinctly summarizes, "Emotional arousal is regulated primarily by others early in life as caregivers monitor and regulate the baby's distress, promote positive affect, and direct the emergence of self-referent emotions. . . But emotional arousal becomes increasingly self-regulated as the result of neurophysiological development, the growth of cognitive and linguistic skills, and the emergence of emotional and self-understanding."

Emotional Development and Emotional Regulation

If we borrow sociocultural models of emotion to use as templates for understanding anger, our focus necessarily broadens to encompass the embeddedness of anger within a larger environment or stage. In this way, our focus rests upon the actors and the very obvious, visible ways in which they seem to affect each other's use of anger. This perspective becomes obvious in statements such as "women's anger is affected by social mandates" and "children learn about acceptable emotional expression from their parents' modeling, reinforcement, and overt teaching." But how does their choreography, the dance between the actors in this socioemotional scenario, happen to result in real intrapsychic change? Where is the vehicle for substantive alteration of one's emotional response, the parts of the person that move as directed, that take seriously these social demands and become qualitatively changed because of them? For these answers, we must look at developmental theory for close, "between the lines" scrutiny that reveals the substances binding together large-scale, external events with microlevel, internal, largely unconscious shifts and balances that culminate in something obvious, like a silent snowstorm dramatically changing our panorama through the night.

In this section, we briefly trace the developmental course of emotional display and expression, as well as the interrelated concept of emotional regulation. Thompson (1991, p. 271) defines emotional regulation as "the extrinsic and intrinsic processes responsible for monitoring, evaluating, and modifying emotional reactions, especially their intensive and temporal features." In her discussion of the socialization of emotion, Saarni (1993) lists five elements of emotion that are socialized over time: emotional elicitors, emotional receptors, emotional states, emotional expressions, and emotional experiences. All these aspects are seen as embedded in learned, cultural scripts, acquired through the mechanisms of direct instruction, contingency learning, identification with role models, imitation, and communication of expectancies. These cultural scripts include "folk theories" of emotion, or our tacitly acquired rules that govern interactions between people and help us to understand them. These perspectives implicitly acknowledge that emotions are both regulated and regulatory (Campos et al., 1994). The next question becomes, "What do we know about how these processes develop?"

Beginning in infancy, nonverbal expressions are thought to be reflective of emotional states, and to have survival value. Smiling and crying are the two primary ways in which infants communicate this basic positive/negative emotional dimension. These fundamental affect displays are thought to be largely innate and reflected in cross-culturally recognizable facial displays in infancy (Izard, 1994; Izard & Malatesta, 1987). Recent evidence also shows that positive displays may be more consistently recognizable than negative expressions (Oster, Hegley, & Nagel, 1992). Perhaps positive displays are more consistently reinforced than negative expressions (at least in American culture). According to Lewis (1993), infants may have a variety of emotional states, and parents say they can recognize these states in the earliest months of their children's lives; indeed, different emotional expressions can be readily seen in infancy. However, Lewis argues that infants do not experience their emotions, in the sense of being self-aware of these states, until roughly the second half of the second year of life.

Infants can self-soothe to a minimal extent by sucking, rocking, or visual avoiding but must count on adults to remove sources of distress if emotional arousal is high or otherwise uncontrollable. Adults may accomplish this via direct interventions such as cuddling, giving toys, or pacifiers. These earliest parental interventions also serve to begin the learning process, through selective reinforcement and modeling, concerning emotion, its expression, and strategies for regulation of affect (Thompson, 1991).

As the infant develops, socialization experiences begin to further shape the expression of emotion. Display rules begin to be learned regarding what emotions to display, at what level, to whom, and in which situations. Lewis (1993) believes that very early in life, emotional states and emotional expressions are likely to be congruent. However, by about the second year, "children very quickly learn to dissociate expression from internal states" (p. 231). In other words, by age 2 years, a child can, to a certain extent, mask his or her emotional displays and perhaps even generate chosen emotional displays in order to make desired shifts in her or his social environment. Masking becomes significant later in our discussion of socialized anger as we try to account for the rift that often separates a person's core emotional experience from his or her visible behavior, as well as between that core experience and more surface awareness.

Malatesta-Magai (1991) reports that in the first year of life, positive displays increase in frequency, followed by the development of facial expressions that regulate negative emotion in the second year. In the third year, there seems to be a general decrease in the intensity with which emotional behaviors are displayed. Indeed, the socialization process seems to be one of increasing control over emotional display (Camras, Malatesta, & Izard, 1991). Thompson (1991) notes that parental approaches to emotional regulation become more multifaceted and emotion-specific and start to include explicit verbal instructions. This lattermost development obviously is tied to the child's emerging language abilities. Once children begin to grasp language, parents can directly give them instructions, threats, warnings, and so forth. Emotions now can be explained and interpreted, specific strategies can be taught verbally, and children can learn about emotion from overhearing the conversations parents have about their own emotions. Children begin to develop a conceptual network of emotion-related terms and ideas, including an understanding of emotional situations in terms of causality and consequences (Denham, Zoller, & Couchoud, 1994; Dunn & Brown, 1994). These researchers also find clear links between cognitive-language ability and emotion understanding.

Lewis (1993) notes that primary emotions such as joy, surprise, sadness, disgust, fear, and anger are seen in the first 6 months of infancy. In the second half of the second year, with the attainment of self-awareness, young children develop the experience of self-conscious emotions: embarrassment, empathy, and envy. Slightly later (around age 3), as the child develops an ability to evaluate himself or herself against a standard (such as parental guidelines), the "self-conscious evaluative" (p. 234) emotions arise: pride, shame, regret, and guilt. Again, we speculate that some metaemotional process does the work of adding a new layer of feeling to that already in place. For example, we learn to be embarrassed about or feel shame regarding not only what we do but, often, what we feel.

Throughout early development, infants and children learn about emotion via what Thompson (1991) calls "affective induction," or exposure to caregivers' own emotional tone and reactions. These cues may accentuate, dampen, redirect, or delay the child's emotional behaviors. Children also use social referencing to understand emotion. Social referencing is when children look to adults, siblings, or peers to gain information about unfamiliar or ambiguous situations. Social referencing appears as early as 12 months and is evident thereafter (Klinnert, Campos, Sorce, Emde, & Svejda, 1980; Walden, 1991).

Children perform increasingly well with age if asked to produce particular emotion displays (Field & Walden, 1982), and the ability to control and master such productions appears to develop over the span of middle childhood (Saarni, 1989). Durkin (1995) notes that these developments parallel childrens' increasing abilities in perspective taking, as well as in fine facial muscle control. In particular, children learn to produce an expression that is socially desirable for a particular context (Masters, 1991). Children also become better at decoding others' emotions over time, as they develop the ability to abstract others' feelings from their own emotional experience (Harris, 1989). Thus, social-cognitve development parallels (and is inextricably interwoven with) children's experience of and understanding of emotion and emotion-related behaviors in self and others. Strategies for emotional self-regulation (versus dependence on caregivers and others) expand significantly in complexity and size during middle childhood (Thompson, 1991). Children begin to master such skills as internal emotional redirection, redirecting attention, deliberate distraction, changing emotion by focusing on rewards and consequences, reframing situations, or acting in ways that provoke different emotions. Again, this close perspective adds depth to positions taken by Markus and Kitayama (1994), Lazarus (1991), and Averill (1997), who all attend in some way to the complex interplay between person and environment in learning emotional response regulation.

Throughout development, emotions are also regulated by control of opportunity (Thompson, 1991). *Control of opportunity* refers to the manipulation of the physical or interpersonal environment to influence the frequency, duration, or intensity of emotion. The degree of control that a parent, child, adolescent, or adult may have can vary depending on the family's socioeconomic circumstances, their child-rearing values, their cultural values, and the physical ecology of the home itself (e.g., it would be difficult to choose withdrawal as a way to cope with negative emotion if the entire family lives in one room). Thompson notes that control of opportunity is a life-long emotional regulation strategy, but that it becomes increasingly under self-control with maturity. Adults typically have greater control over their physical environments, schedules, and relationships than do children and adolescents.

To the degree (which is debated; see Durkin, 1995) that adolescence is experienced as a sexual awakening, a period of stress and storm, of identity crisis, of increased peer influence, and of parental conflict, it certainly would seem to afford numerous opportunities for emotional exchange and growth. Thompson (1991, p. 293) sees the major aspect of emotional regulation in adolescence as one of developing a theory of personal emotion—"an understanding of how emotion functions and is managed within oneself." This personal theory is thought to be a consolidation of self-referent beliefs and to constitute an aspect of the self-schema. It is based on the increasingly complex, differentiated, yet integrated developmental aspects of emotional regulation reviewed in the previous few pages.

Other developmental researchers note that as both boys and girls physically mature in adolescence, the frequency of expression of negative affect by both mothers and fathers rises (Montemayor, Eberly, & Flannery, 1993), as does adolescent expression of negative affect, especially toward mothers. We speculate that as self-definitional processes emerge in adolescents' behavior, unconscious efforts to control or shape those processes simultaneously emerge in parents' behavior. Parental expectations about emotional changes, as their children reach puberty, also may play a role in adolescent emotionality (Freedman-Doan, Arbreton, Harold, & Eccles, 1993). This study shows that parents who believe that they are influential in their childrens' lives and who report having positive relationships with their children have less concern that their children will get into trouble in adolescence. However, fathers expect their children to become more moody and emotional after reaching puberty, a phenomenon that can become self-fulfilling prophecy, suggest the authors.

Stapely and Haviland (1989) discovered that in self-reports of emotional experience, adolescents of both sexes and at all ages find the positive emotions of joy and interest to be most salient. In their research, anger is the most salient negative emotion. Gender differences emerge in that surprise, shyness, shame, guilt, sadness, and self-hostility are more often reported by girls and contempt more often reported by boys. Girls report these emotions to occur in relationships more often than boys; boys cite school, sports, and hobbies to be strongly associated with emotions. The authors report that adolescent boys also deny having memory of emotional experiences to a greater extent than do girls. It seems that gender-role socialization factors are well entrenched by this point (Stapely and Haviland interviewed fifth, seventh, ninth, and 11th graders). In keeping with this explanation, Sayfer and Hauser (1994) also report that adolescent girls express both more sadness and more affection than adolescent boys. Early adolescent girls often show themselves to be more at risk for depression than boys (Kenny, Moilanen, Lomax, & Brabeck, 1993; Nolen-Hoeksema, 1987).

A number of researchers note that a secure attachment base between parent and adolescent is crucial if teens are to successfully cope with the emotion-provoking challenges of adolescence (Blechman & Culhane, 1993; Cooper, Shaver, & Collins, 1998; Kenny et al., 1993; Liddle, 1994). A family atmosphere that is emotionally competent and positive can shield adolescents from deleterious life events, risks, and affective negativity. Similarly, McDonough, Carlson, and Cooper (1994) find that in families with early adolescents, more individuated (free of excessive negative emotional reactivity) spousal units are associated with more positive affective tone, better conflict resolution, lower hostility and cynicism, and greater optimization of individual development within family relationships. Likewise, Bronstein, Fitzgerald, Briones, Peiniadz, and D'Ari (1993) find that non-hostile expression of emotion within families appears to provide a buffer against psychological problems in adolescents, and to be associated with popularity and positive self-esteem (for girls) and positive social behavior (for boys). Parents' and childrens' levels of emotional expression relate highly, suggesting that parents model a level of emotional expressiveness that they support or allow in their adolescents.

On the other hand, "negative emotion" (defined variously) within the family has been consistenly linked with problem behaviors in adolescents. Negative emotion within the family detours problem solving by eroding relationships, creating less motivation to work on solutions, and impairing ability to focus on solutions (Liddle, 1994). Insecurely attached adolescents often react to events with sad (more often girls) or angry (more often boys) affect, even if the events are controllable (Blechman & Culhane, 1993). These negative emotional coping styles also affect peer relationships unfavorably, engendering rejection, loneliness, and poor self-esteem. Similar trends are described by Cooper et al. (1998), who find that adolescents with anxious-ambivalent attachment styles are the most poorly adjusted (compared with those with secure and avoidant styles), with high levels of psychological symptoms, poor self-concepts, and high levels of risky or problem behaviors. These anxious-ambivalent adolescents report experiencing high levels of negative affect, particularly hostility. We further speculate that the interfering negative affect has more to do with unresolved anger, or projecting, blaming anger, than with the experience of difficult feelings per se, a piece of the emotional development picture that deserves more specific address in future research.

Little theory or research has been devoted to emotional development in adults. In an early study, Ekman (1978) reported that in adults, the control of facial display has been refined and appears to take three main forms. These include covering a feeling by expressing a different one (masking), demonstrating a feeling even if it is absent (simulation), and suppressing emotional display although one is actually feeling something (inhibition). Thompson (1991) notes that emotional experience in adulthood is likely to become regulated in increasingly idiosyncratic ways, to become more emotion specific, and to focus more on controlling the environment. Averill (1984) believes emotional development in adulthood is subtle and nonspecific and need not be tied to particular events in childhood. Rather, he cites social transitions in adulthood (such as from home to work, family life-cycle events) as key points during which adults are challenged to "get in touch with" their feelings. Likewise, Cornelius (1984) discusses how the social rules for regulating, structuring, or constituting emotion may shift in adult developmental transitions, but mentions that, "Perhaps the most interesting kind of changes observed in adult development . . . involve changes in individuals' awareness of their emotional performances" (p. 231). He believes that an awareness of the "metarules" that govern emotional meaning and action in an individual's life likely develops in adulthood. Perhaps this awareness is demonstrated in such studies as that by McConatha, Lightner, and Deaner (1994), who found that adults at age 30 years engage in greater rehearsal of negative events and inhibit their emotions more than persons roughly a decade younger.

Emotional development in the elder years is a sorely neglected topic. For example, it is striking to note that even in very recent work (Schulz & Heckhausen, 1996), models of "successful aging" fail to mention emotion explicitly in any context. Shulz and Heckhausen's model focuses on four types of control of self and environment (primary, secondary, compensatory primary, and compensatory secondary) as essential for successful aging, but the relationship of control (or lack thereof) to emotion is not mentioned, unless one imagines that references to unspecified positive or negative "outcomes" might include emotional experiences, or that the cognitive appraisal aspects of control might be linked to emotion (as previously documented). Carstensen (1987, cited in Thompson, 1991) sheds some light on the relationship of control to emotion, by noting that older adults increasingly select settings and relationships that maximize positive emotion, ensure managable and predictable socioemotional demands, and conserve physical energy. By controlling these opportunities, older adults create situations that are most supportive and congenial to them.

At virtually all developmental levels, the mastery of emotional regulation within one's culture constitutes a fundamental aspect of social competence, with wide-ranging implications for postive or negative adjustment. For example, a preschooler's ability to understand emotions has a lot to do with her or his social competence and relationships with peers, both of which are crucial for positive adjustment (Denham et al., 1994). These emotional competencies come under the broad label of "emotional intelligence," as suggested by Goleman (1995). Goleman summarizes five basic domains of emotional intelligence: (a) knowing one's own emotions, (b) managing one's own emotions, (c) motivating oneself, (d) recognizing emotions in others, and (e) handling relationships. Although these domains may look a bit different for a 9-year-old versus a 79-year-old, the basic tasks appear to be consistently important. Goleman notes that adult men who are high in emotional intelligence are more socially poised and outgoing, cheerful, committed to people or causes, responsible, ethical, sympathetic, and caring. Adult women high in emotional intelligence are assertive, express their feelings directly, feel positive about themselves, note meaning in their lives, are gregarious, express feelings appropriately, adapt well to stress, easily reach out to new people, and are comfortable enough with themselves to be spontaneous, sensual, and playful. Low emotional intelligence is associated with social anxiety, guilt, fearfulness, and rumination in both men and women.

Along similar lines, Saarni (1993) speaks of "emotional competence." Emotional competence requires (a) an awareness of one's emotional state, (b) an ability to discern others' emotions, (c) an ability to use a (sub)culturally appropriate vocabulary for emotion, (d) a capacity for emotional involvement with others, (e) an awareness that inner experience and outer expression of emotion need not correspond in self or others, (f) an awareness of cultural display rules, (g) the ability to consider unique personal information in judging other's emotions, (h) an understanding that one's emotional behavior may affect another and to take this into account in self-presentation, (i) a capacity for coping adaptively with distressing or adverse emotion, (j) an awareness that relationships are at least partially defined by the degree of emotional genuiness and symmetry involved, and (k) a capacity for emotional self-efficacy or acceptance of one's emotional experience.

Gross (1998) takes an insightful, integrative approach to the research literature on emotional regulation. He notes that in the research on psychological health, emotional regulation has been associated with decreased stress and psychological benefits. In contrast, much of the work in the domain of physical health shows that emotional regulation leads to increased physiological activation and poorer physical health. Gross resolves this apparent paradox by suggesting that the psychological literature in large part refers to emotional coping strategies that occur before the emotion is triggered (antecedent-focused emotion regulation), and that the physical health literature has been largely concerned with coping strategies that occur after an emotion has already been experienced (response-focused emotion regulation). Antecedent-focused emotion regulation includes such strategies as situation selection, situation modification, attention deployment, and cognitive reevaluation. Response-focused emotion regulation includes strategies that would curtail, diminish, prolong, or intensify an already existing emotional experience or the physiological response associated with the emotional experience (e.g., suppression of emotion, which is linked to negative physical health outcomes).

Presenting a series of experimental studies that give credence to this model, Gross (1998) finds support for the premise that in negatively arousing emotional situations, antecedent-focused emotional responding, such as reappraisal, can be successful in relieving distress, but suppression not only fails to relieve distress but heightens sympathetic tone (physiological arousal). Gross's integration goes a long way towards helping to clarify the discrepancies between the physical health literature and the psychological health literature. It distills many complex notions into the idea that it is timing and the type of emotional regulation that makes a difference; broadly speaking, if a person can regulate the situation or his or her appraisal of that situation before it triggers strong physiological repsonses, better psychological health and better physical health will result. If the person fails to do this, and experiences the emotional arousal, trying to cope with this arousal via suppression (trying to ignore it, trying to "not feel it" or "not show it") will lead to poorer psychological and physical outcomes. Another implication of this model is that once an emotion is experienced, it might be best to just allow that experience to occur—to feel what one feels—rather than trying to modify it after the fact.

Gross (1998) is careful to note that his model does not fully capture the complex, social, and recursive and interactive nature of emotional modulation processes. In particular, he warns that there may be some costs even to antecedent-focused emotional regulation, particularly if emotion expression is compromised. If the expression of emotion is lessened, important adaptive social information may be lost. Thus, showing or expressing what one feels is likely to be an important aspect of emotional regulation. What is not addressed here is the more subtle, intrapsychic impact of antecedent-focused coping or, potentially, the long-term effects of attempting to avoid even having the feeling in the first place. We conjecture that still deeper reverberations affect the unconscious self-definitional processes resulting from continuous bids to quiet one's potential "negative" affect. As we strive to calm or move away from negative emotion, namely anger, we tell ourselves something about the worth and meaning of our discomfort, relative to others. Each time we do, we answer dissentingly the question of whether or not this particular, tiny piece of our appraised interest or claim deserves to take its place in our overall distinctiveness.

Attachment

Infancy is the period in which attachment relationships are formed, and primary researchers in this area, such as Bowlby (1988), see attachment as an emotionally mediated process. Attachment is presumed to assure the infant of proximity to and thereby the protection of parents or other primary caregivers. Although thought to have a biological and evolutionary basis, attachment also is linked to temperament and the social-interactional quality of caregiving (Durkin, 1995). In reviewing the research on secure attachment in infancy, Thompson and Lamb (1980) develop the argument that a mother's expressive repertoire (if it is both recognizable and diverse) and its contingency with a baby's expressed cues begin to foster the development of the child's use of "animated" emotional responses and the ability to self-regulate and cope. In terms of the associations between attachment style and emotion, secure attachment is associated with happy confidence, little distress, and an easy return to calm after disruption for the child, and positive emotional tone in the caregiver. Avoidant attachment is associated with decreases in affect and unresponsiveness; resistant attachment is associated with ambivalence, upset, and anger (Ainsworth, Bell, & Stayton, 1971; Kellerman, 1980). Main and Solomon (1986) added a fourth category of attachment that they labeled disorganized, in which infants display chaotic and contradictory behaviors with their primary caregivers. Secure attachment is consistently associated with positive social development (see Durkin, 1995, for review). Attachments to mothers, fathers, siblings, and peers clearly constitute a large chunk of the emotional world of the developing infant and child.

Thompson (1991) notes that if caregivers respond promptly and contingently to infants' distress, "the states of quiet alertness that result foster the child's conditioned association of the caregiver's cues with relief of distress" (p. 280). These early expectations of an adult's reliable assistance are a hallmark of secure attachment. As adults, these securely attached persons tend to adapt flexibly to pleasant and unpleasant emotions, as compared with insecurely attached people, who have either truncated or wildly exaggerated experiences of negative affect (Cassidy, 1994). Infants who have experienced rejection tend to minimize negative affect in order to keep from being further rejected and may reciprocally (and paradoxically) allow the caregiver to be more cooperative. Infants who have experienced inconsistent caregiving become ambivalently attached and may heighten negative affect in order to draw the attention of their caregivers. It is interesting to note that in Cassidy's view, secure attachement is associated with an acceptance of the entire range of emotions, rather than merely being associated with positive emotion. Her point of view appears to be an important refinement over earlier, more simplistic models of the relationship between attachment and emotion.

The idea that early patterns of attachment between parents and children might have consequences for adult development has gained in prominence over the past decade. In particular, the attachment patterns generated in early life are seen most clearly in styles of interpersonal relating and emotion in adult intimate or romantic relationships (see also the previous section on adolescents' emotional development and its relationship to attachment). Adults who have secure attachments tend to show positive emotions (and less depression or anxiety), and those characterized by avoidant and ambivalent styles show a range of negative emotions, such as defensiveness, hostility, anxiety, and shame (Bartholomew & Horowitz, 1991; Hazan & Shaver, 1987).

Magai, Distel, and Liker (1995) describe the relationships between attachment and trait emotions. Trait emotions reflect a personality construct in which there is a consistent tendency to interpret experience with a particular emotion tone (e.g., fear, joy, anger, sadness). The authors found that in young adults (mean age 25 years) secure attachment is associated with trait joy, interest, and absence of negative emotion biases. Avoidant attachment is associated with trait contempt and disgust and decoding biases that involve poor accuracy in identifying joy. Anxiously attached participants show high trait fear, shame, and decoding biases that involve anger. Mikulincer (1998), as noted earlier, also finds that securely attached persons score lower on anger-proneness, report more positive affect and more adaptive responses in anger episodes, endorse more constructive anger goals, attribute less hostile intent to others, and expect more positive outcomes than insecure persons. Insecurely attached persons report high hostility, escapist responses, and a lack of awareness of physiological signs of anger (ambivalent attachment) or a lack of anger control and anger-in, or the use of strategies designed to hide anger or prevent its overt expression (ambivalent attachment). Such findings that seem to link the quality of our relationships with significant people to our overall experience of emotion help to set the stage for discussing anger-in-relation and point to the complexities in social connectedness that reflect in the anger experience.

☐ Summary and Integration of Theory

Given this discourse on theories of emotion, what can we conclude about anger that will help deepen our understanding of women's experience and emotional development? The following elements in theory and research combine to form a clearer picture of the general function of anger in human experience, the place of anger in social order, and the explanations for anger's role in self-definition. We must, however, take these views and draw from them further questions about their application to women.

What is unique about anger? Evolutionary and biological findings regarding anger, integrated with the literatures on socialization and culture, combine to form a coherent depiction of this primary emotion. Far from being antithetical to each other, as classic nature-versus-nurture debates may purport, these diverse perspectives form an overall gestalt. In addition, interactional models of emotion and developmental views support various aspects of this integration. What emerges is the portrait of an emotion characterized by an energized physical state at the service of adaptive sociocultural needs. Anger urges people to communicate, to interact in order to correct a perceived interpersonal injustice, to distinguish the lines around selfhood. Although its expression and experience in men and women is shaped by appraisals and attributions (Berkowitz, 1990), by family, and by the broader context, the underlying nature of anger remains intact.

Anger appears, in neurophysiological research, to be an approach emotion, in keeping with adaptive, evolutionary perspectives that anger motivates our behavior to cope with blocked goals or perceived social injustices. It provides an individual with vigor, determination, and energy to mobilize for action and to counteract fear. The roots of anger seem to be in the evolutionary fight-or-flight response (Goleman, 1995), and its onset triggered by a sense of endangerment. However, more often than not, the endangerment that provokes anger is not physical but symbolic, having to do with our dignities, identities, or goals. These endangerment perceptions trigger the limbic system to release catecholamines, while the amygdala sends messages through the adrenocortical branch of the nervous system to create a state of action readiness. Although catecholamines produce a quick energy surge, the generalized adrenal and cortical excitation can last much longer and provide a setting for further arousal, evident in a variety of ANS indicators such as accelerated heart rate, higher diastolic blood pressure, warmer body temperatures, and other indices.

For example, Levenson (1992) cites 10 studies that support heart-rate acceleration during anger. In distinguishing between fear and anger, 15 studies show a differential pattern between these two emotions, with anger linked to higher diastolic blood pressure, warmer surface temperatures, less vasoconstriction, and greater blood flow in the periphery than fear. These patterns of response fit with the notion that anger comes with an action tendency to "fight." In terms of fighting, anger energizes and organizes behavior and signals relevant interpersonal information. Some writers describe anger as an assertive posture used to arouse, alarm, and inspire another (Heise & O'Brien, 1993).

The generic anger situation is defined as one in which we have the perception of being treated unfairly (Fitness & Fletcher, 1993). Taken a bit further, "other blame," noticing another's culpability and holding them accountable in the angry encounter, has something to do with appraising and becoming angry (Lazarus, 1991; Smith et al., 1993). The experience of anger hinges upon the discernment that the integrity of one's ego identity has been threatened by something or someone, and distinguishing responsibility is a necessary part of this process. Anger depends on our making attributions that another is accountable and in control over what threatens us. There exists cross-cultural evidence to support this notion. In 37 different countries, Mikula, Scherer, and Athenstaedt (1998) find anger to be the emotion most commonly associated with unfairness or injustice, both clearly interpersonal constructs and both related to other-accountability.

What is unique about women's anger? Evolutionary theorists hold that because men and women historically differ in their survival-related and reproductive strategies, differences in emotional development reflect these roles, a position that characterizes women as more sensitive to non-verbal emotional cues—and more likely to suppress anger (Brody, 1985). Although sociobiological theories are powerful tools in conceptualization, little empirical work seems to have emerged from this discipline specifically regarding gender and emotion (a great deal has been done on gender and behavior, however). Traditional psychoanalysts, likewise believing that socioemotional differences have their roots in biology, indicate that men probably experience and express more outward-directed emotions such as anger than women, and women should experience and express more inward-directed emotions such as passivity, shame, jealousy, and masochism (Mitchell, 1974).

In their thought-provoking article on "his and hers" theories of emotion, Pennebaker and Roberts (1992) suggest that men and women use different strategies to perceive emotion. Based on the research on visceral perception, they believe men focus on internal, bodily cues to determine their feelings more than women, who tend to focus on reading and interpreting situational and contextual cues to determine their feelings more so than men. Pennebaker and Roberts interpret data from both biology and socialization research to support this perspective. On the socialization side, they note that males and females undergo quite different learning experiences in understanding their bodies' signals, and that women's lower status in our culture leads to more attention and skill in understanding social-emotional cues. On the biology side, the authors cite evidence for gender differences in hemispheric lateralization, with males showing greater right-hemisphere lateralization, which has further been linked to accuracy in visceral perception.

Additional data suggest gender differences in brain lateralization. For example, the right cerebral hemisphere may mediate facial recognition (Ekman & Oster, 1979) as well as more spontaneous aspects of emotional behavior (Buck, 1982). The left hemisphere is associated with more cognitive, analytic aspects of emotional function. Though it is suggested that women rely more heavily on right-hemisphere and men on left-hemisphere processing, much related investigation yields equivocal results (Brody, 1985). Smith et al. (1995) suggest that emotional stimuli produce higher levels of arousability in women, that emotion is more salient for them, and that "the female brain is more focally organized for the processing of emotion" (p. 153). These authors also hypothesize that such differences arise because of the differential socialization experiences of men and women.

Pennebaker and Roberts (1992) also note that men in general have a more reactive physiology than do women. Supporting this idea, Kring and Gordon (1998) found that men have stronger physiological responses to emotion than women. Kring and Gordon's study shows men to be more physiologically reactive to fear and anger, women having greater reactivity to sadness and disgust. It should be kept in mind that these are differences in magnitude, not in the overall patterns of autonomic responses across different emotions. In other words, the physiological patterning is the same for men and women, but the intensity of reaction varies by gender. Kring and Gordon's findings thus echo those of Levenson (1992), who reported no sex differences in patterns of emotion-specific ANS activity. All these bits of data support the idea that men and women have somewhat divergent experiences of emotion and perhaps do different things with it. However, though differences seem to emerge between men and women in terms of visceral emotion response, it is important to distinguish physiological reactivity from the subjective sense of having experienced intense emotion. Gross and John (1998) demonstrate that women obtain higher emotional impulse intensity scores than do men, a measure of subjective (not physical) affect intensity. So, women's felt experience may be more powerful than that reflected in traditional somatic anger indices.

Turning to the cognitive side of the anger experience, appraisal analyses of emotion tend to ignore gender in favor of basic appraisal dimensions or information-processing models thought to be used by everyone. However, the socialization and culture literature strongly suggests that gender-appropriateness or gender-relevance has a lot to do with appraisal. How we account for anger elicitors has something to do with our gender, and whatever rules or training support this phenomenon become transmitted via caretaking and schooling practices, social scripts for everyday behavior, religious practices, the media, and everyday language (Markus & Kitayama, 1994). Different behaviors are modeled for boys and girls, such as to whom one should give direct eye contact and for how long, how firmly or falteringly one should state one's opinion, how squarely or apologetically one should request assistance. We speculate that a barrage of gendered emotional material forms a filter through which appraisal is strained for many people, and that much of this process occurs outside of conscious awareness.

Early feminist authors such as Chodorow (1978) and Miller (1976) note that girls, parented by their mothers, learn an orientation towards affective-relational issues, resulting in a sense of self as in relation to others. Boys are said to require differentiation from their mothers in order to develop a sense of separate, masculine identity. More recently, Cross and Madson (1997) argue that "an interdependent self-construal and early socialization in sensitivity to emotion go hand in hand" (p. 14). These authors note that girls are socialized to be more attuned to emotions than are boys, internalizing the emotional awareness that has been emphasized by their parents.

As is well articulated by authors such as these, women are taught to focus on relatedness and to take responsibility for maintaining relationships (Gilligan, 1982). Women in mainstream Western culture have been socialized to value emotional experience more than men, to be more emotionally expressive than men, to attend to emotion in others more than men, and to be better at decoding nonverbal emotional expressions in others (Cross & Madson, 1997; McConatha, Lightner, & Deaner, 1994). Women recall both more negative and more positive life events than do men and encode these affective events in more detail (Seidlitz & Diener, 1998). In addition, women's sense of self as in relation to others may lead them to vicariously experience both positive and negative emotions of persons close to them, as well as to experience more relationship distress (Cross & Madson, 1997). However, Kring and Gordon (1998) report that although women express both more positive and negative emotions than men as registered facially and dispositionally, they do not report experiencing more emotion than men. Thus, women are not "more emotional" than men but are socialized to be freer to express the emotion they feel; men more often mask their emotions.

We further suggest that this "freedom" granted to women for self expression generally includes only certain aspects of emotional experience. Recent research (Wood, Christensen, Hebl, & Rothgerber, 1997) shows that for women (and men) who judge sex-role norms to be salient to their self-concepts, positive feelings result from sex-role norm-congruent behaviors. That is, if sex-role socialization has been internalized to a point at which sex-appropriate behavior becomes an integral and highly valued part of the self-concept, women report feeling good if they act to maintain communion; men report feeling positive if they act in a dominant manner. Further, in spite of the research finding emotional expression more acceptable for women than for men, a major exception seems to be in the expression of anger. It is less acceptable for women to express anger and more acceptable for women to express fear and sadness than it is for men (Brody, 1985; Brody & Hall, 1993; Cross & Madson, 1997; Sharkin, 1993).

Cross and Madson (1997) report that mothers avoid talking about anger with daughters, encourage their daughters more than their sons to resolve their anger in conflicted relationships, and note that girls mask anger more than boys (even if they feel every bit as angry). Cross and Madson tie these results to their theory that girls' and women's interdependent self-portrayals lead them to be more hesitant to display anger because it is seen as having the power to destroy relationships. In a recent study (Rusting & Nolen-Hoeksema, 1998), further evidence supports the idea that women downplay feelings of anger. Women are more likely than men to distract themselves after the induction of an angry mood.

Sharkin (1993) notes that social perceptions of angry men and angry women are likely to vary, given current socialization patterns. Similarly, the entry requirements for anger that Averill (1997) proposes have to do with power. In general, persons who have more authority receive sanctioning to feel, visibly display, or act on anger more than those who have less authority. This double standard seems to apply to any power difference: parent/child, male/female, high socioeconomic status/low socioeconomic status, minority/majority, boss/worker, or those resulting from specific occupational roles (a drill sergeant is Averill's example). Miller (1991) sees these socialization patterns in women's anger as a result of power differences perpetuated by patriarchal culture, which encourages women to feel as if they have no cause for anger, that something is wrong with them if they feel angry, and to see themselves as weak and unworthy. A woman's anger is only allowed in defense of someone else (e.g., her children). Being in a one-down position in the patriarchy, women likely feel a great deal of anger but are educated in the ideology simultaneously that anger is destructive and that feeling it in response to one's own needs or blocked goals is less than desirable. With this review of anger and emotion in mind, as well as the peculiarities of anger's social uses and cultural rules, we now delve deeply into the issue of its enigmatic place in women's emotional development.

The Formation of Socialized Anger in Women

Self-development is a higher duty than self-sacrifice.
—Elizabeth Cady Stanton

Recent clarifying portrayals of girls and women resisting sociocultural pressure to dampen their own voices or give up power (e.g., Brown, 1998) show a kind of struggle against the very forces that we hold up as salient in this discussion of socialized anger in women. These question the emerging stereotype of girls and women as shrinking away—as handing over authority to give voice to their own experiences—and offer much needed alternatives, images of strength, stubbornness, willfulness, and instrumentality. In our present exploration, however, we wish to push the theoretical envelope a bit further to continue some dialogue about the more covert, insidious aspects of women's anger socialization. Our aim in returning to this (arguably well-worn) discussion is to revisit gender training for another honest look at the very camaflouged processes occurring there. Another concentrated shove allows us to view anger itself as the unsuspecting victim—an unwilling tool in the often intense battle between social comfort and women's self. Anger as a weapon for self-defense becomes turned against the self in an ironic socialization twist. Anger itself, rather than just anger suppression, becomes a vehicle for gender socialization. Something evolutionarily developed to promote self and well-being becomes the unwitting participant in a nonconscious social conspiracy.

Reviewing models of anger and the history of its understanding and portrayal in Western culture generates several observations about its survival-related and motivational function in human experience. Combining these formulations with our current knowledge about human emotional development provides an even clearer picture of the emergent complexities in emotional experience. A broad-based view of emotional development incorporates both the gradual increase in the amount of emotion-management behavior and the social survival-related necessity most likely motivating this process. Viewing anger as both a social phenomenon and a motivator for adaptive behavior, it follows that feeling intense emotion in the context of interpersonal relationships could have adaptive significance. The direct release of anger appears related to catharsis for its own sake, as well as assertion of individual integrity.

This chapter attempts to synthesize abundant theory and research on emotional development, women's socialization regarding anger, and both the individual and cultural implications involved in those processes. It appears that the development of an identity is difficult, if not impossible, without exploration of the boundaries of self, a phenomenon embedded in the experience of anger. A proposed three-dimensional model incorporates both the elements involved in women's anger experience and socialization and women's development of selfhood.

☐ Anger's Function in the Individual and in Society

Conflict permeates the existing research and theorizing on anger. From the early Greek descriptions through more modern formulations, conflict emerges between acknowledgment of anger's protective function in human behavior and fear of consequences associated with it.

Classicists, Aristotle, Plutarch, and Seneca each remark on anger's informative and motivational functions. To summarize their views, anger is aroused in a person if that individual perceives a slight or injury and its energy directs that person toward punishment of the offending party. However, these philosophers expressed the ambivalence and fear associated so often with anger, writing also about dangers regarding its expression (Schimmel, 1979). Seneca (as cited in Schimmel, 1979) writes in his major work, "On Anger," "We shall forestall the possibility of anger if we repeatedly set before ourselves its many faults and shall rightly appraise it. Before our own hearts we must arraign and convict it, we must search out its evils and drag them into the open. Anger renounces human nature, which incites to love, whereas it incites to hate; which bids us help, whereas it bids us injure" (p. 328).

Much later, Victorian society evidenced the historical conflict between acknowledging and controlling the emotion of anger as a double standard for anger expression emerges between the sexes (Stearns & Stearns, 1986). Anger became decidedly unfeminine and thus prohibited in women, but simultaneously necessary for men to use in business and politics. Herein the picture of anger's psychosocially adaptive function is juxtaposed with the sex-biased cultural mythology forbidding its use or clear experience by women. The larger cultural ambivalence regarding anger plays out in a dualistic notion about male and female experience of such.

Cognitive theoretical ideas about anger involve the individual's response to an assault on one's domain or moral code. Izard (1991) suggests that anger is an adaptive state that interacts with disgust and contempt, mobilizing energy for defense. In this way, the state of anger itself becomes acknowledged for its catalyzing role in human behavior, promoting survival of the individual by virtue of a self-interested alarm system. Markus and Kitayama (1991, p. 236) comment about the adaptive nature of anger by calling it an "ego-focused emotion . . . diagnostic of the independent self." Stated differently, when experiencing anger, the individual notices his or her own rights, needs, or opinions and their violation or dissatisfaction (or threat of such). In so doing, the self comes to the forefront of the individual's consciousness and some inclination to act on one's own behalf becomes manifest.

Anger, then, delivers messages to and about the self (an admittedly Western concept). These formulations on anger, divergent in many respects, each characterize the informational and facilitative nature of this emotion, suggesting its communication value within the individual. However, although anger reminds us of our individual inclinations, a function that appears to have self-preservation merit, history reveals the irony of a rather embattled relationship between humankind and its anger (Kemp & Strongman, 1995). Much societal energy focuses upon restraint and control of this emotion, the experience of anger often being labeled a sin, weakness, or sign of mental disturbance. What is the source of such pervasive difficulty in acknowledging the disagreeing, oppositional, angry aspects of our selves? We suggest that for an aspect of humanity to evoke such prohibitions, consequences, and efforts toward control, therein must lie enormous potential of which we are all subconsciously aware.

Anger Between Individuals

Anger functions as a social phenomenon, according to many theorists. Sullivan (1953), perhaps the first to emphasize anger's interpersonal nature, suggests that individuals' unmet expectations of others produce anxiety. Anger functions to relieve this anxiety, allowing for feelings of increased empowerment in the interpersonal context. Similarly, Solomon (1976) later wrote of anger as a judgment of personal offense. If a person experiences the displeasure of unmet expectations in another, she or he seeks to punish the offender. More recently, Averill (1983) supports this social perspective, finding anger to occur most often between friends and loved ones, precipitated by some perceived wrongdoing.

As the individual takes notice of his or her anger, instantaneous realization of potential outcomes takes place at some level of consciousness, begging a choice. The decision embedded in one's experience of anger reflects a tension between actions taken to preserve the self, creating some form of change in the environment, and actions taken internally to alter one's experience of the emotion. With the former, a realization of some degree of separateness becomes unavoidable. This awareness relates to an experience of self at odds with another, or perhaps with the environment. To act upon this realization with intent to create change (even if only to speak one's sentiment aloud, thereby causing another to take notice of the separateness between the two selves) forces an awareness of the self. Conversely, to take actions internally in rearranging one's phenomenological experience of the anger obscures the realization of the separate self.

A commonly depicted form of acting on one's environment if angry is the use of aggression or violence, often directed toward people of lesser perceived power. Usually characterized as more common in men, aggression often becomes an icon for the fear of anger and its avoidance. However, considering violence as facilitative of a cultural fear of anger raises another question about the possible roots of anger avoidance.

Though aggression often has been linked unfortunately with anger, Western society may have a much more potent, yet unconscious, psychological reason to avoid anger, with a fear that could actually engender the use of violence or aggression to prevent its realization. We contend that individuals fear the potential aloneness that results from our experience and expression of an emotion that brings our separateness to light. Both men and women, consciously or unconsciously, fear the potential highs and lows of separation. The experience of the separateness of the self at once exhilarates and terrifies. The liberating awareness of one's independence brings the fearful and perhaps even horrific realization of one's literal and figurative aloneness. Anger is a cognitive, emotional, affective, and physiological experience of both possibilities. Although the connection with aggression plays a large part in society's alienation from anger expression, this painful awareness of one's self as separate and alone provides stimulus for avoiding anger.

Men typically seem to receive more models for use of aggression in modern culture, as evidenced by popular media depictions. However, even these explosive, externalizing demonstrations fall short in terms of expressed feeling and opinion. Perhaps the same subversion of direct anger expression that supports such externalized behavior also becomes involved in teaching others to internalize or transform anger into self-criticism. In this way, much of Western culture creates a polarization with regard to its anger, keeping men and women on separate but equally unfulfilling ends. Explosion or suppression both reflect and engender isomorphically related phenomena. Though apparently dissimilar, the ends of the anger expression spectrum share similar causes; namely an avoidance of the clear, direct expression of anger.

Recent feminist writers assert that traditional theories of emotional development fail to address unique situations faced by female children growing up in a patriarchal culture (Brown & Gilligan, 1992). Erikson's widely accepted theory shows a valuing of independence and disconnection (perhaps independence via disconnection) as goals for healthy development. Such notions sit alongside arguments against such for women, as this traditional model suggests they develop less "resistance to control," leaving themselves more malleable by relationship forces (e.g., marital partners, children). To address the contradictions inherent in Erikson's model, writers on the subject of emotional development propose different markers of growth for women than have been put forth for men. In the following sections of this chapter, we address these markers at various stages of maturity as well as their implications for women's anger experience.

☐ Anger's Function in Women's Emotional Development: Socialization to Suppress

> *Make sure you never, never, argue at night.*
> *You just lose a good night's sleep, and you can't*
> *settle anything until morning anyway.*
> —*Rose Fitzgerald Kennedy*

In this section, we address empirical findings on the nature of emotional development and anger expression in women at various points in the life cycle. We place the majority of our emphasis on the period between early adolescence and young adulthood, owing in part to the burgeoning litera- ture on girls' internalization of distress and its impact on their develop- ment of selfhood. Additionally, given the confluence of physiological and cognitive milestones reached at puberty, the years encompassing its onset and aftermath form a sort of crucible for the emergent woman and her experience of herself.

In other phases of the life cycle (i.e., early childhood and late life), anger receives comparatively little direct treatment. Investigation instead organizes around various paradigms that include anger as one part of their construction, resulting in a fractured and compartmentalized perspective that only tangentially informs about anger. Thus, anger becomes acknowl- edged in theory and treatment surrounding depression, borderline per- sonality disorder, eating disorders, recovery from sexual abuse, and post- traumatic stress syndrome but is generally not examined as a discrete and independent element. Much may be gained from viewing women's di- lemmas through the lens of anger experience.

Matheson (1992) quotes the familiar nursery rhyme in her discourse on the residential treatment of girls:

> There was a little girl, who had a little curl,
> Right in the middle of her forehead.
> And when she was good, she was very, very good,
> And when she was bad she was horrid.
> She stood on her head, on her little truckle bed,
> With nobody by for to hinder.
> She screamed and she squalled, she yelled and she bawled,
> And drummed her little heels against the winder.
> Her mother heard the noise and thought it was the boys,
> A-kicking up a rumpus in the attic.
> But when she climbed the stair, and saw Jemima there,
> She took her and did whip her most emphatic.

This poem, one of many in which acting-out or angry women are cast in a negative, punitive light, contrasts with presentations of angry men. Lerner (1985) represents the first wave of interest in women's anger as a topic of value for study. She writes that anger in women is not only prohibited but given labels such as "unladylike" and "unattractive." Thus, instead of direct anger expression, women transform such feelings into fears or hurt. Behind this transformation, Lerner theorizes, women hide the unconscious fear of being omnipotently destructive, as well as "sepa- ration anxiety." Women particularly fear the alienation of those with whom they have intimate relationships, and so suppress oppositional feelings to preserve harmony. Expression of anger (especially towards men) takes on such descriptions as "strident," "unmaternal," and "sexually unattractive." Thus, to mitigate the perceived relationship jeopardy resulting from experiencing anger, women tend to undergo an internal questioning process that serves to block or invalidate the clear expression of such feeling. The cost, Lerner suggests, involves depression, guilt, and self-doubt. These negative internalizations represent actions taken against the self.

To explore possible factors underlying the above characterizations of women's anger, we must first look at models of emotional development to find bases for the management of emotion states in general. Traditional approaches as well as more recent formulations provide a backdrop for further clarification of the special developmental tasks faced by women and how these are translated into the experience of intense or oppositional emotion.

As typically conceived, three dimensions make up the emotion system: the physiological, the behavioral or expressive, and the experiential or subjective. As developmental changes take place in all three areas, the experience of emotion, elicited primarily by physical stimuli very early in life, becomes more likely tied to a wider band of elicitors as the individual matures. With development comes more attunement and response to abstract stimuli and thus greater capacity to regulate and manage the outward manifestation of emotion (Brody, 1985).

In other words, we increasingly alter our expression and possibly our experience of emotion to meet requirements placed upon us by the people in our lives. To further clarify, Brody (1985) lists five widely accepted trends in the literature on emotional development, highlighting the movement from simple and instinctual to complex and mediated. These trends presumably represent the tasks faced by all humans as they integrate external, social information with their internal experience of emotions such as anger.

1. A biological preparedness for emotional expressiveness (and, implicitly, experience) exists at birth.
2. This preparedness seems to take the form of either general arousal or discreet emotional states (anger versus sadness), playing a significant part in infant-caretaker interactions and the development of cognitive skills or motivation.
3. As individuals develop, their experience and expression of emotion becomes more differentiated, stable, and both internally and externally regulated.
4. Expression of emotion becomes increasingly subject to voluntary controls as individuals become more aware of social acceptability with development.

5. Each emotion becomes elicited by or associated with an increasing number of different situations.

Given individuals' tendencies toward increased regulation of their emotion states and affective displays, an overlay of processes must be involved in mitigating any social or psychological consequences of intense emotional experience. From a social-constructionist perspective, these complex processes involve the integration of incoming sociocultural information with one's actual internal states. In fact, emotional response itself may be best understood in terms of the social context in which it occurs. With increasing age, children learn to moderate overt expression of feelings in response to interpersonal pressures and norms. Within the emotional development paradigm, girls' social training includes specific elements that serve to alter their experience of anger.

The Relationship Context as Foreground: Autonomy Redefined

Certain theorists emphasize the self as fundamental to relationships (Erikson, 1963); others emphasize relationships as central to the self (Kohut, 1971). The so-called Western notion of self as independent, self-contained, and autonomous relies heavily on internal attributes for explaining human behavior (Markus & Kitayama, 1991). Much traditional developmental theory mirrors this view as well. As mentioned previously, Erikson's (1963) model holds that adolescent development involves detachment from relationship, thereby placing the self opposite another. In this way, autonomy is achieved through the creation of distance from the other.

Such a view is considered by many developmental theorists to be inaccurate for women (Stern, 1991). The emphasis on detachment, however, seems to be the primary source of misapplication to women. Rather, "self-opposite-other" *inside the relationship* provides a conduit through which women's autonomy is cultivated. In other words, a person can operate within the intimate, attached caring of a relationship—while squaring-off and facing the other in disagreement. Autonomy by virtue of *detachment* reflects the larger cultural bias in favor of traditional patriarchal norms for emotional development. Markus and Kitayama (1991) compare an independent view of the self with a very different interdependent view, asserting the former reflects a monocultural, Western, middle-class, male bias. As such, traditional Western notions of the self as detached from its context simply fall short in describing women and their potential for developing autonomy in-relation.

In fact, such traditional notions may fall short of the full meaning of autonomy in general. We propose that autonomy includes not only the exercise of power and control over one's experience (separateness), but also a form of self-knowledge only attainable through the process of exploring the self opposite the other, in-relation. Women's experience of achieving autonomy through the self-discovery that relationship offers includes both striving for independence and increasing depth of understanding of the internal self as it interacts with and is reflected back by others.

Miller (1976) put forth a theory of women's development called *self-in-relation*, having as its premise that all humans begin life as a self connected to a primary caregiver and sensitive to this person's emotional state. Miller asserts that though all infants begin life this way, women continue as primarily relational, in large part because of gender socialization. Thus, a discussion of women's emotional development "in relationships" makes sense in terms of gender socialization. Women's emotional experience and expression in the context of significant relationships represent important components in their overall development. Because an awareness of and sensitivity to others is paramount to the psychology of women, it follows that self-esteem depends on fostering and sustaining relationships as well as other, more independent markers of success (Markus & Kitayama, 1991). In contrast to Erikson's ideas wherein autonomy is achieved by disconnection, girls tend to gain self-knowledge within the bounds of close connections to others, and perhaps the acquisition of autonomy by virtue of the relationship.

However, this potential for development of autonomy often becomes truncated in girls as they develop. This happens as a paradoxical double bind begins to operate in girls' relationships with others. Several writers on the topic of girls' emotional development offer insightful formulations of this occurrence. As we shall see, the very relationships in which girls could practice autonomous anger expression provide an environment in which girls must extract a portion of themselves in order to remain connected.

Reconstructing the irony between anger's adaptive function and its societal prohibition for women, Gilligan (1990, p. 527) calls anger the "political emotion par excellence—the bellwether of oppression, injustice, bad treatment, the clue that something is wrong in the relational surround." Debold, Wilson, and Malave (1993) write that for most working-class women and women of color, anger is an almost omnipresent defense that tells the world to watch out. They further suggest that almost all women have lost the righteousness of anger, the empowerment embedded in the experience of anger to demand change. Similarly, Brown and Gilligan (1992) describe a cultural pressure for White middle-class girls to bury or disown their anger in the name of femininity.

To continue the juxtaposition of female anger, relationship, and autonomy, we find that a progression of feminist and other developmental ideology leads to some conclusions about the perplexities of women's experience. Some early feminist reconceptualizations of women's emotional development describe a fear of anger based on its potential for disruption of relationships with men. In these portrayals, women redirect their anger from male antagonists to themselves, to women in general, or to less powerful persons (such as children). Female anger becomes subverted into indirect hostility, irritability and dependency, options chosen over the risk of lost support and approval from significant males. Women expressing oppositional feelings, or behaving in other than completely empathic, non-aggressive, other-serving ways, arouse stereotypical images of the "bad mother" (Bernardez-Bonesatti, 1978; Bernardez, 1987).

Object-relations theory provides a possible explanatory framework for Bernardez's formulations. In this view, the attachment basis of emotion predisposes women to experience more shame, and men more guilt. Two complementary forces act to create women's internalization versus clear expression of distress: women's low sociocultural status, which causes them to feel inferior, predisposing them to experience more shame (internalizing others' negative views of them); and women's more affiliative orientations, wherein shame is more easily induced than it is in men. In other words, women experience more negative feelings about themselves because of the emphasis they place on others' approval or disapproval. Further, because girls are parented primarily by their mothers, they learn an orientation toward affective-relational issues, resulting in a lack of separateness in relation to others. Conversely, boys must clearly differentiate from mothers in order to develop separate masculine identities (Lewis, 1983).

Therefore, if girls are socialized toward affective-relational orientations, others' feelings in general take on increased significance for them in comparison to boys. In turn, if others' feelings include low status appraisals for girls, these too become internalized by the developing woman. Women experience more negative emotion directed toward the self, as predicted by psychoanalytic, object-relations, sociological, feminist, and feminist-psychoanalytic theories, and paradoxically may be even more expressive of emotion, as predicted by certain feminist and psychoanalytic theories. However, this expression tends to be restricted to feelings that are socially sanctioned for women or perceived as relationship-enhancing. In other words, although perceived as more "emotional" than men in stereotyped portrayals, women redirect angry or oppositional feelings to more self-effacing or other-promoting expressions. Further, if women experience more shame, helplessness, vulnerability and anxiety because of their low social status, the likelihood that they express emotions such as anger, which may be more self-protecting and self-interested yet perceived as less relationship-enhancing, decreases sharply (Brody, 1985).

It is precisely these prescriptives toward overemphasis on others' feelings that we suggest confuse the boundary between self and other for the developing woman. Such a blurred distinction, born of the requirement to suppress outrage at the other, robs the woman of an opportunity to develop this kind of autonomy. Instead of experiencing the exhilarating and terrifying separateness of the self at odds with another person, a woman's focus must be drawn away from herself, into the needs of the other or the perceived requirements of the social surround. This distraction process takes place via cultural requirements that she be, among a host of other things, beautiful. Because "beautiful" has an external referent as its definition, she becomes further carried away, outside her internal, authentic experience.

Girls in Early and Middle Childhood

Given our cultural avoidance of addressing anger in a straightforward manner, we find no surprise in the relatively sparse study of anger in children, as opposed to anxiety or depression, which yield abundant analyses. The complexity of the interaction between socialization, gender, and attitudes about anger reflect in the conflicting research on early and middle childhood years. Researchers generally agree, however, that boys and girls do differ in their expression of anger and in other relationship-oriented behaviors. In anger studies, 4- and 5-year-old girls exhibit prosocial behaviors and respond with expressions of social connection and cohesion more than boys of the same age. However, conflicting results show both higher and lower levels of anger expression in girls as compared with boys (Zahn-Waxler et al., 1994; Zahn-Waxler, Cole, Welsh, & Fox, 1995).

It is notable that behaviors serving to maintain social connections exhibit themselves in girls at this young age, given the relationship orientation central to girls' development of autonomy as outlined elsewhere in this chapter. Further research on anger expression in this age group will serve to illuminate the roles of intrinsic need-based drive and socialization as genesis for girls' unique involvement with relationship and consequential behavioral and attitudinal differences.

Such differences impact school, social functioning, and success, as pointed out by Cole, Zahn-Waxler, and Smith (1994). These authors report that experimenter-manipulated disappointment in 5-year-old girls resulted in altered behavior on the parts of these children, according to the presence of the adult experimenter. Such behaviors differed from that of boys in that girls at higher risk for maladjustment displayed less negative emotion in the absence of the experimenter than did girls at lower risk, who increased their expressiveness after the adult left; high-risk boys showed no significant alterations in their expressiveness. Further, this minimization of negative emotion predicted attention deficit and conduct-disorder symptomatology in girls.

Gender differences continue into middle childhood, according to some studies (Cox, 1997). Again, girls seem to suppress anger expression more than boys, as measured by facial-expression masking (Underwood, Coie, & Herbsman, 1992). They also tend to respond with a higher correlation of childhood maladjustment to anger, among other measures of conflict, in family relationships (Jaycox & Repetti, 1993), and to exhibit higher levels of anger at males than at other females (Brody, Hay, & Vandewater, 1990). Girls' greater tendency to internalize anger yields no greater likelihood of clinical depression, however, at prepubertal ages (Allgood-Merten, Lewinsohn, & Hops, 1990). The prevalence of girls' depression increases dramatically somewhere between childhood and adulthood (Rutter, 1986).

Gender differences in emotional development may result in part from the qualitatively different exchanges made between parents or caretakers and boys versus girls. Girls receive generally more attention than boys in the area of their appearance, both in terms of physical beauty and neatness of schoolwork (American Association of Univeristy Women [AAUW], 1991; Sadker & Sadker, 1994). Early work by Block (1973) suggests parents encourage sons toward aggression with nonemotionality, and they encourage daughters toward emotionality with nonaggression. Birnbaum and Croll (1984) report that parents show more acceptance of anger in boys than in girls—with greater acceptance of fear in girls than in boys.

Likewise, school and other related professionals often advocate for the teaching and modeling of appropriate anger-management skills to children of both sexes, introducing boys and girls to anger-control methods at early ages. More recent writings emphasize the importance of recognizing some type of appropriate anger expression along with instruction in behavioral inhibition and control (Marion, 1994; McClure, Miller, & Russo, 1992).

Girls to Women at Adolescence

Research indicates adolescence is a time of great psychological danger for girls (Petersen, 1988). Compared with boys, adolescent girls manifest more depression and poorer emotional well-being (Ebata, 1987; Rutter, 1980), appraise themselves more negatively (Grove & Herb, 1974; Kandel & Davies, 1982), and more likely experience their first psychological disturbances (Ebata, 1987). Often, these disturbances continue into adulthood, developing into more serious problems later in life (Rutter, 1980).

The AAUW (1991) conducted a survey that polled 3000 boys and girls nationwide on their attitudes toward self, school, family, and friends. The students, spanning ages 9 to 15 years, were asked to provide comments and were interviewed in focus groups in some cases. Results show passage into adolescence to be a treacherous time for girls, marked by loss of confidence in self and abilities (especially in the areas of math and science). Adolescence brings a highly critical attitude among girls toward their own bodies and an overwhelming sense of personal inadequacy. Teenaged girls reported much more vulnerability to depression and hopeless feelings than boys, being four times more likely to attempt suicide. They experience a reduction in their expectations for success and a self-censorship of their creative and intellectual potentials.

Regarding school issues, the AAUW (1991) study shows gender bias in the classrooms of adolescents, where both boys and girls believe that teachers encourage more assertive behavior in boys, who also receive more teacher attention in general. Girls report feeling diminished by their teachers when they are angry and observing those teachers to become hypervigilant to boys' anger but consider angry girls to be "petty" (Cox, 1997). Girls' interest and achievement in math and science drops precipitously during these years, but researchers have long known that loss of confidence in math precedes a drop in achievement, rather than the reverse (Kloosterman, 1990).

The AAUW (1991) survey reports an interesting variation among ethnic groups in the loss of self-esteem. Although all girls report consistently lower self-esteem than boys, more African American girls retain their overall self-esteem during adolescence than White or Latina girls, with a corresponding sense of personal and familial importance.

In a large-scale study of Minnesota adolescents, Harris, Blum, and Resnick (1991) found girls to display a picture of "quiet disturbance." Boys act out in the form of fighting, vandalism, and substance abuse; girls tend to internalize distress. The adolescent girls in this study reported significantly more negative body image, chronic dieting, and bulimic behavior than boys. Girls in this study also reported more emotional stress, depression, and suicidality than the boys. This difference tends to widen with the age of the adolescents, as twice as many post-seventh-grade girls in Minnesota attempt suicide when compared with their male counterparts. Further, Harris and colleagues found far more teen girls to report physical or sexual abuse in their histories than boys, a substantial number having never discussed the abuse with anyone.

These findings parallel those of many other studies on gender differences in adolescent psychological well-being (Earls, 1987; Gjinde, Block, & Block, 1988; Seiden, 1989). Across a variety of populations studied, females tend towards internalized expressions of distress and loss of self-efficacy feelings versus more externalized symptoms. Further, Harris et al. (1991) assert that these differences reflect gender socialization from an early age. However, as these authors point out, characterizing adolescent females as more prone to internalizing stress may be an oversimplification of the issue.

With the onset of formal operational thought in the Piagetian tradition, adolescents begin to comprehend the hypothetical consequences of their behavior with others, inferring general principles from specific instances or encounters with social norms (Stevens-Long, 1990). In this way, girls at or around puberty begin sizing up the potential political damage of their uncensored expressions of distress or outrage. More cognizance of unspoken cultural expectations filter through a girl's awareness, motivating almost constant efforts to attain the embodiment of ideal physical images and elusive behavioral paragons.

Gilligan's (1991) qualitative study of adolescent girls yields insight into a relational crisis faced by girls as they enter adolescence. She calls this crisis an "impasse" in development, wherein for the sake of important connections with others, girls must remove themselves from those very relationships in certain significant ways. Girls begin to feel the conflict between the necessity of relating and the necessity of personal feeling (particularly individualistic or oppositional feeling). Therefore, some compromise must be created. Eleven- or twelve-year-old girls are said to speak with clarity of knowing and seeing, based on their use of personal judgment (Gilligan, Lyons, & Hammer, 1990). Adolescence brings about new rules, wherein girls must maintain relationship by denial of information about the self.

Compared with boys, whose desire for relationship tends to be less articulated and more associated with early terror and loss, girls' desire for relationship takes on a much different flavor (Gilligan, 1991). Following years of experience with the complexity of deeply connected friendships, girls' desire for relationship remains less contaminated, more resistant to the hardships faced as they approach adolescence. Thus, as girls approach adolescence, and a dominant culture of relating that favors separation as the optimal dynamic for individuation, they must resist the expected disconnection. This resistance forces a sort of double bind, requiring the girl to remove certain aspects of herself from relationships, a compromise designed to protect such connections with people.

Brown (1991) considers this necessary compromise to take the form of a "giving over" of one's thoughts and feelings. Stern (1991) suggests that "viewing the female self as completely congruent with its relationships highlights a problem inherent in the process of gendering emotional development. Ironically, viewing the self as completely able to absorb the agendas of others becomes the mirror image of seeing the self as completely outside of relationships" (p. 113). Stern seems to be saying that denying one's own agendas by solely focusing on others' actually keeps one *outside* the interactions of a relationship that would be made possible by a more self-interested engagement with the other. Recent empirical evidence using a scale based on Jack's (1987, 1991) "silencing the self" theory seems to support this notion. Thompson and Hart (1996) report women who score higher on the Silencing the Self Scale (Jack, 1991) to correspondingly experience decreased intimacy, insecure attachment patterns, and depressive symptomatology.

By disavowing the self, a girl attempts to avoid the choice between self and others. Denying her conflict-laden feelings helps her avoid criticism or attack she is certain would follow their revelation. To disregard or devalue one's experiences allows a girl to avoid jeopardizing those sacred connections so familiar from earlier childhood. They also allow her to strive toward gender-prescriptive images of the perfect girl or woman, with which she is inundated. However, such internal disregard comes not without a cost to the developing self. As several studies point out, adolescent girls begin paying the psychological price for the attainment of an illusory goal, with tolls on the self continuing well into adulthood.

Gilligan (1982) and others (Bernardez, 1988; Brown, 1991) describe the interaction between female emotional development and gender-specific ideals that become translated into expectations for behavior. As boys are pressured to emulate hero images in early childhood, Gilligan (1991) hypothesizes that girls are pressured in adolescence to take on images of "perfection" as goals for becoming. The perfect female in gender-socialization mythology is completely empathic and agreeable, one whom everyone likes and wants to be with (Brown & Gilligan, 1992; Gilligan, 1990).

Brown (1995) writes about this female standard against which others are measured. She describes this image as recognizable to anyone who opens the pages of a typical teen fashion magazine: beautiful, tall, long hair, perfect skin, pretty eyes, nice figure, talented, obtaining good grades, having a personality to match her looks, humble, nice, and loyal. Brown makes reference to the regulatory power that this "phantasmic ideal" (Butler, 1991, p. 21) wields among groups of girls, even though they know of no girls who can perfectly emulate her. She further writes of idealized femininity as endorsing "silence over outspokenness, passivity over active resistance, a pleasing ignorance over knowledge of the complexity and difficulty of lived experience and relationships, weakness over physical strength and aggressiveness" (Brown, 1995, p. 13).

Further, Gilligan (1991) writes that in order to achieve this goal of feminine perfection, girls must resist knowing what is happening in a given moment. In other words, girls must learn to censor the incoming information to which they attend. Stern (1991) suggests that some girls who demonstrate a solid sense of self in preadolescence begin to devalue their perceptions, beliefs, thoughts, and feelings during adolescence. This disavowal of self, although allowing for relationship maintenance, also relates in some studies to psychological symptomatology aspects of socialization, including eating disorders and depression (Jack, 1987, 1991; Steiner-Adair, 1986).

Psychoanalytic theorist Horney (1926) linked this subtle devaluation phenomenon to dysphoric feelings that correspond with a woman's adoption of male-defined values and goals. Other early writers (Deutsch, 1944; Thompson, 1942) noted female adolescents' shutting down or suppressing affect but conceptualized this in terms of female passivity or masochism, as theorized by Freud. Although this perspective has been criticized as endorsing a view of traditional masculinity as the norm for all human behavior, their observances of girls coincide with observations made by contemporary researchers. Brown (1989; as cited in Stern, 1991) and Gilligan (1984) report decrements in self-confidence among girls aged 11 to 15 years that go "beyond the usual adolescent uncertainty and questioning to indicate a deeper conflict about the validity of what they were experiencing and seeing" (Gilligan, 1984).

Focusing on self-esteem as a marker in gender socialization, Orenstein (1994) writes that girls with a healthy self-esteem feel a sense of entitlement, a right to occupy space in the world and to be heard, expressing a full spectrum of human emotions. On the flip side of the emotional development coin, Brown (1994) writes about how girls must deal with inherent contradictions in middle-class notions of femininity, and how these contradictions undermine their strong feelings, particularly feelings of anger. She further asserts that this struggle to handle the inconsistencies in expected feminine behavior contribute to girls' disconnection from themselves and public life. Brown's qualitative study of adolescent girls uncovers the issue of class as endemic to this struggle, as working-class girls display more intense and sustained, less hidden or disguised forms of anger. She notes, however, that like middle-class girls, these girls choose, at times, to suppress strong feelings, apparently because of the potential for ruining supportive relationships.

Gilligan (1990) asserts that for girls to remain responsive to themselves, they must resist the conventions of feminine goodness; to remain responsive to others, they must resist the values placed on self-sufficiency and independence. Presented with this dilemma, choices of either appearing selfish or selfless, many silence their distinctive voices. They appear less confident, more tentative, punctuating their speech with "I don't know" rather than firm declarations of opinion.

In summary, viewing emotional development through a gender-specific lens clarifies some particular dilemmas faced by girls and women. Emotional development becomes further elaborated by women's more relational orientation and gender socialization messages involving perfection as the ultimate goal for becoming. A large portion of female emotional development centers around close interpersonal relationships and more attunement to the needs and feelings of others. Also, girls come under increasingly heavy influence by societal messages suggesting a more passive form of feminine ideal, focused on external attributes rather than on internal processes that involve expression of divergent or angry feelings.

These dilemmas, dramatically played out in adolescence, emerge in the form of a suppressed or silenced self. Both in literal expression of opinion or intense feeling and, symbolically, in terms of covert self-disavowal, girls learn to diminish themselves as a way of protecting valued connections with others, living up to the ideal image given them by gender-socialization norms. Correspondingly, girls experience more depression and other forms of internalized distress and self-abnegation upon entering adolescence than their male counterparts.

Using the foregoing conclusions, together with insights generated through traditional developmental models, it is argued that with maturity, girls learn to suppress strong or oppositional feelings via reinforcement and feedback from significant others and society at large. As girls develop increased capacity to monitor their emotional experiences and expression, they increasingly silence themselves, resulting in reduced feelings of self-efficacy or self-worth. Depressive or other symptomatology indicative of internalized distress may tend to manifest in girls who demonstrate this cumulative and selective "control" over emotional expressiveness.

Women in Adulthood

As we continue through the life cycle, adulthood brings different tasks for self-definition. Tangible markers such as relationship, career, and parenting issues come into focus, as well as less directly observable psychological processes that serve to propel the developing adult forward. Stevens-Long (1990) summarizes the major developmental theories and their treatment of adult tasks, using the categories of motivation, emotion, cognition, and behavior. These tasks appear different at each stage in adult life, but each shares the common thread of a deepening self-awareness within the context of relationships. For example, the young adult emotional task of "ma-

ture love" involves the complete identification with another, while maintaining a strong sense of self. Similarly, the young adult motivational task
of "self-actualized intimacy" integrates self-sufficiency with intimacy, as
the person resolves conflict between individuation and fusion. These tasks
become particularly treacherous for women who are diverted from the
individuation experiences that come with complete access to their anger
response.

Collier (1982) writes that society routinely teaches women not to
express anger and in some instances, not to even feel it. Thus, she believes
most women learn to hide anger or release it indirectly. Lemkau and Landau
(1986) view women's difficulty with anger as reflecting a selfless attention
to enhancing relational ties with a corresponding cost to self-awareness.
Crawford, Kippax, Onyx, Gault, and Benton (1992) offer one of the few
existing feminist analyses of emotion, suggesting that anger involves judgments about rightness and wrongness but also is related to fear. Connected
with being hurt, anger in these writers' view is disallowed for women, as
evidenced by the common ridicule or teasing of women for its expression.
Kopper and Epperson (1991) write about cultural taboos against women's
experience and expression of anger culminating in a milieu that reinforces
women's hiding, suppressing, or indirectly expressing anger. Their study
shows sex-role orientation, versus sex per se, to predict anger-expression
style, feminine orientation corresponding with controlled or internalized
expressions.

Anger suppression or internalization, the topic of more direct inquiry
in the literature on adult females, corresponds with a variety of conditions
and situations. For instance, suppressed anger relates to the experience of
unipolar depression (Sperberg, 1992; Thomas & Atakan, 1993). However,
some studies show that the *expression* of anger correlates with the experience of depression for women (Biaggio & Godwin, 1987; Frank, Carpenter, & Kupfer, 1988; Thomas, 1989). Because anger expression varies in
definition from study to study, determining behaviors and their impact
becomes difficult. However, some evidence suggests that the relationship
in which these women's anger occurs and becomes manifest may mediate
between their anger and their depressive symptomatology. Sperberg and
Stabb (1998) found that lower levels of mutuality in women's relationships contribute to the level of depression they experience relative to their
suppressed anger. Given women's relational orientation, it follows that
levels of reciprocity in the expression of emotion between partners mediates between their satisfaction in talking about anger and their subsequent
symptomatology.

Perhaps Miller and Surrey's (1990) assessment of women's use of
anger helps to further explain this phenomenon. These authors suggest
that the expression of anger per se in women's relationships pales in sig-

nificance compared with its use in identifying things that need to be changed about the connection. These authors further write that women's anger is accompanied by other feelings such as sadness, disappointment, betrayal, guilt, worry, or fear that may go unexpressed. However, they acknowledge that safe expression occurs only in a supportive relationship context. This reflects the complexity of internal processes that accompany the female experience of anger and helps explain the genesis of women's angry tears. Women typically identify aspects of their intimate relationships that need altering far more readily than they may outwardly express the singular emotion of anger. Observing a woman's tears as she attempts to deal with dissatisfaction without sanction to request desired change (i.e., to express opposition) one must notice the irony of her work. The problem appears to be that the woman, held socially responsible for relationship maintenance, is simultaneously required to refrain from the very emotion that would prove her most useful tool in this endeavor. She cries because her anger causes her great pain.

Women in Late Life

Evidence for the continued importance of "self-in-relation" among older women comes from Heidrich's (1994) study of elderly females and the relation between the self, health, and depression. She reports that positive relations with others seem to be the most important dimension of the ideal self for these women. Women appear to experience less anger in the later years of their lives, according to some studies (Bleiker, Van der Ploeg, Mook, & Kleijn, 1993; Gueldner, Butler, Ray, Rickets, & Schlotzhauer, 1994; Weiner & Graham, 1989). However, cultural expectations in relation to anger suppression fall even more heavily upon women of age than for women at other points in the life cycle. Given societal ageism, messages about the denial of oppositional feeling become even stronger for this undervalued group.

Research that seems to indirectly illustrate anger suppression in the elderly points to continued body dysmorphia in older women (Hetherington & Burnett, 1994). This study shows no significant difference between younger women (18–31 years old) and older women (60–78 years old) in dietary restraint and eating attitudes. Although younger women report greater dissatisfaction with their bodies than older women, the persistence of efforts to control one's weight by diet restriction suggests a lifelong retention of social messages about perfection. We postulate that disordered eating in late life reflects the continued presence of a connection between women's anger and eating.

In another intriguing glimpse into the possible continuation of gendered anger in late life, Pang (1990) describes a Korean disease called *Hwabyung*, theorized to relate to the suppression of anger. This affliction manifests in somatic symptoms, particularly those involving the abdomen, which, as the center of the body, is said to be the source of life energy. Further, *Hwabyung* only affects elderly Korean women, a phenomenon attributed to the fact that they suffer the accumulated stress of years of suppressed anger.

Although research directly relating to older women's anger experience is lacking, the passage of time may be postulated to contribute to the effect of cultural forces documented in earlier life periods. Women of more advanced age have had the opportunity to practice anger suppression for scores of years, and there is little in the existing literature to indicate a major change in patterns established in childhood, adolescence, and young adulthood.

☐ Resulting Dilemma for the Development of Self

From an object-relations perspective, children of both sexes receive unconscious messaging in the form of attachment style from immediate caregivers who also have received those messages (under which they now operate as parent figures) from their immediate caregivers. These messages involve, among other things, expectations regarding the management of intense feelings. As these messages become internalized, the developing child alters her or his management of the feeling, contributing to a culture wherein the emotion is seen to be handled in a particular way. Regarding the expression of anger, an emotion that holds the potential for the distinguishment of the individual as separate, social restrictions fall differentially for female and male children.

As mentioned elsewhere in this chapter, the difficulty in developing a sense of self without the full experience of anger lies in its embedded reminders of our separateness. If, then, anger is diagnostic of the self, if one discovers and maintains who one is by pushing up against the boundaries of others to feel the edge of selfhood where it bumps and scrapes against the world, then what happens to women who are taught that they are not angry, must never become angry and should never have been angry? Aspects of the self become severed and opportunities for the development of a sense of separate self become at least momentarily lost. Social training involving parent-child interaction serves to facilitate or contradict the larger cultural imperative to ignore anger. If parenting mirrors society's anger-suppression prescriptive, a form of self-amputation necessarily occurs.

Our model of women's anger includes four points with a triadic base, a triangular pyramid (see Figure 3). The base incorporates three points representing anger, gender socialization, and emotional development. The psychosocial issues of anger, gender socialization, and emotional development interact with movement between all three points. Stated differently, societal expectations of women in their experience of anger inform their development, their use of anger, and, subsequently, continued gendered expectations for behavior. These in turn play a substantial role in the generation of the peak or fourth point in our pyramid, the development of self. Lines connecting each point with the other three symbolize the bidirectional interaction among factors and the impact of all factors upon each other.

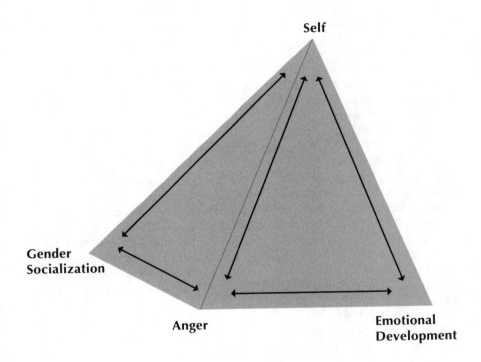

FIGURE 3. Pyramidal Model of Anger Socialization

The bridge between anger and selfhood consists of the very possibility of autonomy created by anger's experience and so very tentatively embraced in Western cultures. Development of a sense of self implies some kind of autonomous awareness of one's existence as individual. Therefore, this model of women's anger experience encompasses a socialization process inclusive of an overall cultural fear of anger, female sex-role prescription, and the resulting predicament for selfhood.

The "relational orientation" in this model seems to imply not only concern with connection to others, but also a kind of permeability or penetrability wherein the woman is rigorously trained to allow others' influence to become a part of her. In turn, relational orientation in this model implies malleability, wherein the woman's training includes practice at being changed by those influences. An openness to being changed by another rests at the heart of friendship, allowing women to cultivate strong bonds with each other. In much of Western culture, however, the permeability and malleability promoted in women also implies unidirectionality of influence. Stated differently, women become highly skilled at absorbing the impact of others' statements of opinion or feeling, but less practiced at creating similar impact in the form of directly stated feeling, especially if that feeling is at odds with the other.

Therefore, the social construction of emotional experience for women is primarily *receptive* in nature, giving rise to a problem in the experience of the self as instrumental in creating a portion of the perceived reality. Anger, as a more individually orienting emotion, has the potential to draw out those aspects of the woman's self that receive less endorsement in her social context and thus engenders fear of emotional and perhaps physical abandonment. Given "mainstream society's" quarantine of groups of women perceived stereotypically to be angry (e.g., angry lesbians, angry feminists or "women's libbers," angry Black women) it follows that a fear of this form of social desertion would accompany women's experience, however subtle or unconscious, of the emotion of anger.

Such harsh psychological consequences to open expression of divergent feeling renders its suppression something of an adaptive behavior. Although ample evidence suggests adverse physiological and psychological effects of internalizing anger (Goldman & Haaga, 1995; Greer & Watson, 1985; Mills & Dimsdale, 1993; Spicer, Jackson, & Scragg, 1993; Tennant & Langeluddecke, 1985), the developing woman perhaps chooses the apparent lesser of evils in protecting her social connections by swallowing her rage. The losses she faces in terms of self remain unnoticed for the most part until she must deal with some symptom related to her practice of this form of self-disavowal. According to some studies, this symptom likely resembles clinical depression (Beutler, Engle, Oro-Beutler, Daldrup, & Meredith, 1986; Thomas & Atakan, 1993; Tschannen, Duckro, Margolis, &

Tomazic, 1992). More is said in Chapter 5 regarding the clinical symp-tomatology associated with women's anger suppression.

☐ Summary

Emotion, specifically anger, constitutes an adaptive, behavior-modifying process moderated by the social context in which it emerges. Thus, a cir-cular and recursive process evolves among emotion, behavioral manifes-tation, and requirements of the social surround. Implications embedded in this process are gender-sensitive. By examining formulations on women's emotional development, it becomes clear that as all individuals' experi-ence comes under increasing influence of its social context, women's ex-perience carries specific diminishing or suppressing influence via pre-scribed images of ideal femininity and cultural messages prohibitive of their anger.

If anger informs the self, facilitating a sense of individual survival-related behavior, it becomes also a politically relevant emotion. If anger fosters ego-focused adaptation and a sense of one's individual rights and integrities, its suppression necessarily ushers in the potential for problems with self-protection. Research in fact points to a variety of psychological and physiological problems as being related to the suppression of anger, such as depression and lower levels of assertiveness.

Women experience a critical juncture at adolescence wherein cul-turally prescribed messages about proper femininity begin to interfere with their more self-promoting developmental tasks. Teenaged girls report more depression, negative self- and body image, eating disorders, hopeless feel-ings and suicide attempts than teenaged boys, with adjustment problems relating to internalization of distress; their male cohorts appear more likely to externalize. Because of this internalization, gender-socialization mes-sages catalyze the evolution of girls' emotional adjustment difficulties. Suppressed anger as a vehicle for gender-prescriptive behavior carries cog-nition-emotion sets to inform and paralyze the development of self. Such a process occurring individually in girls contributes to the circularity of anger, its expression, and its psychosocial environment, thus directly in-fluencing the continued social prohibition of female anger.

The apparent irony between anger's adaptive function in human experience and its social condemnation in women is owed in part to the very nature of its adaptive or ego-enhancing influence. Society's overall fear of an emotion that potentiates the choice between self and other has its roots in a long history of ambivalence about anger, misgivings that have been translated into a polarization of suppression and aggression, extremes that each fail to characterize a person's natural anger response. Rather, these polarizations give rise to continued fear and exile of human anger, particularly in women. The girl, then, becomes a part of the overall social reinforcement for women's anger suppression as she learns to quiet the stirrings of her self.

CHAPTER

Clinical Issues in Women's Anger

Of the Seven Deadly Sins,
Anger is possibly the most fun.
To lick your wounds, to smack your lips over grievance long past,
To roll over your tongue the prospect of bitter confrontation to come—
to savor the last toothsome morsel of both the pain you are giving
and the pain you are getting back,
in many ways, it is a feast fit for a king.
The chief drawback is that what you are wolfing down is yourself.
The skeleton at the feast is you.
—Unknown Author

The therapist faces a dilemma that is not often articulated. From many psychotherapists' perspectives, anger can be a vital life force to be studied in the person and channeled into growth and self-knowledge. Conversely, reflecting the poem at the start of this chapter, anger for much of the world (and much of the behavioral sciences) is a threatening and sinister force to be controlled, diminished, or even punished in individuals. If the woman informs her therapist that she hates herself when she gets angry, she could be referring to a mood that needs to be bridled for her own best interest, or, instead, something that could help her grow if she approached and became more familiar with it. Many of the clinical decisions made concerning women have to do with a resolution of this issue, which rests upon the helper's world views and assumptions about healthy emotional development. Resolving the dilemma means debunking the myths that surround the expression of strong, clear, and direct anger.

The subject of this chapter, clinical issues in women's anger, involves an exploration of a variety of presenting and underlying concerns which relate to women's anger. We examine the causes of some most commonly reported forms of women's psychological distress from the perspective of socialization as discussed in Chapter 3, tracing the path of symptom development within gendered culture. In keeping with feminist philosophy, we use a continuous, nonlinear approach to clinical anger issues, employing symptom clusters as a means for understanding various forms of distress as opposed to traditional diagnostic categories (Brabeck & Brown, 1997). Although most sets of symptoms correspond in some way with diagnoses listed in the *Diagnostic and Statistical Manual of Mental Disorders* (American Psychiatric Association, 1994), our approach to them attempts to steer the practitioner toward inductive dialogue with clients and other professionals.

The model we propose was developed in harmony with central tenets of feminist therapy, including the use of a gendered self, promotion of a feminist consciousness throughout the therapeutic process, and purposeful emphasis on the importance of power, control, and authority issues in women's lives. Its genesis lies in practical, applied experience that parallels our respect for the experience of women who take on the challenge of therapeutic work in order to examine and bring change to their lives. We also embrace the importance of consistently addressing gender roles and socialization in practice, modeling awareness of these issues as central to women's experience within relationships and within larger systems. In our attempt to firmly ground our practice in feminist philosophy and political theory, we strive to find a point of balance from which to offer something more than a static collection of techniques, without engaging in an abstraction that overpowers reality (Brabeck & Brown, 1997; Goodrich, Rampage, Ellman, & Hallstead, 1988).

This chapter also represents our conscious effort to widen the boundaries of discussion concerning the practice and application of feminist psychology beyond standard academic discourse. We endeavor to bring in the voice of the practitioner, to add a slightly different way of knowing and speaking about these issues in order to enrich the development of theoretical approaches and to create an integrated perspective. It is our goal to offer a combination of scholarly consideration and therapeutic experience throughout the following pages (Brabeck & Brown, 1997).

☐   Development of Anger-Related Distress

Symptomatology

The term *emotional deviance* functions as a label leading people to believe that they or others are mentally ill (Pugliesi, 1987). In other words, we tend to see ourselves or others as abnormal if we or they experience feelings that appear outside the range of acceptable feelings for persons in our social group. Thoits (1985) asserts that if efforts fail to bring deviant emotional experiences in line with normative expectations, people see themselves as sick. Lerman (1996) asserts that much of women's experience, if falling outside the bounds of prescribed behavior and feeling, becomes diagnosed as an illness. Here, the normative expectations are reflected in women's scripted nonexperience of anger, sexuality, and instrumentality. Historically, open sexuality in White women has received the labels of "psychopathic," "hypersexual," "nymphomaniac," and "fervor uterinus" (Lerman, 1996; Lunbeck, 1987), just as their open expression of anger is identified as narcissistic or borderline.

Gender-group membership defines pain and how it is expressed or silenced. Chronic fatigue syndrome and compulsive eating seem to predominantly affect women (Burke, 1992; Droppelman, Thomas, & Wilt, 1995); intermittent-explosive disturbances occur most frequently in boys and young men (American Psychiatric Association, 1994). Other sets of symptoms predominate in people of various ethnic or subculture backgrounds, as with depression, which often exhibits in primarily somatic ways for people of Asian heritage (American Psychiatric Association, 1994; Maser & Dinges, 1992–1993). Although factors such as physiology, development, and folklore necessarily enter into the overall picture of health and disease, the manner in which distress emerges within a given group of people has something to do with the way fierce emotion interacts with unique cultural prescriptions for behavior. Applied to women, the symptom-selection process implies a fit between the woman and her culture in terms of her presenting distress, begging the question of how acceptable a certain form of discomfort is for women in a particular group, as compared with other forms. Or, more specifically, how acceptable is a woman's panic, as compared with her rage?

Olivia is a 50-year-old Japanese-American woman who has always lived in the United States. She is married to a successful business executive and is the mother of three grown children. Olivia attends community college and presents to counseling because of a persistent inability to write in public.

She writes at home when no one else is around, composing letters and paying bills. However, when she goes to her English class at the college, she can neither take notes nor respond to questions on an essay examination. The debilitating problem has been with Olivia for as long as she can remember, causing her to be retained in the early elementary grades and be classified as "slow." Because she knows she has the ability to write in private situations, she fights a constant bewilderment about "freezing up" in environments in which she might be watched. She tells about feeling horrified at the thought of her instructor observing her as she puts words to paper and suddenly experiencing her hands as clumsy, the pen a useless stick in her hand, while her memory is bankrupt of letters or words.

As Olivia continues to tell about the experiences she has had with her writing problem, she remembers an additional trauma that began when she was about 6 years old. She recalls being abandoned by her natural mother, raised by an aunt, and treated as if she were despised in this relative's household. Olivia's aunt lavished her own children with gifts and attention, virtually ignoring the niece who was now in her charge. She was deposited at school in a new town, with no nurturance or support from home, having lost her own dear parents with no explanation or opportunity to grieve. She tells the story with budding empathy for her small first-grade self. She grieves fiercely now and begins to see how the experience of being treated as someone who had nothing to say for so many years now creeps into her adult life wherein she only utters those things which she knows are safe.

Adult Olivia marries a powerful but cowardly man, who becomes easily threatened by her quiet displays of wisdom. She learns quickly not to outshine him or threaten him with her quick wit and resourcefulness. In the past, she has been met with more rebuff and ridicule after disagreeing with her mate. He has told her not to bother thinking, that her mind is useless. Although she has owned three thriving businesses in her adulthood, she has never once written down her thoughts or feelings. Now she wants a formal education more than anything and must learn to unlock her inner wisdom for use in her endeavor. As Olivia continues to explore her feelings about these family relationships, her writing problem begins to worsen.

Olivia's case illustrates the complexity in women's presenting symptoms, and how easy it is to lose anger in the tangle of other issues presented in therapy. Olivia continues to wrestle with her right to speak and be heard, and as she does, she recognizes that the same adaptive muffling that has kept her silent enough to survive so many years in less-than-mutual relationships is the muffling that works to render her apraxic in the presence of others.

Women's nonpsychotic psychological symptomatologies may be conceptualized as most often revolving around the following clusters: (a) depressive features, (b) anxious features, (c) somatic features, and (d) problematic consumptive features (problems with eating, spending, sex, and substance abuse). These features overlap each other and often coexist to produce significant despair.

Though these primary disturbances tend to propel women into psychotherapy by virtue of their pernicious effects on overall functioning, some element of relationship despair usually resides within and around them, becoming the focus of a woman's psychotherapy. Often, these relationship issues involve strong emotion that is ignored or condemned, giving rise to compensatory emotional states that serve a woman's felt need to rid herself of the more primary but less tolerable feeling. In other words, women come to feel something besides their anger in relationships in which anger is prohibited or ignored. Anger or some variant thereof (jealousy, resentment, frustration, indignation, outrage) often comes to the forefront in therapy as women uncover the origins of their panic, binge eating, fatigue, or melancholy.

In Droppelman, Thomas, and Wilt's (1995) study, 91% of women reported avoidance of direct anger expression to the target of their displeasure, favoring instead denial of their own hurt in order to protect the feelings of others. This sample of women describes deliberate attempts to overlook injuries by others, a habit these authors suggest compromises both their emotional and physical well-being. The authors list several physiological and emotional conditions that relate empirically to lack of direct anger expression, including hypertension, coronary heart disease, breast cancer, depression, migraine headaches, and obesity. Taking the issue a step further, we add that women's attempts at avoidance of emotion makes necessary (i.e., adaptive) the use of some fundamental diversion of anger. Women become ill or symptomatic in spite of the resultant stigma, pain, and losses experienced, rather than directly knowing and seizing the forbidden feeling of anger. From a sociological perspective, assessment of emotional well-being and the meaning we ascribe to certain symptoms and conflicts emerge as a product of both interpretive and interactional processes (Emerson & Messinger, 1977). Relational problems frequently become redefined as individual ones, as a woman takes full responsibility for the relationship problem by becoming sick instead of angry. Symptoms therefore appear quite personal on the surface, camouflaging the underlying relational despair.

Are these symptoms real entities or mere emblems promulgated by a culture that assigns diagnoses to the emotions it refuses to tolerate? Rather than offer an absolute or arbitrary answer, we turn to the authenticity of women's voices for understanding. Their stories compel us to treat these disturbances as real and as obstacles to achieving fulfilled and enriched lives. Later in this chapter, these clusters of symptoms are detailed and explored, but first we look at how anger is currently assessed and measured.

Anger Evaluated: The Measurement of Anger

We can learn a lot about women's anger by looking at attempts that have been made to measure anger and related constructs in both men and women. In reviewing tests designed to assess anger, we face ideas born within traditions of thought that have prevailed for the past 60 years or more. Tests reflect the culture in which they are developed. Professional socialization, the invisible aspects of training embedded in culture, depends largely on theoretical and clinical construals of emotion as well as prevailing standards for what is considered normal and abnormal. Although work recently has been undertaken in this vein, no unified definition of healthy or normal anger yet exists in the clinical literature. Looking at available assessment instruments highlights the artificial dichotomies and quantifications present in general anger theory (e.g., anger internalized versus externalized; amount of tendency to respond angrily), which manifest in research and clinical practice as well as public opinion. Our brief review of these instruments suggests that explosive behavior and emotional suppression, opposite ends of the anger expression spectrum in both sexes, receive attention, but assertive, nonexplosive options and positive uses of anger often go unrecognized in research, theory, and clinical practice. Historically, efforts to quantify, describe, and define anger for purposes of assessment often confuse constructs, mixing the notion of aggression or explosiveness with simple anger and its expression. Most measures focus on anger-related problems, and only a few address positive or adaptive aspects of the emotion, allowing a necessary conceptual distinction between feelings and behavior, as well as between explosive or aggressive displays and more constructive outward forms of expression (Müller, Rau, Brody, Elbert, & Heinle, 1995). Thus, the instruments available today, described more fully subsequently, appear to focus more on the types of anger experience that we have come to call diversions of anger. In pursuing the definition of a constructive, instrumental, and assertive anger expression, we find very little by way of assessment that is applicable.

Most available anger indices fall into two categories: those that measure responses to specific anger-provoking situations, and those that contain items intended to measure anger in a more general, less situationally bound manner (Knight, Ross, Collins, & Parmenter, 1985). For example, Novaco's Anger Inventory (Novaco, 1975) uses situation-based items to elicit self-report measures of anger with items such as "watching someone berate another person to excess," and "someone ripping off your automobile antenna." In contrast, the Buss-Durkee Hostility Inventory (Buss & Durkee, 1957) and, more recently, the State-Trait Anger Scale (STAS; Spielberger, Jacobs, Russell, & Crane, 1983), both detailed later in this chapter, represent approaches to anger as an underlying trait, with less use of contrived situations for drawing responses. The two primary scales of the Zuckerman Inventory of Personal Reactions (Zuckerman,1977; Zuckerman & Mellstrom,1977) combine the situational approach with a state-trait distinction. The trait scale of this instrument taps into five categories of affective response (fear arousal, positive affective, anger and aggression, attentive coping, and feelings of sadness); the state scale measures how respondents feel at the time of administration, without the use of situation prompts.

Another distinction between various anger measures has to do with the language used to define constructs being appraised. Most often, a very broad term such as "hostility" is used to mean the feeling of anger and any related observable behaviors, usually depicted as explosive or aggressive. Buss and Durkee's (1957) instrument, one of the earliest attempts to measure anger, uses the term hostility to indicate several different portrayals of anger, some of which reflect much more of an internal feeling state than an overt expression of volatility. This nonspecific use of terms creates implications not only for the accuracy of particular instruments, but for overall conceptualizations of anger adopted within the discipline of psychology, as well as within society.

The Buss-Durkee Hostility Inventory (1957) blurs the boundary between anger and hostility by using a generalized definition of the latter and employing a broad range of feeling states and described behaviors. Still widely used to assess various views of anger, its authors aim to provide both a global measure and several subclasses of the phenomenon, including assault, indirect hostility, irritability, negativism, resentment, suspicion, and verbal hostility (some of which are instinctive internal states potentially helpful in identifying situations of danger or other negative impact on the individual). Each of these subscales contains a mix of behavior-related items and those that describe feeling-states, such as, "I often feel like a powder keg, ready to explode." Although some items tap into feeling responses without associated behavior, the instrument yields no separate scores for feeling states, independent of behavior. Thus, the inventory as a whole obscures the important distinction between the emotion of anger and its possible behavioral sequelae. Buss and Durkee acknowledge that their instrument assesses only personality components "generally regarded as being socially undesirable" (p. 345), which is the usual stance taken with regard to hostility.

The construct of hostility, a set of behaviors or attitudes related to anger, is generally thought to involve some degree of antagonism or enmity (American Heritage Dictionary, 1982). Commonly regarded as pathological, hostility encompasses many subcomponents, and its definition has engaged the efforts of many theorists. Voluminous research during recent decades results in inconsistent findings, perhaps because of complications with defining hostility and the incompatibility of various scales. Cook and Medley's Hostility Scale of the Minnesota Multiphasic Personality Inventory (Cook & Medley, 1954; Hathaway & McKinley, 1943) represents another attempt to accurately define hostility. The scale measures suspiciousness, resentment, frequent anger, and cynical distrust of others—a combination of factors called "cynical hostility" by Smith and Frohm (1985).

Some evidence links the hostility scale with subjects' trait anger (Smith & Frohm, 1985; Spielberger et al., 1983) and with resentment (Buss & Durkee, 1957). Smith and Frohm suggest that the hostility scale measures a rather specific form of hostility, which renders individuals more likely to be vigilant, calculating, and manipulative in their social relationships, but not necessarily to use more physical aggression. High scorers are likely to feel more dysphoric, more isolated, and to experience more health problems than low scorers on the hostility scale.

Developed primarily for use in clinical assessment, the Reaction Inventory (Evans & Strangeland, 1971) measures anger in individuals approaching clearer definition in its use of the terms anger and aggression. Using a situational-elicitor approach, the instrument asks subjects to rate from 1 to 5 how much the event depicted in each item angers them (e.g., "people pushing into line"), with items falling into the following categories: minor chance annoyances, destructive people, unnecessary delays, inconsiderate people, frustration in business, criticism, major chance annoyances, people being personal, and authority. This inventory seems to attempt quantification of all possible anger-elicitors in the interest of predicting aggression. The authors assert that "theoretically specific stimulus situations as measured by The Reaction Inventory result in anger, which in turn leads to aggressive behavior" (p. 413). This assumes that feeling anger causes one to act aggressively (or act at all).

In contrast to all the above, the Anger Self-Report (Zelin, Adler, & Myerson, 1972) attempts to distinguish between the awareness of angry feelings and the expression of aggressive impulses. Using a Likert format, the instrument yields separate scores for awareness of anger, expression of anger, guilt, condemnation of anger, and mistrust, allowing for the assessment of negative metaemotion relative to anger. In other words, a person's own thoughts and feelings about his or her anger can be evaluated with the Anger Self-Report. Under the expression subscale, separate scores for general, physical, and verbal expression may be obtained. As with the

Reaction Inventory, no gender information is reported for the Anger Self-Report's norming samples.

As mentioned previously, another situationally based instrument, Novaco's (1974) Anger Inventory measures the degree to which a person becomes angered in various provocative scenarios (e.g., "being called a liar," "someone spits at you"). Originally designed for use in both Novaco's research and clinically as a screening inventory for admission to an anger-treatment program, the Anger Inventory provides an index of the disposition for anger as well as the types of stimuli that provoke anger in a person through the use of a five-point rating scale. Novaco provides gender differential information on his norming sample that indicates that men give higher ratings of anger for items having physical content, and women give higher ratings for items involving unfair or unjust events. In regard to anger's constructive and destructive potential, Novaco's cognitive, self-control–based treatment program purports to regulate not only angry behavior but the very arousal of anger itself in individuals. We discuss the ramifications surrounding this therapeutic perspective with regard to women's healing.

The Subjective Anger Scale (Knight et al., 1985), a more recent attempt to use situation referencing to measure propensity for anger responsiveness, employs anger terms in a more specified manner than most of the other scales. The Subjective Anger Scale asks for individual response to such cues as, "You have just found out someone has told lies about you." Knight and colleagues clarify their use of the term "anger" by distinguishing it from aggression and hostility, assigning it solely to the subjective experience of angry feelings. They further report women in their norming sample to indicate somewhat greater degrees of anger responsiveness than men.

The Clinical Anger Scale (Snell, Gum, Shuck, Mosley, & Hite, 1995) attempts to measure the syndrome of "clinical anger." This instrument addresses the following symptoms: anger now, anger about the future, anger about failure, anger about things, angry-hostile feelings, annoying others, angry about self, angry misery, wanting to hurt others, shouting at people, irritated now, social interference, decision interference, alienating others, work interference, sleep interference, fatigue, appetite interference, health interference, thinking interference, and sexual interference. Nearly all of these factors reflect one's discomfort with anger or a negative experience with anger and present a range of potential areas to be affected by clinical levels of anger. In this model, clinical anger consists of symptoms varying in strength and intensity that exist in a variety of contexts. Additionally, the authors assume that clinical levels of anger involve a person's social relationships. High scores on clinical anger show correlations with other measures of symptomatology and "unhealthy behaviors," according to preliminary investigation. Snell and colleagues report similar clinical anger scores for men and women in their norming sample.

Another approach widely used in current research allows for the assessment of styles of anger expression using a continuum of possible expression modalities. Quite a number of studies employ one of the measures designed by Spielberger and colleagues. The STAS (Spielberger et al., 1983) contains two subscales relative to (a) the amount of anger a person is currently feeling, and (b) more enduring, chronic feelings of anger. By design, the STAS assesses the intensity of anger as a state and measures individual differences in anger-proneness.

Spielberger et al.'s (1985) Anger Expression Scale assesses individual differences in anger as a personality trait. Constructed as part of research principally focused on the etiology of hypertension and coronary heart disease, the scale yields three scores for (a) anger-in (suppressed or internalized anger; e.g., "I boil inside but don't show it."), (b) anger-out (anger expressed outwardly, most often depicted in explosive or aggressive terms; e.g., "I strike out at whatever infuriates me"), and (c) anger-control (attempts to contain the expression or experience of anger).

Originally, it was expected that anger-in and anger-out on the Anger Expression Scale would represent opposite ends of an expression spectrum, one predicting the other. However, factor analysis indicates each of these two dimensions are, in fact, discrete, a puzzling phenomenon if one assumes a dichotomous approach to understanding individual expression of anger. Martin and Watson (1997) point out that "anger-in" may represent a larger, more complex set of individual differences in emotionality than simply suppression of anger, and the two dimensions indexed may more closely parallel the ideas of emotional experience and overt behavior. Spielberger and colleagues (1985) report both higher state and trait anger for men in their norming samples, as compared with women, on the STAS. They also report moderately high correlations between state anger and state anxiety for both men and women on the STAS (Spielberger et al., 1983) a finding the authors suggest results from people's anger and aggression being punished in childhood.

A later instrument, the Pediatric Anger Expression Scale (PAES) developed by Jacobs and Blumer (1985), measures children's use of anger-in versus anger-out in anger expression with the addition of a scale that reflects the use of assertive and constructive problem solving. This scale, modeled after the State Trait Anger Expression Inventory (Spielberger, 1988) yields four different scores relative to anger expression: (a) anger-out, (b) anger-in, (c) anger reflection, and (d) anger control. This final subscale focuses on behavior intended to control angry reactions as well as attempts to resolve the conflict or the upset with strategies that are more cognitive in nature. Anger reflection or control, corresponds to items such as, "I try to calmly settle the problem" and "I keep my cool." Although this instrument is still being developed and its psychometric properties with regard to anger reflection still call for further refinement, it contributes to our ability to understand children's anger expression styles and possibly their use of options other than either extreme of explosive or repressive expression.

Another important aspect of anger experience and expression involves a person's comfort level with her or his own anger. Sharkin and Gelso's (1991) Anger Discomfort Scale measures negative feelings about one's own anger. In Sharkin and Gelso's conceptualization, individuals high in anger discomfort feel both threatened by their experience of the emotion and worried about others' reactions to it. Questionnaire items are rated on a four-point Likert scale in terms of how characteristic they are to the person (e.g., "I am embarrassed when I get angry"). Although the Anger Discomfort Scale deals primarily with troublesome feelings, factor analysis reveals a clustering of items expressed in positive terms and indicative of comfort with anger (i.e., "I believe it is natural and healthy to feel angry"), an ease with anger's place in one's working set of emotions. Sharkin and Gelso (1991) report a positive relationship between anger discomfort and trait anxiety for their norming sample. Further, in this study, anger discomfort correlated with both anger suppression and expression, giving rise to the speculation that discomfort with anger is both an antecedent and a consequence of other aspects of anger experience. In other words, a feedback loop develops between the feelings of anger and other kinds of discomfort that accompany it. If we feel angry, we often get immediately anxious and uncomfortable because we are angry.

Specific to women's anger, Van Goozen, Frijda, and Van de Poll (1994) offer the Anger Situation Questionnaire (ASQ), a vignette-driven approach to measuring "anger-proneness" in women. The authors conceptualize anger-proneness as a low threshold for angry action readiness, a disposition to appraise situations in angry ways, or both. Citing the large body of data showing sex differences in aggression and causes for anger, Van Goozen et al. set out to gather information relative to "experienced emotion," "felt intensity," and "action readiness." The authors also argue that compared with traditional questionnaires (e.g., the STAS), their 33 vignettes represent situations more clearly relevant to women's anger. For each scenario women are asked (a) which emotion would be felt, (b) how intense this feeling would be, and (c) what action they would want to take. The authors of the ASQ set out to capture anger proneness, instead of overtly aggressive behavior as an index of likelihood to become angry. To accomplish this, Van Goozen and colleagues combine "assertive" and "aggressive" tendencies into one scorable construct (anger-proneness).

The consolidation of these two tendencies makes sense in light of the fact that this research compares women's aggression with men's. However, the overlapping of assertive and aggressive anger expressions, and the assumption that their combination makes up a trait that could be described as "level of likelihood to become angry" may oversimplify the very complex experience of anger, its storage, and its outward manifestation. Van Goozen and colleagues equate "anger-proneness" with the materialization of some kind of self-interested response. The woman who endorses no need for taking action with her anger, nor much awareness of the feeling itself, would receive a less anger-prone score even if she were smoldering much of the time just outside her own conscious awareness. It appears that even though women respond in terms of both feeling and action on the ASQ, the construct being defined is a quality that encompasses them both. This becomes problematic if we talk to women who store anger inside, hiding it from others and themselves, without demonstrating any kind of assertive or aggressive behavior.

What exactly is anger-proneness? Are only certain people anger-prone at certain times and in certain situations? What does it mean to suggest that some women are more prone to anger than others? Do some women feel anger more intensely or in more situations than others? Perhaps the notion being chased here is a tendency to acknowledge anger in a conscious way versus the inclination to ignore internal and external signals that convey the meaning that "I am furious." Would we expect two different women to both experience some kind of anger at being insulted or cheated in some way? Although each woman's experience is unique and no two women can be expected to experience the same affective spectrum given the same scenario, we can be reasonably certain that many or most women would feel some degree and kind of anger in those situations.

Perhaps then, anger-proneness (in whatever obvious or not-so-obvious form) can be some form of instrumental awareness, a likelihood to act in one's own interest if angry or at least a likelihood to know that one is angry. Conversely, perhaps less anger-proneness is a kind of longer-term storage issue resulting from internalized, unvoiced, untouched anger that is never trusted to speak or emerge from the shadows of the unconscious. Anger-proneness could be less an index of likelihood than a statement of misdirection. Finally, because Van Goozen et al. (1994) argue anger without assertiveness is a less anger-prone reaction than is anger with assertiveness, it seems they may mesh internal response and desire to act with what a woman actually allows herself to do relative to that feeling. We speculate, however, that inwardly wanting to shout at someone (or just noticing some unnamed discomfort) is quite different from actually doing so. A very crucial difference resides between instrumental awareness of feeling and overt action on that feeling, a point acknowledged by these authors. To get at the notion of assertiveness in concert with readiness, one would need to use actual behavioral records (e.g., journaling, peer ratings) to more accurately assess the assertiveness of the outcome. Because the ASQ moves our assessment repertoire closer to encompassing women's tendencies, additional research is needed to provide confirmation of its predictive validity. For these reasons, the addition of some dimension to address actual behavior alongside readiness could illuminate the tension that lies between a woman's internal readiness and the action she permits herself to take. This lack of differentiation in the ASQ is indicative of the general obfuscation of subtleties involved in the measurement of anger.

Each of the aforementioned scales attempts to quantify, confine, and define anger for the sake of psychometrics and empirical research. However, our dialogue suggests a need for more inductive, open-ended assessment procedures. For example, if we view anger as a universally reflexive emotion, we become less interested in placing a numeric value on tendency to react angrily. Instead, we become much more interested in how often that feeling is translated into conscious acknowledgment and tangible behavior. Using this approach, we assume some degree or quality of the emotion is present within all individuals at some time or another, given evocative circumstances. So, instead of assigning a value to someone's tendency to be angry (a value that may reflect more their circumstances than their actual psychological difference from other people), we closely examine the relationship between eliciting context and what the person knows and does. What happens in this woman's environment that injures her? How much injury does she allow herself to feel? What does she do with that feeling?

How well do commonly used assessment tools measure a woman's level of anger, or her tendency to respond to it in a certain way? Moreover, do these approaches allow for a deepened understanding of her anger as it evolves within the relational atmosphere in which she lives? Do they take into account the interactive conditions in which the anger emerges? Do these tests discern her more visceral responses and make those distinct from her socialized responses ("I feel" versus "I should or shouldn't feel"). The use of such testing to measure anger and the implied constructs of "good" and "bad" that come from these tests serve only rudimentary research and clinical needs, and the cost of this approach may be that anger, as it is variously packaged for the sake of assessment, loses some of its essential meaning as individuals' own most salient triggers and unique responses go uninvestigated. The emotion becomes construed as, and limited to, the potentially frightening and aversive features to which clinicians are asked to attend and are socialized to diagnose. In particular, the complicated internal stories of a woman's anger in-relation may be obscured in the effort to assign some level or type to her anger.

Additionally, how culturally sensitive are these measures of anger? Do indices of anger-proneness or readiness tap the same characteristics in people across ethnicities and subcultures? These instruments measure various pieces of the anger spectrum and which pieces fit together differently for women and men. How would these aspects of anger experience compare if measured across cultures? Most of these questions represent unexplored issues for research and theory. Yet, as we accumulate cross-gender and cross-cultural data on anger, we learn more about both the universality and the uniqueness of individual anger experience.

Other important questions raised by an examination of these instruments are: What constitutes a clinical level of any emotion? What differences exist between men and women in the experience of measurable anger-related despair? What predictions arise out of measuring aspects of women's anger (both in terms of symptomatology and growth-promoting traits, behaviors, and so forth)? What gains can women expect to make intra- and interpersonally through a deeper familiarity with their own anger? What healthy and constructive experiences do women have with their anger in relationship? How are socialization factors inhibiting our professional and societal recognition of healthy anger?

The scales measure different portions of the overall gestalt of human anger. Recognizing them as such, we can identify potential oversimplifications and misclassifications embedded in them (e.g., "expression" versus "nonexpression"). Because we know relatively little about anger expression in terms of its nature and effects (Martin & Watson, 1997), it seems imperative that we return to a more inductive, exploratory approach to understanding anger expression, especially in individuals or groups for whom solid empirical information is sparse.

Anger Diverted

For this discussion, we define anger as a form of emotional energy that is directed or applied in a number of possible ways and typically depends upon an object or target for its materialization. It must be consciously or unconsciously directed at someone or something, although many of us feel anger without real clarity over its target. Note the relationship inherent in this idea. Feeling angry involves at least two individuals, as illustrated in Bowlby's (1973) conjectures about attachment and anger. Bowlby held that anger could be *functional*, as in anger that engenders the hope of change or transformation. This kind of anger occurs if individuals are both securely attached and have learned that anger can be released or acted upon in constructive ways. In contrast, people who have insecure attachments most often experience a *dysfunctional* anger, according to this model. Dysfunctional anger is an anger of despair, wherein individuals have learned to expect unsatisfying, perhaps even devastating outcomes if they are angry.

We, the authors posit that women's dysfunctional anger, the type of anger that creates women's despair is relational in nature, and involves one or more of the following diversions: suppression, internalization, segmentation, and externalization. These categories of misapplication denote the process by which anger makes its way to the root of a woman's presenting problem. If writers suggest a link between powerlessness, victimization, and later symptomatology (Epstein, Saunders, Kilpatrick, & Resnick, 1998; Goodman, Dutton, & Harris, 1997; Leserman, Li, Drossman, & Hu, 1998; Perrin, Van Hasselt, & Hersen, 1997; Whiffen & Clark, 1997), they speak of the antecedents to the disturbance, not the route through which those antecedents become a disturbance. Powerlessness and abuse precede emotional reactions in the person that can later evolve into patterns of distress. Because it is reasonable to assume that women in positions of low power and higher vulnerability to victimization experience anger in response to being dominated, it also becomes imperative for those seeking to more clearly understand these women's situations to pursue the trajectory of that anger.

Similarly, if authors point to gender-socialized behaviors or attitudes that relate to symptoms or diagnostic categories, a closer inspection must follow to show how these behaviors transform themselves into actual disturbance. For example, Munchausen syndrome by proxy (MSP) has been characterized as a "woman's disorder" (Robins & Sesan, 1991), as it involves primarily mothers, who knowingly induce or exaggerate physical symptoms in their children for purposes of obtaining medical attention. These authors review studies in which mothers with MSP are evaluated to have difficulty with autonomy and self care. However, we view the characteristic sacrifice of self in mothers with MSP as a surface layer of behaviors situated just above a restricted expression of self-interested, ego-focused emotions, one of which is anger. Jack (in press) asserts that efforts to diminish anger lead instead to its continued arousal as, paradoxically, the socialized internal tyrant (gendered standards) inflicts judgment upon its own angry self. The double bind of self judging self makes it necessary to divert one's anger pathway, in this instance toward the direction of exaggerated caretaking roles that themselves become receptacles for anger that must not be voiced. This necessary act of redirecting the flow of anger energy can lead to certain kinds of suffering, and if it cannot be directly voiced, anger must live elsewhere in the woman (i.e., her repertoire of roles and behaviors). In the case of MSP, she turns to the mothering role, which becomes a place for her to both express and suppress her own needs.

What follows here is a look at symptom development for women within each area of socialized diversion of anger—leading to an exploration of the symptom clusters and their roots in the silencing of women's real emotion and avoidance of the self. We hold anger to be an essential, adaptive part of human experience and note that some problems that present in psychotherapy originate in the socialized degradation of the emotion. What develops into awareness in the woman and demands attention looks like a cluster of features such as difficulty sleeping and finding pleasure in ordinarily pleasurable activities—perhaps combined with some kind of gastrointestinal discomfort. Beneath the presenting despair lies some kind of diverted anger to which clinical attention may be focused. Is anger the core issue for every woman who seeks therapy? Certainly not, but if anger is present, it is often unacknowledged or under-acknowledged as a source of both pain and possibility. Therefore the authors attempt a careful scrutiny of the processes by which symptomatology develops from anger experience.

Viewing anger diversion as a complex process with many possible forms reflects our intention to move beyond conventional dichotomies in personality and affect. For example, notions of "instrumentality" as masculine and "expressivity" as feminine derive from the traditional use of Spence and Helmreich's (1979) Personal Attributes Questionnaire and appear regularly in the literature. Typical descriptions of expressivity are paradoxical in that they involve nurturance, tenderness, and caring, leaving out the expression of anger and assertiveness. As usually conceived, a higher score on the expressivity or "femininity" scale has nothing to say about how likely a person is to stand up for his or her own rights or make a statement of his or her displeasure. Given this kind of contradiction, as well as our foregoing discussion of ways in which anger has been measured historically, we attempt to break away from dichotomous models of instrumentality and anger management (anger-in and -out; expressed or not expressed; masculine and feminine) into a multidimensional model of anger direction or diversion. We present categories of diversion for ongoing discussion. In more ways than one, anger is expressed either overtly or covertly to an audience of self or others. However, the precise direction and nature of that expression depends on many factors and is not limited to the categorizations presented here.

Suppression

The act of suppression begins our list of diversions. Although the term *suppression* is used in a variety of ways both in anger research and in emotion theory, we electively use the term for the duration of this book to indicate somatic or physiological concomitants with the avoidance of direct anger expression. If anger is expressed in a manner other than direct action taken on the environment with intent to create change (e.g., discussion with target), certain physiological events take place that accompany suppression, the conscious (albeit most likely unnamed), phenomenological experience of "holding back" or "swallowing" one's anger.

Droppelman et al. (1995) describe bodily concomitants of general anger as increased cardial output and peripheral vasoconstriction with elevations in blood pressure. These changes make up a physiological response of arousal (Smith & Allred, 1989) hypothesized to contribute to disease, if prolonged, by producing adrenocortical hyperresponsivity (Williams & Barefoot, 1988; for a more thorough review, see Thomas, 1993). It follows that a suppression of this emotional experience, by means of keeping one's feelings hidden to self and others, is actually not suppression at all, but prolonging of response on a more muted level. Suppression most likely prolongs and exacerbates these physiological changes by thwarting a release or catharsis, encompassing the act of not saying how we feel, and the accompanying bodily changes. However, there are other possible vehicles for "not saying," discussed subsequently. We use the term suppression specifically in reference to the use of physical response to the silencing of felt anger.

In part, our rationale for pinning the label "suppression" on these prolonged physiological anger correlates derives from recent research done by Gross (1998) in which antecedent- and response-focused emotion regulation are separated into "reappraisal" and "suppression." In Gross's work, reappraisal is a cognitive process by which emotional experience itself is moderated through thinking differently about a situation (a concept not unrelated to our use of "internalization," to be detailed next). Conversely, suppression in this study is the act of hiding an already-evoked emotional response or display, as illustrated by increased sympathetic nervous system activation in response to watching a disgust-eliciting film. Gross proposes that using suppression to regulate affective response actually sustains the physiological activity generated in the emotional experience because it entails the added task of containing what one is already feeling. In fact, "anger suppression," as variably defined in the literature, relates to an assortment of physiological processes including hypertension (Cottington, Matthews, Talbott, & Kuller, 1986; Mills & Dimsdale, 1993), atherosclerosis (Tennant & Langeluddecke, 1985), and colorectal cancer (Kune, Kune, Watson, & Bahnson, 1991). Such phenomena appear to involve biological correlates of stress, namely increased autonomic arousal, endocrine, and immunological responses (Greer & Watson, 1985).

If both sexes are studied with regard to physiological anger symptoms, women tend to report more symptoms than do men (Durel et al., 1989; Thomas, 1989). Women experience the tangible distress of anger suppression as a tightness in the chest and lungs; muscular tension (especially in the upper back, neck, and shoulders); nausea and abdominal cramping or diarrhea; headaches, including migraines; insomnia; muscle spasms; and general, nonspecific feelings of discomfort. The authors theorize that true somatic anger can become so well hidden in the body that links to its emotional and relational precursors fade into oblivion. Women's bodies declare lost anger at others, but their focus remains on individual, physical symptoms; shortness of breath becomes self-recrimination for "too little exercise," cranial throbbing is excused as "overstress."

Mary, a 74-year-old great-grandmother has the distinction of having undergone 13 different surgeries during her lifetime. She has had surgery for gall bladder removal, hip injuries, heart problems, hernias, and bowel obstructions. She has survived a hysterectomy, several sprained joints, migraine headaches, serious colitis, and chronic major upper-respiratory problems, just to name a few things. Mary talks at length about her physical predicaments and the doctors who have treated them. She gets to know her treating physicians well because she sees them often and for lengthy visits. Mary is not a psychotherapy client, but her adult daughters are.

Mary's daughters, Janine and Sarah, describe their mother's life in terms of her unremitting focus on medical problems, both hers and those of her children. They are quick to point out the impact this has had on their own development and parenting, saying it is difficult now to remember what happened between people in their family, and what they felt as girls, except for when it comes to being sick and receiving attention from their mother. As adults, they have discovered that Mary was physically and emotionally abused by her mother and an uncle who lived in their home. She was once locked in an outside garage for an entire day as punishment for grimacing when she was told to give up her own toy to a neighbor child who wanted it. Displays of negative feeling were not tolerated in this household, where adults were frightened of losing control. Paradoxically, Mary was allowed to express physical pain and discomfort and was in fact rewarded for such behavior by being allowed to stay home from school and help her mother if she (Mary) appeared ill.

As Janine and Sarah's mother, Mary brought forward the same tradition and consequently punished the appearance of anger in her daughters. She survived a 28-year marriage that included regular infidelity by her spouse. Her girls knew of her feelings only because she warned them constantly about the diabolic nature of men. She kept their house impeccably clean, dressed her girls in the finest clothes, and played bridge each week with her friends. Whenever either daughter appeared to be in any physical discomfort, Mary lavished her with attention and care.

Janine and Sarah initiated family therapy, and Mary attended on one occasion. In the course of asking about her life the subject of anger was raised, and Mary asserted that she was angry with her daughters for digging up the past. What emerges from Mary's clinical picture is not only her extensive and involved medical history, but the notable absence of overt anger acknowledgment. Ironically, Mary gives voice to her irritation if prompted but directs this toward her grown children, who are insisting she address anger issues.

Internalization

The principle differences between suppression and internalization as used here have to do with both level of awareness and point of focus. To address the former, women may hold back overt anger by keeping quiet and thus experience the sustained physiological changes (suppression), while having a sense that they are angry but in no safe place to articulate or act upon that anger. Internalization takes the notion of suppression and goes a bit further to acknowledge parallel cognitive and emotional reorganization that become necessary to accommodate storage of the emotion. The principle difference involves the point at which women focus their energies on reversing an affective response. In other words, internalization can be used to prevent the actual experience of the emotion, instead of simply squelching its display to others, as in suppression. Here, internalization denotes the personal absorption of both cognitive and affective elements involved in the experience of anger. Gross's (1998) use of the term *reappraisal* is similar in that it describes the cognitive activity designed to accomplish internalization. Reappraisal is a way of altering one's cognitions around an experience, so as to think differently and thereby preclude the anger experience.

Women who internalize lose awareness of their anger at others but tend to carry many negative feelings about themselves. In contrast, direct action taken to release and express one's anger includes talking about it, writing about it, perhaps yelling and screaming about it, or maybe even doing something physical with it—all with some intention involved. If anger expression does not take some form of direct action, a reorganization of elements occurs, resulting in a redirection of cognitive and feeling factors within the individual psyche. Internalization clearly demonstrates misdirection of anger if women experience self-blame or self-loathing instead of acknowledged anger at another person or entity. Symptoms of internalization show themselves in cognitive ways, as in distortions of self-concept. Beliefs that one's body or appearance is deformed or unappealing, or that one is inherently shameful or disgusting, replace the original outrage. Cognitively, these beliefs develop through unconscious messaging as women's attributions for anger elicitors shift. "I am less worthy as I am deconstructing my personal experience to fit the needs or expectations of an other or others." Although such a statement is rarely made fully consciously, women must continuously and unconsciously reattribute (or misattribute) meaning to situations in which they cannot claim their angry voices. This diversion epitomizes the thinking aspects of anger turned inward, upon the self.

Similarly, internalization of anger results in affective symptoms, as in depression or anxiety. Beck's (1972) cognitive theory of depression highlights distortions in thought processes and content as major contributors to depressive syndromes. This link may be the connection between widely noted "anger suppression" and depressive symptomatology (Thomas, 1989; Thomas & Atakan, 1993). In fact, anger emerges as a mediating factor between locus of control or attributional style and depression in some studies (Lester, 1989; Young, 1991). If we perceive ourselves to be in a less powerful position with regard to others and feel unable to express anger toward them, we are more likely to become depressed. Cognitive reorganization becomes necessary to fit knowledge of an offense or threat (anger elicitor) into a framework reflecting that we have not responded assertively, a failure to defend the boundaries of our selfhoods. Almost immediate shifts occur wherein the offended party takes some share of responsibility for the offense. Jack (1991) theorizes that the depressed woman has self-images directing her behavior in relation to others, leading her to subordinate her own internal needs to those of her partner, and to assume that doing otherwise will jeopardize the relationship. Thus, a cyclical process forms between internalization of responsibility themes, depressive symptoms, beliefs in the inherent harmfulness of personal impulses, and further alienation of the self.

> Rochelle is a 33-year-old, White teacher who lives alone and works in an agency with children who are disabled. She has a slight build, with very fair hair and skin and large blue eyes that speak volumes about her pain. She presents to therapy, a quiet and demure (almost muffled) picture of moderate dysthymia, which has been with her as many years as she can remember.

> Rochelle tells a story of sadistic child abuse by her father, a surgeon, during which she was beaten with various objects and forced to contain her tears and other expressions or experience sustained battering. The events she manages to relate in the initial two or three sessions of counseling, although

traumatic in nature, are not her expressed reason for seeking treatment. Rochelle believes herself to be extremely ugly. She experiences her face as tremendously misshapen and her body as disgusting. Although some part of her knows that these are distortions, she continues to feel intense pain when viewing herself in the mirror and avoids any type of dating or romantic involvement with others because of her expectation that they find her appearance revolting.

Over the course of several months, Rochelle begins to approach her feelings about how she was treated by her father. As if instinctively, she moves from her preoccupation with the appearance of her face to memories of a particular ordeal she experienced as a 7-year-old girl, hiding from her father as he went on one of his many tirades throughout the house, turning over furniture and shouting insults at Rochelle's mother. She remembers abject terror, the feeling that at any moment she would become the target of his rage if she were discovered cowering in her closet behind the dolls and toys. She also remembers fearing for her mother's safety and wondering how she could help her escape the onslaught of this explosive and dangerous display. These things are painful but nonetheless accessible to Rochelle as she digs through her memory of events in her childhood home. The last pieces to come together for Rochelle, the more difficult to claim, are the other kinds of feelings she experienced then. The feelings that now seem alien as she speaks them aloud, the outrage, the bitter hatred, the constant, unrelenting anger toward this man who was supposed to be her protector and was instead her captor and torturer—all come forth with an unfamiliar strangeness that shocks Rochelle and forces her to reckon with something she has carried unconsciously for more than three decades.

What this young woman slowly learns is that she incorporates beliefs about herself by virtue of her inability to assign hatred to its true objects. Rochelle begins to understand shame and self-loathing as part of her own rage, a burning energy directed out, not in. If there is no hope of being released toward its true target, the anger ricochets between inner walls, weaving together thoughts, convictions, and beliefs about her self. It is safer in some ways to hate her own image than to recognize her hatred of an all-powerful father who refuses to allow acknowledgment of the pain he causes.

Shame-proneness contrasts with guilt in that it reflects a tendency to experience the self as bad or unworthy in some way (Tangney, Wagner, Fletcher, & Gramzow, 1992), versus experiencing remorse over some specific deed. Tangney and colleagues review literature pointing to shame as a catalyst for anger that typically is directed at the self. As a defensive maneuver, shame can be experienced instead of aggression at a target so that "the individual moves from an active stance to a passive state, taking refuge in the passive and disabling shame experience, escaping aggression by dismantling the active self" (p. 670). So adaptively, women like Rochelle who have been victimized by powerful others and thus shamed twist their own instrumental anger into a hatred for themselves in some way. This transformation allows them to survive the double-bind of forbidden rage.

Segmentation

Here, segmentation refers to an attempt at amputation of or separation from some aspect of self as a result of intolerable emotional experience. Like the dissociative symptoms noted in trauma survivors (Anderson, Yasenik, & Ross, 1993), signs of sustained effort to take leave of the angry self appear as rigid overcontrol, anxiety, or agitation, as well as some markers of blocked emotional development, often labeled as personality disorders. Other ways to segment the personality involve behaviors stamped "passive-aggressive." Passive aggression involves triggering anger in another as a means of indirectly asking that person to carry and express one's own anger. The recipient of passive aggression often recognizes an element of manipulation along with their feeling of frustration and irritation, but it may be difficult to figure out why.

How does segmentation happen? For safety, for social acceptance, or because of internalized acceptance of cultural dictates concerning the evils of anger, women often resort to a conscious denial of anger in contexts wherein it is provoked. If a woman uses segmentation to deal with this double bind, she creates a barrier between herself and her anger, shutting out what she cannot tolerate. The authors posit that at this point a permeable emotional barrier is constructed, through which subtle aggressive impulses necessarily escape. Because the amount of energy needed to section off any part of the self is typically greater than that available to the individual, leaks in this barrier allow telltale signs of anger to trickle through, though they remain unacknowledged. If individuals learn to overuse this kind of chronic dismemberment as alternative means for coping with intolerable feeling reality, the maturational process of the self is thwarted. Thus, segmentation affects not only how a woman sees herself in the moment, but who she becomes over time. In this way, anger diversion powerfully redirects women's identity development. The woman's personality becomes affected by the same process that forces her distress, a process that ironically helps her adapt to the demands of her social environment. So is segmented anger good or bad? Is it helpful or unhelpful? Sectioning one's conscious, waking images of self away from those aspects that feel anger accomplishes the task of relationship maintenance, indeed. Yet, we must question the intimacy and mutuality levels of relationships maintained in this way.

Carl Jung's notion of the shadow (Von Franz, 1993) provides a metaphor for this splitting of selves. The shadow side of each person is theorized to contain the darker elements of humanity, the lust, greed, and aggressive impulses that we need as balance, but that we routinely hide away out of fear. Far from needing to be excised from the self, the shadow, according to Jung, is an aspect of living to be acknowledged and used. It is powerful and important in that it contains information about the self that is not always directly apprehensible during waking. However, Jung asserts that most individuals cannot conquer their own fear of these powerful forces in order to achieve a synchronous balance between "light" and "dark." If anger, specifically, is relegated to the shadow, the angry self becomes an alien from which to hide or run. Alien anger also frightens us if we glimpse its appearance in others.

In psychodynamic terms, segmented anger often parallels Freud's conception of reaction formation in its appearance. A woman can so carefully and completely avoid her anger that she comes to hate the very suggestion of aggressive impulses in self or others. Thus, the woman who learns by necessity to overuse her system of affect denial becomes agreeable and compliant in an exaggerated kind of way, leaving those around to wonder if she is genuine. She continuously offers her pleasant countenance in exchange for the approval of others without overt resistance to their unpleasantness. This is accomplished through the segmentation of the self, only one section of which is given conscious voice. The abandoned side is treated with contempt—illegitimized. Those in her presence who intuit darkness feel the pull of the lost side wherein she must dispose of vague feelings and thoughts she is unable to tolerate in herself.

Jack and Dill's (1992) Silencing the Self Scale includes a subscale called The Divided Self, which taps into aspects of this kind of splitting. The Divided Self measures the experience of inner division made necessary through a woman's living out of societal prescriptives for her passive compliance. Items such as, "Often I look happy enough on the outside, but inwardly I feel angry and rebellious," reflect the experience of hiding away one's authentic self and presenting something known to be acceptable instead.

Myra, a 58-year-old, White, middle-class mother of two adult sons, lives with her spouse of 36 years and her younger son, who at 29 years of age has returned home to live with his parents while saving money for a large fishing boat. Myra presents to therapy with a desire to change careers after 40 years as an office manager for an accounting firm.

She experiences vague distress around leaving her job but primarily explains this distress in terms of worry about her employer's having to find a suitable replacement for her in the office. She seeks career counseling and assessment and stresses that she feels no other need for counseling, as her marriage is intact and she feels close to everyone in her extended family.

When queried about this extended family, Myra reveals that she takes care of both her aging mother and her grandmother, each with degenerative diseases that make them unable to return affection or engage in lucid adult conversation. She tirelessly visits, bathes, grooms and feeds the two women in her care (both of whom live about 20 minutes' distance from her home) and then returns home to repeat the processes in slightly different ways for her husband and grown son. She takes care of all the cooking, cleaning, and other household work in her own home, works a 40-hour work week at the office, manages the family's finances, and performs countless other unacknowledged duties for her family on a routine basis (e.g., laundry for her spouse and son, repair of household damage done by her son, errands to the grocery store and the mall requested by her son, and preparing tax returns for almost everyone in her immediate family and social circle). Myra recently has gained about 25 pounds and expresses some discomfort with her weight. Often during session she keeps her arms tightly folded across her waist, as if to hide her stomach, while maintaining a taut posture and facial expression. Early in therapy Myra responds to a question about anger and resentment in the following way:

> What do you mean [smiling]? I'm not sure I understand. I mean I have a lot to do, but I love everyone so much who's in my family and care what happens to them. Anger, well, I don't like angry people at all. I know a woman in my church who always looks so angry. I've never wanted to be like that, and I just refuse to let things get to me. You have to have faith in God and learn to love people.

As we work together, Myra repeatedly faces the puzzle of why she feels so bad if nothing "gets to" her. Slowly she begins to allow herself to explore the possibilities for change, and when she is ready, we turn together to revisit the issue of anger. In our perspective, her use of segmentation serves to protect the status quo of her relationships by divorcing herself from the angry feelings she experiences on some level, in relation to her family's constant demands and seeming expectation of entitlement to her faithful service. These feelings seem foreign to her, something outside of her sense of who she is. Myra can relate the question to someone she knows, whose demeanor is unacceptable to her. At the same time, she has great difficulty owning the parts of herself that might become instrumentally angry and lead to requests for change from her family. Our approach views these same angry feelings as holding potential for energy creating career change or finding gratification in learning something new, which would take emphasis away from overeating and ruminative self-consciousness about her body. However, at the present time, they remain hidden, lopped off and discarded as unconscious waste material.

Externalization

Finally, diverted anger sometimes takes the form of externalization, the disowning of one's anger by casting it onto another through emotional, physical, or verbal assault. Here, the same underlying process, avoidance of the angry self, results in a behavior pattern that appears to do just the opposite. Although people who externalize their anger seem to be acting on the environment to create change, the process is indirect, leaving personhood behind in an attempt to escape contact with self at odds with another. Conversely, a direct, assertive action involves some acknowledgment of feeling residing in the self. "Borderline" and "narcissistic" rage often fall into this category, as persons with extremely fragile images of self (Rhodewalt & Morf, 1998), those who tend to exhibit very labile emotional reactions that seem ungrounded by a personal sense of "who I am," often find it difficult to claim the integrity of their own feelings.

The woman who externalizes anger with verbal abuse of a child appears to be directing her affect toward the source of frustration. However, she sacrifices the immediate experience of her own person as instrumental, angry and related to her child, in favor of an indirect release of tension. On the other hand, if she allows herself to realize the force of feeling in her own body, as an element of selfhood in the moment, she gives herself the opportunity to experience her own instrumentality rather than exclusive focus on her child as an irritant or obstacle. The externalization of her own emotional response obscures the separateness of mother and child, paradoxically hiding the relationship between them, placing her child at considerable risk. On the other hand, if she claims and gives voice to her own internal state, she does something to make herself heard (perhaps even to create change in her child) and something that protects the integrity of her self as distinct from her child. The child, or partner, or whoever becomes a target for her unclaimed anger, cannot literally embody her distress. Rather, her own internal response to that person is the piece of the picture that deserves recognition and articulation, however painful that process may be.

Kathryn is a 55-year-old professor of anthropology and divorced mother of three. She presents to psychotherapy for the stated purpose of wanting to lose weight and regain control of her eating habits. She reports that her children recently have begun talking with her about the impact of her "temper" in their relationships with her over the years. Although she insists these current developments have nothing to do with her weight problems, she readily acknowledges her resentment and stress over having to hear about the damage she's caused.

Much later in her treatment, Kathryn's grown children report during a family-therapy session that their mother's history includes striking them about the face and head when they were growing up. The middle sibling, Trevor (age 26 years), recounts a time when his parents were sleeping in separate rooms and his mother, although basically invested in his well-being, would scream at him for minor annoyances, shaking him and telling him that he was "horrible." Trevor remembers each of his two sisters being slapped in the face and told that they were "arrogant little bitches" for misbehaving in some way.

Kathryn remembers this period in her life. However, the anger she recognizes is directed toward her now ex-husband, Matthew, whom she could never please. She has great difficulty acknowledging to her adult children that she was wrong in hitting and insulting them. This awareness appears to cause her significant pain, and she refrains from contact with these issues as much as possible. She is more able to connect with the devastation she felt as a young mother unable to reach her husband for any mutual connection. She finds the part of herself to grieve, the frantic 32-year-old who was enraged with her mate, but appears unable to tolerate the anger she experienced toward her children at that time or the regret and sadness she might feel now if she could hear her children's pain and anger and recognize the part she's played in it. This extremely difficult emotional task was given over in the past, to be replaced by rage flying outward, quickly removing her from her inner experience.

Externalizing masks anger at more powerful others, which then usually is deflected onto less powerful others. For instance, women who are angry with their partners or other adult family members, but unable to express these feelings inside a nonmutual relationship, can find themselves ventilating at children, who make for safer, more available targets. Externalizing anger also masks other kinds of symptoms (depressive and so forth) that become a focus of treatment in many instances. Often, women present to therapy with concerns about their own outbursts. Along with the externalization, however, is usually some other misapplication such as segmentation or suppression that serves to make the experience of direct anger appear insufferable. An unfortunate cycle begins that places the woman at risk for externalizing by virtue of her chronic internalization and suppression. As somatic and emotional pressures mount, the need for some kind of release grows exponentially, crescendoing to an explosion of tumultuous rage.

Although women commit fewer violent crimes than men (Harvey & Pease, 1987), such potent forms of externalized anger become more pathologized in women because of women's prescribed abstinence from externalized force (Heidensohn, 1991). Perhaps because mainstream society can tolerate the potential for agency found in each anger episode only if it is accessed by men, modern social, legal, and medical systems combine to pathologize women's violent expressions of anger to a greater degree than they do men's. Such acts become labeled as products of uncontrollable psychological forces that render a woman helpless, thus stigmatizing her as sick rather than angry or instrumental. Another hypothesis about recent increases in women's violence, arising as a reaction against modern feminism in the 1970s, suggests liberation leads to criminality—in other words, women are becoming like men in every way, including their violence-proneness. Both notions avoid acknowledgment of the possibility that women, like men, sometimes use anger to act in self-interest and to attempt solution of a problem. Both forbear any possible medium of instrumentality in women's externalized anger by undercutting its legitimacy as compared with men's.

Violent behavior is unacceptable in women, as it also should be in men. Rarely, though, does men's violent behavior ignite the same social and media response seen in cases involving women. For example, the recent notoriety of mothers who have killed their own children stands in shocking contrast to the lack of attention given the many cases of men committing such acts every day. Such untenable acts of violence against others may be more likely to occur, however, because the extreme social restrictions placed upon women's anger and aggression leave no room to maneuver in conceptualizing appropriate and acceptable expression.

Anger Transformed: The Symptom Clusters

An early lesson for the clinician in training is the fluid continuity between diagnoses and sets of symptoms. Emotional disturbance is not discreet. Therefore, let us acknowledge at the outset the absurdity of symptom categorization. We have punctuated subjectively the list of features into groupings that make discussion possible and correspond with current research. However, as with the four anger diversions outlined previously, these groupings of clinical features overlap and mutually influence each other, arguing for a continuous approach to understanding the primary nonpsychotic anger-related areas of women's discomfort that present themselves for mental health treatment. Symptom clusters rarely exist in isolation from one another and instead combine to form meaningful mosaics for client and therapist to interpret.

The Depression/Anxiety Symptom Cluster

We begin this section by considering the question of how depression has become twice as prevalent in women as in men. Could depression be an index of what happens uniquely in women as a group (although present in the population as a whole), the evolution of which follows a distinct route through the minefield of gendered emotional development? The realms of depression and anxiety merge here because of their relatedness in both research and clinical practice. Symptoms of each so often coexist that clear differential diagnosis eludes the clinician and is only approachable if a response to medication distinguishes the physiological effects of each. Women experience and are diagnosed with both depression and anxiety more often than men, according to Mirowsky and Ross (1986) as well as others (Aneshensel, 1992; Dick, Bland, & Newman, 1994; see Culbertson, 1997, for a thorough review). Women's depression-proneness predominates in the literature, regardless of occupation, income, education, or race (Droppelman et al., 1995). Many studies point to women's greater likelihood of experiencing unipolar depression, with ratios as high as two to one (Nolen-Hoeksema, 1987; Weissman & Klerman, 1987; Wetzel, 1994).

Adolescent girls also report more self-consciousness, negative body image, and poor self-esteem than their male counterparts (Algood-Merten et al., 1990), each of these often a marker of depression or anxiety. Female adolescents tend to experience more depressive suicidality than males (Harris et al., 1991) as well as more anxiety and general difficulties with adjustment (Street & Kromrey, 1994). Linking the depression/anxiety cluster with internalization and suppression of anger, girls more likely show tears as evidence of their rage than boys, who more likely aggress (Jones & Peacock, 1992). In analogous fashion, girls tend to score higher on dimensions labeled "worry" and "sensitive-emotional" than boys, who conversely score higher on conduct problems (Beitchman, Kruidenier, Inglis, & Clegg, 1989).

Elderly women in Gueldner et al.'s (1994) study of nursing-home residents demonstrate higher anger/hostility scores than their male counterparts. Gueldner and colleagues suggest that these women's greater anger and hostility, which correlates with their higher levels of depression/dejection, indicates a diminishment of their anger expression. The authors offer learned helplessness as a way to explain the women's reticence, stating that apathy of expression and passivity relate to a perceived lack of control. In other words, these elderly women ceased to give voice to their oppositional feelings as they learned either that no one was listening or that nothing would be done.

It has been pointed out that no singular existing theory is adequate to explain the prevalence of depressive illness in women (Jack, in press). In Nolen-Hoeksema's (1990) book, *Sex Differences in Depression*, she suggests that the culture of a country plays a major role in gender-discrepant depression, and she reports significantly higher rates of depression for women in developed nations, as compared to low-income nations in which no such discrepancies exist. Kessler, McGonagle, and Zhao's (1994) National Comorbidity Study confirmed Nolen-Hoeksema's (1987) previous two-to-one ratio for depression in women and found female adolescents to be more depressed than male adolescents. White girls in this study had the highest levels of depression; Black girls showed the lowest.

Jack and Dill's (1992) Silencing the Self Scale includes a subscale for externalized self-perception, which measures the absorption of external standards for womanhood. Jack (1991) uses the fairy tale of Rumpelstiltskin to illustrate how women's use of their own feminine power and instinct frees them to employ anger as an ally in reclaiming the authentic self from the grip of socialized inner oppressors (the adopted standards). If women are allowed to develop the use of their own internal emotional states, and open outward display of those states, they will learn a comfortable familiarity with the self in all its forms. Going back to the auto mechanic to demand amelioration of an inferior repair job, or shouting about atrocities suffered in an abusive relationship, the angry self becomes an instrument to effect change. The angry self protects women from the paralyzing effects of depression.

Getting to know the outer boundaries of the self in an active way produces greater facility in use of the self for instrumentality, and a kind of self-defining authority develops through use of the full range of emotions as expressed in interpersonal relations. Alternatively, self-alienation often requires anxiety to fuel the vigilant watch that is kept to guard against inadvertent breaks in the internalization or segmentation processes. All these factors combine to make up the principal components in women's depression. Bromberger and Matthews (1996) found that middle-aged women who are low in instrumentality and who hold angry feelings inside became more symptomatic in a variety of ways during the course of a 3-year study. An important focus for these researchers is the "passivity" (in contrast to assertiveness) demonstrated by more symptomatic women in this study. In addition, they found that women who are "nurturing," "concerned," and who possess other more sensitive, "feminine" qualities did not show distress. Instead, higher levels of qualities relating to passivity and restraint were more highly correlated with depression, suggesting instrumentality's key role in the maintenance of mental health. This process of finding and using the angry voice (in spite of feminine norms) not only offers women more empowerment, it also contributes to development of an identity that is inclusive and authentic in its embrace of the total female experience.

Research addressing what usually is called "anger suppression" links the phenomenon with depression (Beutler et al., 1986; Culkin & Perotto, 1985; Jones, Peacock, & Christopher, 1992; Sperberg & Stabb, 1998). Typically measured with instruments like Spielberger's State Trait Anger Expression Inventory (1988), these studies survey individuals' tendencies toward externalization versus internalization of anger states. Mirowsky and Ross (1995) find that keeping one's feelings to oneself relates to feeling more anger, rather than less—as well as to higher levels of depression.

In Begley's (1994) study, anger-out, measured by the Multidimensional Anger Inventory (Siegel, 1986), moderates the relationship between responsibility for people and depression. This study points to both extremes of anger expression in the development of symptoms. Anger-in relates to three health complaints, anxiety, depression, and somatic problems; its interaction with responsibility for people relates to depression and anxiety. Anger-out in this report interacts with responsibility for people and also correlates with depression. Although Begley's study indicates stronger support for the health-compromising role of internalized anger, both ends of the spectrum are shown to relate to symptomatology. We suggest that neither anger-in nor anger-out really helps people avoid the anger diversion that compromises individuals' ability to use their emotion in instrumental ways. Begley calls for further work in clarifying the full process by which anger works inside relationships to result in emotional distress. He also, unfortunately, argues for reduction of anger itself as the key to solving the dilemma between two options that each appear problematic. A step in the direction of exploring ways in which anger works inside relationships has been taken by Sperberg and Stabb (1998), who found that both low levels of mutuality in relationships and high levels of suppressed anger were associated with depression.

Rather than targeting the emotion itself, a natural response to the unhappy or conflicted circumstances that arise in relationships, the authors point to the ways people avoid and disown their anger, because of the lack of a healthy cultural norm for processing and expressing it. In this view, Jack (in press) contends that women's internalized "eye," which represents cultural standards for their behavior, includes the critical misnaming of anger as selfishness and works to silence the parts of self that could inspire movement out of depression and assert the needs of the living self. Thus, Begley's (1994) push for anger reduction amounts to throwing the baby out with the bath water, as we rid ourselves of a catalyst for change. Again, if anger is reduced, the opportunity to learn about a specific, aroused part of one's personhood is also lessened, and identity formation is minimized accordingly.

Although it is difficult to trace a direct path from diverted anger to anxiety, we speculate that an anxious or agitated depression as well as more generalized fearfulness often stems from efforts to keep oneself contained. Some theorists suggest women's greater tendency toward anxiety stems from greater arousal levels necessary to manage affective intensity (Fischer et al., 1993). Combining the paralyzing quality of depressed affect with the fear of being "found out," women become their own captors in participation with socialized depression and anxiety. The noted relationship between anger and panic (Morand, Thomas, Bungener, Ferreri, & Jouvent, 1998) further illustrates these interlocking pieces of the story.

Clary, a 34-year-old marketing executive, lives with her lesbian partner of 7 years. It is evident that she is extremely bright and motivated, both in terms of her career and in taking care of her parents who live in a nearby town. Clary describes how her partner and her family, constantly at odds with each other, vie for her attention, time, and loyalty. She feels pulled apart by her love for each of them and her fear that she cannot perform adequately for either. Clary's experiences with "coming out" in her family include having a group of priests sent to her home to tell her the evils of homosexuality, being told by her mother that she is an embarrassment to her parents, and seeing her partner markedly excluded from family functions, reunions, and holidays.

Queried about her relationship with her partner, Clary becomes tearful and has difficulty talking. Though she loves Susan, she admits difficulty living with her. She feels she must dutifully call at midday and then again in the late afternoon to let Susan know when she will be arriving home for the evening. If she does not call, she can expect to find her partner crying in front of the television when she comes home, refusing to talk or move. Clary recalls this pattern beginning slowly in the early years of their relationship and escalating in frequency and intensity for the past 2 years. Along with feeling manipulated, Clary reports being physically threatened by Susan, who flies into verbal rages when she finds Clary disloyal.

At present, the most disabling and alarming symptom Clary experiences is panic. She describes driving toward home one evening and feeling as if she were having a heart attack. She began to hyperventilate, with her pulse racing and her body becoming drenched with perspiration. Clary pulled off the road and called her mother. This scenario has been repeated four times in the past 7 weeks, along with a sensation of "shuddering" that occurs when Clary tries to talk with Susan or her mother. The shuddering does not appear related to body temperature or blood sugar and instead seems to be triggered by the topic under discussion at the time. She characterizes herself as feeling afraid during these moments but cannot say what it is she fears.

During the course of therapy Clary gradually begins to connect with her own outrage at being manipulated from both sides of her family. She begins to listen to and embrace the part of herself that is weary of explaining and cajoling and eventually desires to defend herself, to act in her own best interest instead of submerging her needs and feelings to protect the status quo of her relationships. She approaches her experience of panic, including the shuddering, to discover that its ultimate purpose lies in its clever camouflage of her fury. Clary also notices that she is terrified of bringing up this rage, that the thought of talking about it with loved ones sets off the shuddering as she rehearses her declarations in session.

The Somatic Symptom Cluster

In many relationships and families, the experience of physical problems garners more acceptance and support than does outrage. Could messages of disease, pain, and discomfort in a woman's body communicate anger's transformation into more socially acceptable forms of distress? If so, just how do women translate opposition into physiological distress? It has been demonstrated consistently that people who routinely use a repressive or inhibitory coping style instead of talking aloud about various types of upsetting experiences show higher rates of illnesses such as heart disease (Pennebaker, 1989; Shedler, Mayman, & Manis, 1993). Although it is beyond the scope of this chapter to provide in-depth coverage of the physiology of anger (see Chapter 2 for additional background), this brief segment addresses correlates of diverted anger as well as some ways to make sense of the research in this area.

We purport to show how some diseases that primarily affect women intersect with diverted anger. Droppelman et al. (1995), in their review of research pertinent to women's anger, list several conditions that relate to some form of anger process, highlighting the multifactorial nature of disease. Among them are hypertension, heart disease, systemic lupus erythematosus, breast cancer, headaches, stomach pain, nausea, diarrhea, shakiness, weakness, and premenstrual syndrome. These authors note that although a number of these conditions predominantly affect women, little research has been done to explore their specific relationship with anger.

What is more, many studies on the role of anger in disease rely on data gathered solely from men.

Irritable bowel syndrome (IBS), characterized by bowel dysfunction and alimentary symptoms, relates to lack of assertiveness, according to Nyhlin et al. (1993). These authors find patients with IBS to experience significantly more difficulty in expressing negative feelings towards others (an index of assertiveness in this investigation) than do controls. Further, anxiety and depression ratings for patients with IBS in this study exceed those of the control group, in spite of the fact that no substantial difference between patients with IBS and controls was noted in the area of major life events. Breast cancer in women relates to concealing anger as well as stifling emotions in general (Bageley, 1979; Jansen & Muenz, 1984). These findings illustrate the interdependence of affective and somatic experience, hinting at their mutuality in women's psychological health.

Anger is associated with several other physiological conditions and states, by virtue of its immediate nervous system involvement. However, the literature specific to anger's enmeshment with somatic symptomatology, again, creates an interpretation dilemma. Although many studies point to suppression of anger as a cause of physiological disturbances, some also show feeling anger at all, and some, various forms of anger expression, to be related to illness. An example of this seeming contradiction appears in a study done by Keinan, Ben-Zur, Zilka, and Carel (1992). In this report, expressing anger outwardly and intensely relates to fewer health problems except if the outward expression is frequent. Here, frequency of outward anger expression relates to more physical complaints. Although this study samples only men, it illuminates some of the complexity in how people display anger and how that display works its way into overall health.

Both extremes of this artificial anger-expression dichotomy (internalizing and externalizing), have been shown to relate to adverse conditions physiologically and psychologically. Suarez and Williams (1990) report anger-out, defined as antagonistic hostility, to relate to greater systolic blood pressure, forearm blood changes, and poorer systolic blood pressure recovery to harassment. These authors also note anger-in as related to greater forearm blood flow changes to harassment, suggesting that physiological stress is associated with both theoretical extremes of anger processing. Goldstein, Edelberg, Meier, and Davis (1989) report that the family tendencies of individuals toward either suppression or inhibition have to do with greater cardiovascular reactivity to stress.

It would be easy to become bogged down in this kind of inconsistency in reports about anger's role in somatic distress. Nonetheless, anger diversion seems fundamental in the etiology of these disturbances, and the grouping of diversions offered here may help by reflecting anger's complexity. Most research examining anger and physiology relies on this black-and-white approach (anger-in versus anger-out) for pairing the emotion with physiological variables of interest, leaving subtleties of affect management eclipsed. Both extreme options for handling anger represent opposite ends of an expression spectrum, which in pure form are fairly unrealistic in actual experience. However, both present problems that can manifest in physical ways. The key issue here is that the fact that these extremes are associated with symptoms does not necessarily mean anger itself is to blame. Because most women rely on more than one means for diverting anger, clinicians must ask questions that uncover those intricate processes. What happens if angry energy is felt and verbalized to another but is followed by intense self-doubt at having behaved assertively in relationship? What becomes of a woman's sense of herself over time if as she periodically voices her unrest she becomes dismissed, diagnosed, or given another label that diminishes her own authority to say what upsets her? It follows that prolonged physiological stress that accompanies this kind of process bears directly upon a woman's health, and it is an oversimplification to suggest that happens in only one of two ways.

It is important for practitioners to be aware of not only the medical issues that relate to diverted anger, but also the likelihood that inappropriate diagnostic labels become assigned to women when they reveal their anger to others. Let us look at some ways in which women's other-than-compliant behaviors have been pathologized historically. Pugliesi (1992) offers a discourse on the medicalization of women's strong emotion as she reviews the literature on premenstrual syndrome (PMS). Primarily, the most troublesome symptoms reported by women who suffer from PMS involve anger, irritability, and depression. Though little agreement exists about the definition of premenstrual syndrome, much has been written about this dreaded disturbance, most concerning its clinical features, pharmacological treatment, and relation to other variables like stress (Steiner, 1997; Woods, Lentz, Mitchell, Shaver, & Heitkemper, 1998; Yonkers, 1997). With prevalence rates of PMS ranging from 30% to 90%, and the fact that emotional symptoms of PMS (primarily anger-related) typically receive the most attention, the question arises of where exactly is the disorder? Does it reside in the individual woman, her usual barriers of suppression and segmentation giving way at certain times, allowing once neatly packaged anger to flow unencumbered from her? Conversely, does the disorder reside in a societal misunderstanding of her process? With such large numbers of women experiencing the "disorder," how appropriate is it to give this cyclical turmoil a diagnostic label? Who has the most trouble with this periodic stirring that seems to allow a woman to voice what she otherwise keeps silent? Is it the woman herself, or those in relationship with her?

Women's angry behavior as well as much of their sexual behavior often becomes construed as medical illness, as their passion becomes labeled "lesbianism," as "man-hating," and as "feminism" (an interesting juxtaposition if one considers the development of feminist identity, to be discussed in Chapter 6). Historically these aspects of women's lives have been tied together, as their anger, hostility, and aggression once were regarded widely as a form of insanity, caused by the menstrual cycle (King, 1990; Showalter, 1985). Pugliesi (1992) suggests that women and intimates become concerned about PMS if emotional experience or conduct falls outside of normative expectations or disrupts the fulfillment of role obligations (such as being a wife and mother). Further, she argues that the ready acceptance of PMS by professionals and society at large could reflect a covert reaction to the women's movement—a reaction against women's efforts to change their lives by getting angry.

The Consumptive Symptom Cluster

Consider the symbolism of disordered eating, a phenomenon much more common in women, especially white women living in industrialized nations, than in men (American Psychiatric Association, 1994). Our treatment of disordered eating revolves around research conducted with primarily White female samples. Recently, however, eating disorders have increased among Black and Hispanic individuals, lower socio-economic status groups, younger and older individuals, and males (American Psychiatric Association, 1993; Phelps & Bajorek, 1991). The connection between anxious, depressive, somatic, and eating symptoms indicates the probability of a common emotional substrate. How does emotion, specifically anger, become involved in the development of anorexia nervosa, bulimia nervosa, and other problematic eating? Perhaps if we see a woman caught in these confinements, we actually are looking at her anger intertwined with a societal prescription that she be reduced physically, and her struggle to be contained within social imperatives for thinness. Both thinness and obesity can become dangerous outward manifestations of revolt if women have no other viable means for expressing anger.

First we examine the symbolic meanings that exist for women's emotional development in the hunger strike of anorexia. Along with the preoccupation with weight that usually accompanies this sort of consumption problem, anger and other intense feelings play important roles. Exploring anorectics' difficulties with experiencing intense or oppositional emotion, Manassis and Kalman (1990) review the cases of four adolescent girls whose symptoms begin with their fear of vomiting following a viral illness. Interestingly, assessment of family dynamics reveal significant restriction in the range of affect demonstrated by the individual girls as well as their families, with particular avoidance of anger expression.

Relationships between major depression, diverted anger, and disordered eating are further documented in research literature (Herzog, 1984; Riley, Triber, & Woods, 1989; Snaith & Taylor, 1985). The presence of depression and anxiety-related symptoms along with consumption problems illustrates how our four symptom clusters appear to nest one within the other (Keck et al., 1990; Toner, Garfinkel, & Garner, 1986, 1988). Rubinstein, Altemus, Pigott, Hess, and Murphy (1995) report comparisons of women with obsessive-compulsive disorder (OCD), bulimia nervosa, and no psychiatric history using a variety of measures of obsessiveness and compulsivity, depression, and anxiety. Women with bulimia in this study score midway between those with OCD and controls on these variables. Women with both OCD and bulimia score similarly and higher than controls on measures of depression, anxiety, and anger. Steinhausen and Vollrath (1993) report that adolescents with anorexia nervosa show increased depression and obsessive-compulsive symptoms. Many of these girls also demonstrate extreme compliance and seek to achieve perfection in their self-standards and achievements (Phelps & Bajorek, 1991).

Further, patients with eating disorders show greater intropunitiveness (punishing the self) and hostility than controls according to Tiller, Schmidt, Ali, and Treasure (1995). These researchers link impulsiveness with an extrapunitive style (externalization of anger) and depression with an intropunitive style, the former being more likely in bulimia and the latter more characteristic of anorexic patterns. Rebert, Stanton, and Schwartz (1991) report greater state depression and hostility if subjects binged and purged on a daily basis. We conclude that anger surely is being expressed by girls and women with disordered eating, but in very indirect ways. Each major criterion of disordered eating relates to at least one type of anger diversion. For anorexic and bulimic individuals, anger becomes suppressed (in somatization or the experience of a distorted body image), internalized (in the acceptance of requirements for women to maintain a hard, lean, adolescent body), or externalized (bulimic punishment of the body as an external target).

If we examine research linking anger with eating disorders we also notice the complexity of symptoms in people who have developed an overtly anger-diversive process. For instance, Fava, Rappe, West, and Herzog (1995) report the phenomenon of "anger attacks" in persons of both male and female gender with bulimia, consisting of feeling out of control, feeling like attacking others, feelings of panic, and tachycardia—features not unlike those of panic disorder. Although these symptoms bear a likeness to externalization, the panic felt by these individuals suggests a more complicated process than simple projection of rage. Once a concerted effort is made to experience something other than anger, a diversion process begins, leading to some degree of anxiety and pressure to continue camouflaging the anger. The interrelatedness of symptom clusters is further seen in Fava et al.'s finding that persons with disordered eating who experience anger attacks also show higher depression scores than those without such attacks.

Observations of affective involvement in consumption problems provide a backdrop for the development of the Emotional Eating Scale (Arnow, Kenardy, & Agras, 1995), a measure designed to assess a person's consumption of food as a means to manage difficult feelings. One finding reported by these authors in their psychometric evaluation of the scale is that each of the subscales, anger/frustration, anxiety, and depression, correlate significantly with recall of days during which binge eating occurred and with scores on the Binge Eating Scale (Gormally, Black, Daston, & Rardin, 1982). Rather than make difficult feelings known to others, women may find a safer alternative in the soothing but temporary relief they experience when eating. Yager, Rorty, and Rossotto (1995) report women with active bulimia nervosa to be significantly less likely to seek emotional support or to focus on and vent emotions compared with recovered women and those with no history of eating disturbance. Obese binge eaters in the Gormally et al. study report the most difficulty coping in situations that elicit higher emotional arousal, suggesting that painful affect initiates a reactionary pattern of choosing eating over verbalizing wherein these women feel that they must turn to food not only as companion but as confidante (Grilo, Shiffman, & Wing, 1989).

Renee, a 26-year-old graduate student, exceeds the suggested weight range for women of her height and age by approximately 150 pounds. She has carried this added burden since sometime in junior high school following an incident of sexual abuse perpetrated by her brother. This incest and her parents' lack of response are the more outstanding features in a bleak landscape of emotional sabotage and neglect that filled Renee's early years. It served to reinforce her family's overall message to her, namely that "your feelings, needs, instincts and body are not worth our respect."

As an adult, Renee often finds herself in crippling double binds with her mother, Melanie, who uses every available opportunity to diminish Renee's adulthood by labeling her as incompetent. The unspoken contract between mother and daughter dictates that Renee sign over her rights to think and feel for herself, in exchange for her mother's demonstrations of love. Melanie uses her daughter's weight as a weapon, suggesting that her intrusive attempts to control are only signs of concern for Renee's well-being and health. However, her inappropriate involvement further insinuates that Renee cannot accomplish anything on her own, even the care of her own body. The dynamics between Renee and her mother bespeak an analog trauma history for the older woman, who has learned to segment the honest fire of her anger into barely recognizable sparks of misdirected hostility that often flare out so subtly and quickly, people in their path wonder how they were burned. Renee does not date or initiate any kind of romantic involvement whatsoever. She makes friends in school but keeps them at an arm's length, perhaps to protect herself from what she has learned to fear.

> I think that for me, I was not aware that I could express anger. Other people's impressions were supposedly more important and chancing them seeing me in a bad light was not a possibility. It was okay for me to suffer but not for others to suffer because of something that I was feeling. To chance losing or somehow negatively changing (and that was the only change possible) that relationship, or having someone seeing me in a negative light, was not an acceptable possibility either. The only way to make my suffering okay was to find ways to soothe and protect myself. The easiest protection was distance. If I told myself that a person did not mean anything to me nor I to them, the anger somehow seemed easier to handle because they were not worth it. But that only served to produce anger about the distance and loneliness. I mean, on some level, I knew that they were and that I was important, otherwise I would not be getting angry. To deny the anger and distance myself, I needed an active way to punish me (for needing others) and them (for not needing me). All kinds of people don't like touching a fat person. The food served as my protection from them and me and still does.

Listening to Renee's own words about her experience sheds light on the anger segmentation process necessary in disarranged eating. She tells of her own internal double bind, wherein she must both punish and soothe herself with food. She learned from Melanie (as well as from her father and extended family) that the autonomy that comes with direct anger is more dangerous than losing one's authentic self-interest. Renee needed a protective barrier between herself and others with whom she might exchange anger or intimacy. She also needed this protective barrier between the part of herself that feared rejection and the part that understood the dignity of her outrage. In therapy, Renee steadily becomes familiar with this powerful aspect of her personhood and begins to reclaim it.

In addition to problem eating, the consumptive symptom cluster also encompasses substance-abuse features. In Munhall's (1993) phenomenological study of women's anger, she provides women's descriptions of their anger experiences in their own words and draws conclusions about how anger is transformed in "socially acceptable pathology" (p. 481). Among the sets of symptoms she hypothesizes to be related to the displacement of anger are those having to do with the body, including substance abuse and other patterns of somatic distress. The link between diverted anger and subsequent alcohol or drug problems is further borne out in studies examining the effects of childhood physical and sexual trauma on women's later functioning (Neumann, Houskamp, Pollock, & Briere, 1996; Wallen, 1992). Woodhouse (1990) uses exploratory data gathered from women in treatment for substance abuse to generate life history themes. Common threads running through these women's lives involve being injured while in powerless situations, such as being sexually or physically abused as children; being raped; being physically abused by a partner; or being economically disadvantaged and dependent upon a man for money. Woodhouse goes further to explain how these women contain their many years of anger and self-hate, leading to problems with drugs and alcohol later in life.

In Seabrook's (1993) sample of women, the experience of somatic anger symptoms relates to drinking more. Further, for women in this study the use of alcohol relates to the use of other substances (e.g., nicotine and over-the-counter drugs). Seabrook conducts analyses by age group in this study and finds that in the 36- to 45-year-old category, women's tendency to ruminate over anger-eliciting events correlates with consumption of alcohol; in women older than 45 years of age a relationship exists between number of drinks consumed and level of anger. These women report not only a tendency to drink associated with ruminating about angry incidents, but also physical symptoms of anger, such as headaches and accelerated respiration. In this age group, Seabrook also reports a relationship between suppressed anger and prescription drug use.

How do experiences of abuse and powerlessness lead to later consumptive problems? Again, we must peer between the life event and its later manifestation to discover the vehicle for a woman's distress. If anger is experienced in relation to a powerful other and cannot be voiced, it must be diverted in some way. By and large, consumption problems may be regarded as attempts to medicate or soothe an inner wound that knows no conscious words for catalyzing its healing. Anger that has been internalized leaves the woman with conflicting and self-damaging realities that she can, among other possibilities, either ignore or escape through food, alcohol, and recreational drugs. Segmented anger also leaves a woman vulnerable to continued displacement of the parts of herself she cannot tolerate, through excessive shopping or risky sexual encounters that offer an experience of herself as other than furious, devastated, disappointed, or anguished. Respect for her adaptive use of food or alcohol or plastic credit cards comes from an appreciation of her anger diversion process.

☐ Treatment of Women's Anger-Related Distress

These conceptualizations about diversions and measurements of anger lead one to ponder ways of applying them in session. How then does a therapist incorporate these complex issues into clinical practice? How can we translate appreciation for the value of women's anger in the experience of self and self-in-relation into therapeutic interaction, intervention and growth? Answers to these questions inform primary decisions concerning the direction a woman's therapy will take. Choices about how much anger is to be avoided, minimized, and controlled, and how much it should be explored, processed, and expressed are routinely undertaken. These choices demand movement beyond a historically simplistic model of anger toward recognition of the complexities involved.

Previously, anger's effects were measured and discussed within the framework of a fairly simple model built on the premise that anger works the same way for everyone. Tavris (1989) in her landmark book about anger speaks forcefully about the detrimental effects anger has on individuals and relationships. She criticizes the use of venting, rejects the hydraulic theory of emotional experience, and portrays anger as a destructive force that is tolerated much too freely by both professional psychology and today's society. She states that most often the act of expressing anger makes one more angry and contributes to an overall pattern or habit of being hostile and writes, "If you keep quiet about momentary irritations and distract yourself with pleasant activity until your fury simmers down, chances are you will feel better, and feel better faster, than if you let yourself go on in a shouting match" (p. 159). As we describe subsequently, others now suggest that only some individuals benefit from avoiding anger expression, and that there are healthier alternatives to either suppression or shouting matches, a fact selectively omitted by Tavris throughout much of her book.

In further indictment of anger, she states, "Any emotional arousal will eventually simmer down, if you just wait long enough" (Tavris, 1989, p. 130), and, "It seems to me that the major side effect of the ventilationist approach has been to raise the general noise level of our lives, not to lessen our problems" (p. 129). Although it is easy to agree with Tavris that the noise level of our lives is certainly rising, it could be that the source of this noise is not merely relationship static, but all those aroused emotions that did not simmer down over time in the manner predicted. Perhaps instead these emotions, so crucial and life-sustaining to selfhood, find expression through inner voices that increase in volume if outer expression is thwarted.

Tavris (1989) criticizes anger expression as a significant contribution to physical ill health, citing empirical evidence from earlier laboratory work to support her assertions. Both the design of the studies and Tavris's interpretations often lead to overgeneralizations and misunderstanding of the complexities of human anger experience. For example, the types of anger expression studied in the works Tavris cites vary widely in form and intensity but all are included under the terms "ventilation" and "catharsis," which themselves are used interchangeably in spite of their different connotations. Included under Tavris's "conditions of catharsis" are several items unrelated to either venting or cathartic expression, such as "improved communication with target of anger," "increased feeling of closeness with target," and "getting results from the target of anger." These issues lie outside the process of catharsis, which centers on inner change, not problem solving or negotiating with others. To say that catharsis does not work because it doesn't improve one's situation or relationship to another misses the point.

Tavris (1989) also equates any number of emotional values and experiences with the physiological measures that are reported in studies she cites. In reviewing this research, she moves from defining catharsis as a drop in blood pressure and heart rate to making assumptions about the resultant emotional states of participants not substantiated by the data. This confusion between physiological and emotional catharsis facilitates oversimplification and blanket criticism of the anger experience.

Tavris is joined by others who emphatically condemn anger expression. Whereas she eventually grants grudging approval to a highly controlled, cognitive approach to anger that resembles conflict resolution more than any authentic emotional experience, McKay, Rogers, and McKay (1989) choose to present a model of anger as purely and inherently destructive. They describe the emotion (assuming the everpresent dichotomy) as "an unhealthy habit" (p. 32) and state, "It doesn't matter whether anger is expressed or suppressed. . . It's just plain bad for you" (p. 31), and, "Venting anger rarely leads to any real relief or lasting catharsis. It leads instead to more anger, tension, and arousal" (p. 22).

As we will see, under certain circumstances, for certain people, recent research shows that there is more than one single anger reality, and that clear acknowledgment of the complexity involved in anger diversion or expression is crucial in providing helpful therapeutic treatment. For example, both of the works cited here describe early research by Hokanson (1970) designed to measure the amount of catharsis experienced by male and female participants reacting to a series of shocks administered in a laboratory. Results indicate a significant change in physiological measures, labeled "cathartic relief," in men who respond aggressively (administering shocks in return) and in women who respond in a friendly fashion. Although common sense would indicate the women's relief follows a reasonable assurance that one's "friendly" actions have at least temporarily warded off future painful stimuli, it strains credibility to label that relief "cathartic." It is this ease with which a woman's experience (presenting with submissive pleasantness in order to prevent victimization) is relabeled to match a traditional model of women as naturally anger-avoidant that adds a certain urgency to the call for a deeper examination of the data.

New studies, indeed, do illuminate some portions of anger and its expression, using more complex research designs and more careful interpretation of the results. For example, the work of Van Goozen et al. (1994) in developing the ASQ described previously clearly differentiates between the emotional experience of anger and its corresponding behavioral manifestations. They question the adequacy of laboratory-induced anger, saying it has not been shown clearly that the resulting behaviors (e.g., aggression) are linked to the emotion of anger and point out that the physiological measurements so pervasive in empirical anger research have led to an overemphasis on behavior at the neglect of basic emotional experience. The authors also mention gender differentiated socialization of anger as a significant factor deserving recognition in anger research.

Müller et al. (1995) take things one step further in their discussion of discrimination between emotional and behavioral aspects of anger. They define anger as an emotion that is "neither a necessary nor a sufficient condition for the development of hostile attitudes and the manifestation of aggressive behavior" (p. 70), and importantly, frame anger expression as a behavioral skill. These authors point out that current findings in anger research include data that mix both appropriate and inappropriate anger expression, a practice that certainly confounds results in studies correlating anger and physiological risk factors. Müller and colleagues' own findings indicate higher risk associated with the inability to express anger, which they differentiate from anger suppression. They define the former as a lack of skill or competence in expressing anger, and the latter as a separate and distinct anger coping skill.

In earlier work, Bohart (1980) notes contradictions in findings concerning physiological responses to anger arousal and related risk assessment. By insisting that different types of catharsis, under different circumstances, could lead to widely varying results, he paved the way for more detailed analyses of the conditions under which anger is helpful and those under which it is destructive. Bohart views the inclusion of cognitive work around anger issues and communication of the feeling to another as crucial to healthy expression. He counters absolutist denunciation of anger with statements such as, "Therapies employing catharsis concepts can be, and often are, successful and helpful" and delineates the effects of factors such as repeated practice of anger-release techniques and achieving a balance between cognition and emotion in the cathartic process. His writing suggests that there is no concise way to predict anger reduction by looking at its overt behavioral expression. Instead, anger reduction in research depends on the schemes each participant carries into a situation, and what constitutes "resolution" or "finishing" in relation to those schemes. Looking more closely at these variables opens a door to the reality of anger experience and invites a wider exploration.

One interesting attempt to tease out more of these complexities is Faber and Burns's (1996) investigation of the relationship among physiological reactions, anger-management style, degree of expressed anger, and gender. In examining the impact of anger-in versus anger-out characteristics, gender, and intensity of anger expressed on cardiovascular response to harassment, the authors were able to trace distinct patterns of response for male and female anger-out participants that contrasted with anger-in participants and identified crucial differences in risk factors for each group. Results show that women who identify themselves as high anger-out experience beneficial cardiovascular effects from expressing anger; women who self-report high in anger-in characteristics experience an increased risk of coronary heart disease if they refrain from anger expression, because of their cardiovascular response to behavioral inhibition. In contrast, high anger-out men and men with self-reported high levels of expressed anger manifest riskier cardiovascular responses than low anger-out men and men whose expressed anger level is low following harassment. Thus, anger expression can lead to either increased or decreased coronary risk depending on the gender and anger management style of the individual.

It is noteworthy that increased levels of anger expression appear to benefit women across the board. Women who express their anger freely profit physiologically from it, and women who do not do so suffer some "potentially pathogenic cardiovascular effects" (Faber & Burns, 1996, p. 49). This information supports the inclusion of anger work in women's psychotherapy, specifically anger work that helps women find a voice with which they can release and express anger. Interestingly, Faber and Burns discuss the verbal bias of the tools used in their study, noting that physical modes of expression were not measured. These authors speculate that mode of expression could further influence individual physiological response and subsequent risk level. Both verbal and physical anger work are discussed in more detail subsequently.

In considering the relevance of physiological data to real anger experience, Pennebaker's work with trauma survivors cannot be ignored. Specifically, Francis and Pennebaker's (1992) results show adult participants reporting increased feelings of nervousness and sadness after each of four sessions involving writing about emotions related to trauma (including common life events such as divorce or death of a parent). However, follow-up data collected 6 weeks later reflect significantly lower levels of absenteeism and healthier blood measures; well-being scores show no significant differences from control scores. In a related study, Pennebaker and Susman (1988) find that subjects writing about trauma score higher than controls on anxiety and depression scales each day but report the highest levels of happiness and lowest levels of anxiety and illness at follow-up. The authors comment, "Confiding about traumatic experiences, although depressing in the short run, appears to have positive physical and psychological effects in the long run" (p. 330). In light of these findings, it is troublesome to consider how often anger research focuses on the immediate physiological reactions of the subject to one isolated anger-inducing event without considering the effect of the passage of time, or even more importantly the cumulative effect of repeated anger expression or suppression over time.

A significant contribution to the formation of a healthy anger-expression model is Mikulincer's (1998) investigation of attachment styles and anger experiences. Drawing on attachment literature, Mikulincer develops a model of anger expression and control empirically demonstrated to be utilized by secure, avoidant, and anxious-ambivalent individuals. Securely attached individuals score significantly higher on anger-out, constructive goal setting, adaptive responses, and positive affect, a pattern the author calls *functional anger*. People who practice functional anger stay connected with their intense negative emotion yet associate their experience of anger with feelings of hope and relief, and they are able to communicate in ways that maximize potential for a positive outcome. Secure individuals also attempt to maintain relationships while communicating their anger. Mikulincer states these individuals use anger as "a signal that something is going wrong in a relationship and as a trigger for adaptive actions without overwhelming the cognitive system with negative affect and thoughts" (p. 522).

In contrast, people with avoidant personalities in Mikulincer's (1998) study report unexpectedly high anger control scores and exhibit significantly more intense physiological signs of anger. The author terms this profile *dissociated anger* and postulates that it is motivated by the need to present a positive self-image and a desire to "diffuse the conscious experience of anger feelings without solving the problem" (p. 522). Taken together, these results point to the importance of combining an ability to access angry feelings and live within the anger experience using competent communication skills, in order to form a functional model of anger expression.

Given this evidence, it is noteworthy that even the experience of anger, apart from behavioral consequences, is still seen in our society as harmful and destructive. If one is grieving a loss, it is more or less acceptable for one to choose to cry during designated experiences or ceremonies (e.g., funerals), or perhaps not at all, depending on one's gender and status, but typically no one is enjoined to avoid the feeling of sadness itself. Sadness, like joy or excitement, is accepted as a feeling that is part of the life experience, relevant to reality, and an important contribution to emotional wholeness. If anger is to gain similar status, it must be defined in ways that address individual and social concerns about safety, power, control, and inherent worth and we must provide for authentic identification and processing of anger. Health-promoting, assertive anger must create a space for the emotional experience, including its outward manifestations (the venting side of expression) and concurrently offer regulation of behavior that enhances and empowers relationships with others (the management side of expression).

In the development of these models for assertive anger, the integrity of anger as an emotion in its own right comes to the forefront. In so doing, it moves against centuries of socialization opposing the emotion itself, as well as its behavioral manifestations. Anger control and management have always held a special place in America's community heart. Stearns and Stearns (1986) document the rise in expectations for anger control in family and corporate life in America over the past few centuries. They report that although early colonists appear to have been markedly more permissive and accepting of anger and its expression in various social contexts (perhaps as a result of their recent experiences in England), this rather enlightened state of affairs did not continue. Eventually, Victorian family mores with their focus on self-control and emotional (not only sexual) repression formed a basis for early rules of corporate conduct, which in turn grew to influence the rest of society as industrialization progressed. The development of service-sector businesses contributed to anger avoidance, as unprofitable expressions of anger were expunged from the workplace. Even the emotional release of the 1960s and 1970s did little to liberate anger expression, according to the authors, with T-groups (therapy groups) and encounter groups dealing only superficially with anger. The anger involved in the social unrest of the time was highly criticized, and anger itself was not targeted for revolution, as were sexuality and other socially restricted behaviors. "Mature behavior consists of solving problems without anger. And American society is too immature, it needs control" (Stearns & Stearns, 1986, p. 165).

This view makes sense in recent decades as a response to the increase in concern over violent aggression and crime in our society. Opposition to anger is even more understandable in the context of the fear many majority group members feel in the face of the anger of those who are disenfranchised and underrepresented in our culture. However, we must keep in mind that anger is not aggression, nor does anger consistently cause aggression (Geen, 1990). Thus, these social sanctions miss their mark and would be better utilized in targeting aggressive behaviors perpetrated by majority and minority group members alike.

Anger Applied

At this juncture, we turn to the more clinical applications of these theoretical concepts and this research. In so doing, we introduce the "client," as well as the therapist-client relationship, and begin to discuss tools for facilitating women's journey towards authenticity.

Therapeutic anger work may best be understood within the context of affect congruence in contribution to overall mental health. For purposes of this discussion, affect congruence refers to parity between what is felt and what is shown to others (e.g., facial expression, words, vocal quality). Aside from the sociological issues involved, information about the psychological construct of affect congruence versus incongruence empowers clients who are deciding whether or not to resist social influences on emotional control.

Psychoeducation on anger diversion provides women with information that can help them make deliberate, intentional choices about anger expression. For instance, the costs of maintaining a happy or unaffected demeanor regardless of what internal turmoil is raging, using one or more diversions, can be described to women in terms of the amount of energy required to maintain an "inner wall" that keeps forbidden emotions inside, hidden from others and sometimes from themselves. This energy drain (most likely happening through suppression) can contribute to depression and be accompanied by increased anger or inappropriate acting-out behaviors (externalization). In addition, others misunderstand the true emotional condition of the client because outward cues reveal the opposite of her internal state. This seriously impedes the woman's ability to receive empathy or assistance from others, leading to increasingly painful experiences of isolation and hopelessness.

Once this "inner wall" is in place, it functions as a barrier whose effects reach beyond the intentions of the client in maintaining a socially acceptable demeanor. One cannot uniformly pick and choose which emotions will be inaccessible and which others will be felt and expressed in full force—therefore joy and contentment often become as distant and indistinct as the unwelcome anger and sadness. In addition, the wall works both ways; that is to say it protects the self from incoming stimuli as much as it interrupts outgoing emotional messages. Although this could be viewed as helpful in defending against negative evaluation by others, it also prevents accumulation of important data about self and others that, if tolerated, can contribute to identity formation and maintenance.

The use of the wall metaphor can be generalized to include discussion about boundary development. If a client is unfamiliar with the concept of personal boundaries, information can be offered to explain their importance in maintaining personal integrity and identity in relationship to others. It is particularly helpful to focus on the density of boundaries, presenting this characteristic as one of choice and adaptation. For example, a woman can be assisted in choosing to set a stronger, denser personal boundary with someone who is threatening or controlling, and a more permeable, translucent one (sharing more of herself) in a relationship that feels safer.

Therapy involving careful and detailed examination of ongoing boundary issues in various current relationships often yields empowering results, as clients find the tools to take more control over how and when they reveal themselves. Self-revelation, as opposed to self-presentation, presents another therapeutic challenge to female clients. Because girls and women are socialized to focus so intently on the presentation of an acceptable, appealing self, therapy can provide a much needed space to explore, identify, and make intentional choices in identity development, to perhaps even risk being perceived as unacceptable and unappealing, in order to discover and preserve one's identity. Anger work becomes central to this process, as prohibition of anger is a primary means of arresting personal development in puberty or prepuberty. Anger work in therapy becomes a means through which a woman can continue the process of scaling the treacherous heights of her internal experience that were "off limits" at younger ages.

How then, is anger work accomplished in women's therapy? The answer to this question varies with the age, cultural background, and social class of the client. Markus and Kitayama (1994) present a thorough and thoughtful review of emotion across cultures and Pederson and Ivey (1993) present world views and cultural behavior patterns in a counseling context. Given that women differ in background and thought tradition, the ideas presented may be reflexively applied and subject to modifications as women's special needs arise. Georges (1995) reminds us that in some cultures (Bali, China) there are powerful social sanctions associated with emotional disclosure. Ignoring this cultural context in therapy would be a grave mistake, and the authors expect that application of this model, as with any therapy, needs to be highly individualized.

It is important to remember that the models we present for working with women's and girls' anger in therapy derive from Western theory, research, and practice. As such, they most readily apply to White, middle-class women. One way to judge the potential effectiveness of these therapeutic techniques is to evaluate a client's level of acculturation. Highly acculturated women and girls are more likely to be receptive to psychotherapy in general, and the ideas and behaviors suggested as a part of anger work will not seem so foreign. Less acculturated individuals often require substantive modifications to this therapeutic approach. Some of the many aspects of therapy that might need to be modified include expectations for therapeutic roles and tasks, degree of directiveness, degree of self-disclosure, and nonverbal aspects of communication (Ponterotto, 1998; Ponterotto, Casas, Suzuki, & Alexander, 1995).

In a related vein, the distinctions between an individualist and a collectivist view of self may offer guidance in making cross-cultural adjustments to the therapy models we present. The idea that the revelation of anger to self and then to others can have a positive, self definitional outcome is fundamental to our therapeutic approach. However, exactly how self is defined varies across cultures. In many Western countries, such as the United States, Australia, and the United Kingdom, the self that is valued is an autonomous, individualistic being and the focus of self development is on individual abilities, achievements, and desires. In many of the more collectivist cultures of Latin America, the Middle East, and the Far East, the self that is valued is a more interconnected entity, fundamentally entwined with group, family, and community identity (Markus & Kitayama, 1991). Women and girls from these cultures more likely value group harmony and group identities over individual aspects of self, and for these clients a sense of self does not equate with individualism or autonomy.

In fact, people from both collectivist and individualist countries develop a sense of self in relation to others. However, different aspects of self are highlighted and valued in these different cultures; it is a matter of degree. Such considerations are an important part of any practitioner's application of the principles and techniques we present here.

Anger Revealed

The proposed model for anger work includes two dimensions: first, revelation to self—the release of accumulated anger in a safe and empowering manner; and second, revelation to others—the appropriate and respectful expression, or clarification, of anger to others. These work together to ensure that anger diversion is minimized. In doing this work, it is crucial to create an environment in which women feel safe. Many times the mere mention of anger work brings visions of unrestrained venting or out of control "primal scream" exercises to mind. However, this image differs from the current model in one crucially important way: There is no point at which we consider it helpful or therapeutic for a client to lose control. Each of the clinical interventions described below is meant to be undertaken with clients who are prepared to maintain control during the exercise. Thus the client expresses and releases the anger as the result of an active choice, with responsibility, and without the risk of loss of control. Clients access therapeutic benefit through the realization that they are capable of tolerating such an intense emotional experience and are in charge of how they use its energy.

If a client regularly diverts anger into an externalized, acting-out expression (e.g., raging, abuse), preparation for maintaining control while working on anger may be appropriate. Because of the preponderance of anger management models in the field today, we do not address specific methods for achieving "control over" anger per se, and it is important to note that we see these techniques as only one part of effective therapeutic intervention for such clients. As discussed previously, we theorize that the acting-out behaviors are in themselves a way of diverting anger away from the self onto others, and it is necessary for these women to engage in the same process of honestly acknowledging and giving voice to their anger used by other clients who divert their anger with a more internal focus.

Of course, anger work does not fit every client, and it goes without saying that careful screening and assessment, along with individualized treatment plans, is always indicated. Just as the exclusive application of one singular approach cannot possibly meet all therapeutic needs, we do not advocate the use of our model of anger work with every client. However, if appropriate, anger work can be carried out in various environments. Often, a therapeutic group offers an ideal format in which women can encourage, support, validate and coach each other in ways of physically and verbally expressing anger. As we hear in Chapter 5, this kind of interaction is sometimes sought out informally by women who feel a need to confide in supportive others if more direct anger expression is blocked.

Individually, a woman in the sheltered environment of therapy receives a kind of empowering nurturance from her therapist, who sees the rough and jagged aspects of her rage and values them, in fact encourages her to show more of them, gradually sharing with her how these sharp edges make her more multidimensional and alive. We turn now to the aspect of anger work that focuses on the unveiling of anger to the self.

Revelation to Self: Anger Release

A helpful metaphor in presenting the concept of anger work as anger release to women of any age and background is that of a container full of water. The theoretical container is described to be so full to the brim that the water forms a convex curve at the top. One more drop of water falls into the container and, women are asked, "What happens next?" The universal answer includes descriptions of overflow that are easily applied to the experience of uncontrolled anger expression. Clients often label this kind of expression in negative terms, such as tantrums, losing it, having a fit, or going crazy. Of course, just the experience of getting angry in and of itself is seen as a culpable act, precisely the point at which the practitioner can begin to differentiate helpful and assertive from unhelpful, nonassertive, or aggressive anger expression. If one chooses to empty the container of water, to reduce it to only half full or leave just a bit in the bottom, it is a very different experience from reducing the water level by having the too-full container overflow irrepressibly when one more drop falls into it. In emptying the container through anger release, women take charge of how often, how fast, and how much anger is released. (The authors acknowledge current criticisms of the hydraulic theory of emotion portrayed through this metaphor. However, even Bohart [1980], a confirmed critic of this theory, admits to its "intuitive appeal to laypersons and professionals alike" [p. 197], and we confirm its usefulness in communicating about anger experience.)

Anger release can be accomplished through two means, namely physically acting on the environment and some form of verbalization. Almost every client can benefit from work in both of these media, but many prefer one over the other, and it is important to allow each client to choose based on personal affinity and current need. Physical anger release can take a wide variety of forms. Because socialization has effectively limited this territory for women (and children), clients often find it initially difficult to develop options here or to imagine themselves behaving in physically expressive ways. The therapist can assist by offering suggestions that other clients and families have employed and by making available a workable physical anger-release exercise in session. The latter is typically accomplished by providing instruments that can be safely used to hit, kick, throw, and so forth as a means of releasing angry feelings.

There are many ways to weave anger release-work into therapy so that women feel safe to explore the rich and varied textures of their anger in an overtly expressive way. Depending on the needs and values of the specific client, one can start with exploring anger issues and then develop physical applications, or begin by identifying helpful behaviors and then progress to discovering why these are beneficial. To introduce the option of "getting anger out," practitioners can discuss the client's level of awareness of angry feelings, explore the visceral sensations of anger (e.g., stomach tightening, breath shortening), and inquire about when and how she has made sure these are kept hidden from view. Or, one can offer spoken anger ventilation as an option if a client relates a specific wrath-inducing incident with which she continues to struggle.

At some point, however, the client can be invited to do something very different—to get up, take hold of the bat or bataka, and begin to give physical voice to the feelings she has kept sealed away for so long. Empowering her to take such a step involves the most delicate of therapeutic maneuvering and an accurate sense of timing. The practitioner's ability to tolerate and perhaps model anger expression without fear or judgment is essential, as is a confidence-inspiring level of personal competence in honestly releasing and expressing anger. In other words, the therapist needs to have done her or his homework in resolving anger issues personally as well as professionally. However, no client should ever be coerced into participating if she does not wish to do so, no matter how beneficial the experience would appear to be in the end.

Ideally, the woman finds ways to practice physical anger release outside of session. The steps that need to be taken in order to help her protect herself from negative consequences or shaming depend on the client's age and background, including trauma history. For young women and girls living at home with their families of origin, more negotiation with family members is necessary to find a release that works for all concerned. Family willingness to encounter anger expression varies tremendously, so that no standard suggestion proves acceptable or successful across the board. Each individual and family must work toward their own solution to the problem of ensuring appropriate and safe anger work. In addition to batting or hitting at pillows, cushions, or mattresses, typical options include slamming doors, yelling while alone in a bedroom or bathroom, tearing up old newspapers or phone books (cleanup is the responsibility of the anger expresser), kicking or throwing balls at the backyard fence, shooting hoops, running, biking, or skating around the block, running stairs, and hammering nails into boards. Again, the goal is to define a specific set of activities the client can use when she feels the need, which are safe given her living arrangement and will not put her in further emotional danger. Over time, with these options in place, the client develops the ability to change ingrained patterns of anger diversion and thus accesses information about herself and her relationships with others that can powerfully inform the development of an authentic identity. Her self-knowledge and awareness allows authentic experience.

Clients often find inhibiting any factor they perceive as compromising or threatening to their safety. Therefore, a primary consideration of the practitioner during anger work is to ensure that no action breaches limitations established to support the client's experience of the environment and the exercise as secure. Although these limits vary along with the needs and characteristics of the client, the authors recommend the following:

1. You will keep yourself safe (by not hurting yourself).

2. You will keep others safe (by not hurting them).

3. You will keep property safe (by not damaging anything).

It is a rather startling and profound revelation for clients to grasp that they can engage in a given type of angry and forceful behavior to the limits of their strength and endurance without causing harm or destruction on any level. Besides providing the structure necessary for safe anger work, these rules can also become the starting point for therapeutic work surrounding the concept of anger as helpful instead of dangerous. Additional limitations on the exercises are appropriate for younger clients, as well as for group work. Typically these include restrictions on leaving one's seat, handling a bat or blocker, amount of time allotted to perform the exercise, and spontaneous creative variations of the exercise.

Of course, physical action, as intense and impactful as the experience feels, is not the only way to reduce suppressed or stored anger, inside or outside of a therapy session. Verbalizing is a second method that contributes to release. Speaking honestly and directly about angry feelings during a therapy session represents the simplest form of this communication, yet it remains one of the most difficult therapeutic tasks for women to sustain for any length of time. Parallel with the anger diversion of externalization, emotional socialization encourages us to focus on the faults of any irritating, anger-generating person or thing rather than to dwell on our own personal feeling response. In initial therapeutic explorations of angry incidents, a woman is often unable to respond to a question such as, "And how did you feel when that happened?" with a statement defining herself in the moment.

To continue facilitating verbalization, the therapist can coach the client to identify, name and describe feelings she experienced during the incident she is relating. Clients typically begin with offerings of "upset," "lousy," "pretty bad," "not normal," "down," or similar pseudoemotional labels that often reflect symptom clusters described previously. Encouraging a client to move away from somatic or self-blaming language opens the way for her to use feeling expressions that more clearly reference her emotional experience (e.g., enraged, bewildered, frightened). This is a challenge that is not often mastered initially but brings empowerment and ownership with practice and familiarity. The first few times a client is asked to acknowledge this part of herself by literally saying, "I feel angry," she may actually experience a sense of disingenuousness and only find sincere connection with the word "frustrated" or "upset." Permission to use all the words, to candidly examine her emotional experiences and reconsider their composition and intensity, challenges a client's initial minimizations, and those whose experiences are validated in session not only learn to distinguish between annoyance and rage but eventually are able to own the latter, reclaiming a part of their identity that was given up long before.

Here, the practitioner needs to be especially sensitive to the difference between suggesting and leading. The goal is for the client to feel she has a plethora of rich and varied emotional labels from which to choose in giving her experience a name, and that in the naming process she exercises her own power to designate her selfhood. If she is led to feel instead that there is only one correct word for her experience, and that her therapist has already chosen the right word but will not tell her which one it is, the focus remains on self-presentation and not on self-revelation. The point is not to insist that the client is angry, but to offer up anger as a word that might fit, because very likely it has not been offered to her before, and then to meet the client's response with acceptance and perhaps more wondering questions about when anger fits. To insist a client is angrier than she claims sadly repeats society's wrongful entitlement in naming who and what women are.

Women's anger dialogues take many possible forms, and one of the most well-known is journaling, a method of regularly writing down thoughts and feelings related to therapeutic work. This venue offers clients the freedom to experiment with new types of emotional identification, away from the scrutiny of any other person and with no outside consequences. Although some women find they cannot commit angry feelings to paper in a letter, perhaps because it makes these emotions more visible and concrete, many consider journaling a private enough arena to engender the safe environment necessary for rebelling against social prohibitions on full and honest anger expression.

Journal writing is meant for the client's own use and not for any other audience, as opposed to letters and messages about her feelings that she might at some point intend to use as communication with others about herself and her experience. Journaling creates an opportunity to explore boundary issues and contributes to the creation of a protected space in which the client experiences and owns all of her self and her feelings and chooses which facets she wishes to share and to what depth. Thus, while she is writing, she writes to please herself. However, after the fact, a woman can decide to bring especially meaningful or helpful journal entries into session or dialogue with friends and family about her writings when she feels safe doing so. Consider the following journal entry made by a 34-year-old White woman struggling to love her body. After two years of psychotherapy, she rounds a corner into anger at cultural body-image pressures instead of loathing for herself.

> I'm so angry right now. I'm angry at the patriarchal society [world] that we [women] have to live in. My friend Jenna at work is 19, beautiful, great skin, small waist, large breasts, and she thinks she's fat. I wish I looked like her. My boss has breast implants. Another lady there wishes she had breast implants and will probably get them before it's over with. So we women have all this pressure put on us to have a tiny waist and large breasts, but that's not the way our bodies are made, so none of us are happy with our bodies!! I think most women think my butt's too big and my boobs are too small. . . I am so angry because I feel so powerless!!! I used to want to kill myself because I didn't want to live in this world that puts all this burden on women. We have enough burden—we give and sustain life!! Goddammit we need some RESPECT!! I don't want to kill myself anymore. But I have this horrible frustration I live with everyday!

In making an honest connection with her anger, this client finds it more difficult to sustain narcissistic beliefs that all the wrong in the world lies within herself and the resulting drive toward self-destruction. Having permission to first acknowledge her anger and then explore it, her realization that it is directed outward changes her whole experience of herself. The task now becomes defining ways to express her "horrible frustration" that are constructive, giving her healthy options to the anger diversions that led her toward suicidality in the past.

Sometimes, clients do not feel comfortable with the mechanics of putting words to paper but can still participate in this self-exploration exercise by using a video camera or a tape recorder instead of a pen, creating a spoken version of a journal that can be stored and accessed on tape. This gives them the same kind of permanent and concrete record of themselves without the frustrations of writing or typing if these acts are not facile or fluid. An added bonus is the empathic reaction clients frequently experience upon seeing their own facial expressions or hearing their own tone of voice. Those clients who deny themselves the understanding they would readily feel for others in their situation sometimes find that watching or listening to themselves offers a unique point of view that works to release compassion for the self not otherwise accessible (Arauzo, Watson, & Hulgus, 1994).

Intentionality is a key issue in the safekeeping of an anger journal. Discussions about specific arrangements for ensuring confidentiality are aimed at empowering women to become conscious about protecting their privacy. Inadvertent discovery and examination of journal books and tapes are harmful not so much because the client's anger is exposed, but because this occurs without intention on her part. This problem sometimes arises because someone lacks respect for the woman's boundaries. However, the breach can also occur as the result of an apparent lack of attention to the guardianship of the journal on her part. Careless treatment of it, such as leaving it where it could be easily discovered, would be a way for the client to divert her anger, perhaps achieving some kind of passive release—a manner of expression far more socially acceptable for many women than direct declaration. In encouraging the development of plans for the safekeeping of her journal, the intent is to empower the client to take ownership and responsibility by assisting her in intentionally choosing to share her anger rather than be discovered in it. In the following journal excerpt, a client expresses what she has chosen not to verbalize with her former partner.

Mike,

I can't believe that your big beef with me was that I didn't trust you completely and all the while you lied to me about the porno. I was totally honest with you about my problems. Well guess what, I did trust you. I would have left if I had known. I've tried to work on my problems and one day I will be truly free. I even tried to fix little things like giving you some money when you quit jobs on my account. I fixed a big thing by getting out of the bars. I was cool with the concept of me working a day job and you trying to make your dream come true. I feel that I always supported your music and your dream, I still do . . . I am furious with you for continuing to let me believe you had changed. I hate that you let me make all those changes and did nothing to change yourself. I refuse to tolerate the porn and so I'm letting you go. I will miss you.

Julie

This young woman, Julie, finds a way to juxtapose her anger at this man she loves with her sadness about losing the relationship as she wanted it. The writing gives her a vehicle by which she can carry the grief and anger out into the light and look at it in a new and different way. Besides exercises in physical and verbal anger release, there are other activities that fall somewhere between or outside these two categories. These include anger release through music, dance, poetry, and art. Anger work in art encompasses both works on paper and in other media, such as clay, that provide a visceral experience in the creation of the work as well as an emotional communication or expression contained in the end product.

Clients find another outlet through both listening to and creating music. Sharing tapes or written lyrics of songs can be a meaningful way for younger clients and therapeutic groups to communicate about their anger experience. These more intuitive methods of anger release often yield a certain insight or understanding about the nature of the anger, its composition, its depth, and its links to the past. Many adolescent girls use poetry as a favorite means of self-expression, and it can serve well as an anger release, though it is rarely used for that purpose. This poem comes from the pen of a 16-year-old woman in a struggle with developmental changes that put distance between herself and a long-time friend:

> Anger, it burns inside of me.
> It rips and tears until I cry.
> It makes me feel helpless and hurt.
> Anger just stays inside of me.
> I just want to scream and kick and punch.
> But all I can do is sit and cry.
> Built up inside, the anger won't move.
> Just sit and cry, that's all I can do.

These words illustrate the value of creative modes of expression in working with younger clients. Poetry and music, especially, can be satisfying avenues of expression for adolescents who balk at the idea of "talk therapy." Younger girls often find release they would not be able to otherwise access through art, puppets, or similar therapies. Physical anger expression seems to have an appeal all its own for school-aged girls, who nonetheless require solid structuring of the process in order to ensure safety and a secure emotional environment. This includes an emphasis on the three safety guidelines mentioned previously, and the inclusion of family members in decisions about how anger can be constructively expressed outside of session.

Revelation to Others: Anger Communication

Our focus now widens in scope to include not only the development of clarifying self-realizations and expressions of anger but also the direct, assertive communication of anger to another. These are separate processes, and some of the mistrust of therapeutic anger work in the field today is a result of the historical fusion of the two. Anger communication is a social skill that specifically involves formulating a statement about one's angry feelings in order to convey them to others. In working to achieve this purpose, the form of the statement itself becomes a relevant factor. The goal is two-fold: first, to create an accurate statement concerning one's inner experience that may or may not carry an expectation for change on the other's part; and second to ensure that the message is appropriate, respectful, and given without attempting to dictate the other's response.

Because this act of clearly defining one's inner experience (work that can begin with anger release) moves one through successive stages of self-knowledge, it is a process that contributes to identity discovery and development. In Chapter 3 we discuss adolescent girls' introduction into a dilemma of adult womanhood, in which those aspects of the self identified through the experience of anger as an indication of the difference between self and others are forfeited, in order to maintain the very relationships that generated the anger. Working on anger clarification in therapy addresses not only the manner in which a woman communicates her feelings of anger, but also the need to resolve this dilemma. Once-abandoned parts of self that were sacrificed in adolescent and adult efforts at relationship preservation are reclaimed, and the result is an expanded sense of self and an increased awareness of one's boundaries—hallmarks of personal growth and self-definition.

In the restoration of previously disowned aspects of personhood, a fresh consciousness of the self as separate emerges, and the distinction between the self and others grows increasingly clear. However, this awareness of one's aloneness can trigger intense distress, an effect we postulate contributes to the avoidance of anger. This issue becomes singularly relevant in exercises of anger clarification, as it is through the communication of anger to another that the emotion and consequential self-awareness is made tangible and concrete. If she experiences her own anger, a client takes ownership of those parts of herself she once felt compelled to deny. If a woman chooses to make her anger visible to and heard by another, those parts of her identity then become concrete and real in the world through her act of stating them aloud.

This condition of being concrete, material, and visible with anger is a hazardous one for women. Even the habitation of physical space with our bodies is a tenuous existence in these days of enslavement to dieting and weight loss. The persistence of unreal standards for the body image of women has progressed to the point of the absurd, with images of women in the media now being routinely computer-altered to portray bodily dimensions that are not humanly possible to achieve. In the midst of all these cultural messages loaded for invisibility, therapy that refutes cultural sanctions against anger and acknowledges the importance of constructive anger communication empowers women to move toward visibility and ongoing, tangible confirmation of their existence.

It is precisely this focus on selfhood that ensures anger statements are delivered in a respectful and appropriate manner, the second goal of anger communication. Instead of externalizing by denouncing the other (the conventional portrayal of anger expression), anger communication clarifies one's own experience. Respectful anger expression ensures that the speaker takes full responsibility for her feelings and does not blame, attack, or label others when communicating about her anger. Consideration of the other is paramount in responsible self-expression, which in turn is central to emotional health. Thus, appropriate and respectful qualifications on anger clarification serve to protect clients, as well as the recipients of these communications.

Although it involves interpersonal communication, anger clarification is basically a self-focused act of choosing to utilize rather than divert one's anger. At other points in the therapeutic process, the client may focus on advocating for a change in the other's behavior or negotiating a resolution to a conflict, both of which are important and empowering steps, fundamentally related to experiencing anger. The focus in anger communication, however, necessarily lies in creating a safe space in which the client may develop the courage and ability to choose honest and direct words in communicating her angry feelings to another and thus share her anger outside herself in a clarifying way.

Descriptions from journals or tapes and verbalizations during physical anger release can yield concrete and specific descriptions for use in anger communication. Alternatively, clients can be asked to choose a specific anger-engendering incident and describe their affective experience in detail. In either case, women may fluctuate from affective release involving talk about what happened and what the other person did, said, and so forth, to specific tasks surrounding anger expression. Continuing to listen to and validate the client's experience wherever possible, the therapist consistently addresses anger-release needs apart from anger communication, emphasizing the importance of knowing the difference between the two processes. Anger communication steps beyond anger release to engage a person in the process of relationship transformation. Although focus remains on internal change, the woman's relationships also begin to shift in response to her assertive self-demarcation, as she finds ways to translate her emotional experience into out-in-the-open, two-way exchange.

"I" messages, basic tools of counseling, appear simplistic at first glance. However, these concise statements can be surprisingly difficult to construct, especially if the message is an angry one. Again, this in part reflects the widespread misunderstanding surrounding the purpose of vocalizing one's anger. The typical stereotype of communication about anger is that of a negative but effective means to achieve control, and anger expression is seen as an act of power against another (as it is confused with aggression), with potential for achieving victory in a given conflict (a one-up position), rather than as an act of self-revelation. Anger expression is actually a vulnerable act. An angry person usually feels hurt and opens this wound up for another to see by expressing the pain. In contrast, aggressive behavior attempts to prevail in some way by using force, ending the flow of engagement between people (Miller & Surrey, 1990).

"I messages" about anger present a challenge because the wording requires clients to work on the many levels of feeling in which they may be involved. Because anger is a complex emotion, it often attaches itself to fear, regret, sadness, or guilt by virtue of the contexts in which it emerges and the reactions women have to their own experience of it. The therapist assists the client in forming an appropriate message by helping her to set clear criteria for success in the expression of anger.

First, women are encouraged to carefully and intentionally explore and name their experience when they go through the process of filling in the first blank ("I feel . . . ") in an emotionally honest way. Second, the fact that they own that experience, and that it has become a part of their identity, is borne out in a way not possible if verbalizations focus on criticizing, blaming, or attacking the other ("You are so stubborn it drives me crazy"). Statements such as, "I feel angry when I am alone so often" or "I feel enraged when you stare at other women," all combine to form a clearer, broader, deeper picture of the self, far more complete than if the angry self had been censored.

"How will you know when you've said what you need to say?" In order to avoid setting herself up for failure, the client needs to choose criteria over which she has control, such as describing her angry feelings directly to the person whose actions incited the emotion (rather than triangling in a third person), or successfully resisting pressure to disown her reality or her feelings—in other words holding onto her own experience in the face of argument and resistance from others. This is especially important in relationships in which her power has been diminished over time. If success depends on convincing the other that he or she is wrong or receiving an apology from someone, anger expression disempowers, reinforcing the idea of anger as manipulation and setting the stage for escalating control battles. If instead success entails voicing her anger to the individual who has contributed to its creation, it becomes possible for any woman to succeed, with or without the consent and cooperation of those around her.

Women most often need to identify varied criteria for success within their many relationships. In setting the criteria at different points with different people, a woman can be in touch with the amount of control she has in expressing her anger. Perhaps with a close friend, the client feels successful if she communicates her anger frankly when she feels it instead of waiting until several incidents have accumulated. With a parent, she might choose to write a carefully worded letter about one or two past incidents and for the first time introduce the concept that she is angry about childhood occurrences. At work, she may declare success if she has expressed her feelings to her supervisor at an appropriate time and place using professional language. In all these cases, the response of the other is not pertinent to the experience of success by the client. She succeeds if she expresses her anger as she has planned, regardless of what others choose to do with it.

This part of anger work takes place on a cognitive-behavioral level. Our model includes a necessary, but not sufficient, cognitive component that we find essential in challenging the pressures of socialization against anger and maintaining appropriate levels of control when this powerful emotion arises. Many anger-management approaches are based on similar cognitive and behavioral interventions aimed toward a variety of therapeutic goals. The focus can be on appropriate and respectful expression of anger, resulting in a sense of effectiveness and instrumentality, but often expands to include an unfortunate campaign against the emotion itself, aimed solely at controlling or even avoiding anger experience. We choose to use cognitive-behavioral techniques to accomplish a two-fold purpose. First, we see them as effective in building client skills that can be used as tools for maintaining healthy relationships. For example, in O'Hanlon's (1996) work on brief solution-oriented therapy with couples, careful attention is given to expressive communication skills. Emotions such as anger are to be accepted as valid and acknowledged; beliefs and especially behaviors must be spoken about in very specific and concrete terms. He also teaches clients that understanding a partner's point of view need not be equated with agreement. Similar skills have long been promoted by classic cognitive-behavioral communication skills models such as relationship enhancement (Guerney, 1977).

Second, cognitive interventions are integral to the feminist therapeutic process (Worell & Johnson, 1997). Feminist therapy has long held as a central premise that consciousness raising is a crucial component of change. Learned patterns of belief about gender and gender roles are challenged through direct exploration of power and hierarchy dynamics, socialization messages from family and culture, and experiences of oppression and discrimination.

Although most therapeutic approaches to anger involve these cognitive applications, it is our belief that anger work must go further to embrace affective and dynamic processes as well. We view the experiential elements of our model as indispensable in accomplishing client goals of connection, insight, and change. In this arena, we draw on the practices of other experiential therapies. Gestalt therapy (Perls, 1969) is a primary model for experiential intervention, aimed at assisting the client to become involved in "active expression," which allows access to the state of being in the moment. The physical aspects of this work bring "a deeper awareness that emerges from the depths of [clients'] bodies rather than off the top of their heads" (Prochaska & Norcross, 1994, p. 167). One main focus of Gestalt therapy is to work through "unfinished business." This involves addressing feelings the client has been trying to avoid but that, if expressed, can bring closure to issues that have plagued both the relationships and the internal lives of clients for years. Much of this work is achieved through action-oriented exercises in session.

Emotion-focused therapy focuses on the acknowledgment and expression of emotion as key components in healing and growth (Johnson, 1996; Johnson & Williams-Keeler, 1998). This approach, grounded in attachment theory, considers emotional expression to be an agent of change and central to the therapeutic process. Therapists use experiential techniques to help the client to access feelings, and then to heighten and expand the client's emotional release. Practitioners of emotion-focused therapy believe intimacy in relationships is linked to the level of trust demonstrated by couples who are able to tolerate honest communication about feelings and experiences, including such emotions as anger. Johnson and Talitman (1997, p. 148) explain that intense levels of negative affect are not an inhibitory factor in emotion-focused therapy because "negative affect can be a part of the solution" instead of a source of the problem.

Finally, in combining experiential and cognitive-behavioral intervention, it is important to consider client attributes and how they match with each approach. As part of an evaluation of focused expressive psychotherapy, an experiential group therapy model, Beutler, Machado, Engle, and Mohr (1993) found that clients who externalize their anger and other emotions show more improvement in depressive symptomatology if engaged in cognitive therapy, as opposed to internalizing clients who improved more significantly with focused expressive psychotherapy. By utilizing elements of both, our model aims to address the needs of women who divert their anger either externally or internally, or perhaps even in both directions.

☐ Conclusions

In summary, this chapter represents a blending of research and academic voices with that of the therapist, in understanding and treating women's anger-related distress. Throughout this chapter, we attempted to support the careful and deliberate consideration of traditional versus alternative assessment and treatment for women in psychotherapy, with exceptional attention to the role of anger. We have proposed a model of anger diversion that expands notions of expression from the dichotomous "in" or "out." In a similar fashion, we have moved beyond traditional diagnostic taxonomies by examining symptoms in clusters and by regarding these as manifestations of anger in women that emerge in a society that accepts illness in women more readily than direct anger expression. We further argue for continued and accelerated progress in developing a working model of healthy and appropriate anger expression for women as a means to support each in her struggle for identity and self-expression. For reasons embedded in gender socialization, this work may best be undertaken by those most interested in women's emotional development and treatment.

The idea that anger is a powerful tool for forming an identity and preserving a sense of self in the midst of relationship is central to our clinical model. In this frame, we underline the importance of normalizing anger experience and assisting clients to clearly and concretely identify ways in which their anger can be productive and constructive. By dividing this process into two arenas, the more private act of anger release and clarification through communication of anger to others, the model addresses the full anger experience in ways that neither deny self nor disrespect others. Our approach also recognizes presenting symptomatology as potentially indicative of anger diversion as manifested by depression or anxiety, somatic complaints, and consumptive issues. We present the concept of anger diversion as a maladaptive use of anger energy that includes the processes of internalizing, suppressing, segmenting, and externalizing anger.

In the best of therapy environments, a woman receives a kind of empowering nurturance from her therapist, who can sit with the sharp, bright edges of her rage, value them, and encourage her to express them. Over time, a woman's therapist can help her to incorporate a perspective that places her anger in an integrated, adaptive position within an expanded sense of herself. If this occurs, we hypothesize that many women experience transformational shifts as they accommodate new skills and self images. Women learn to express anger first to themselves, and then to others, in an instrumental way that we hold to be valuable in their recovery from depressive, anxious, somatic, and consumptive features of anger diversion. By extension, far from being the only reasons for therapists to utilize such anger work in women's therapy, these diagnostic markers bear significance for women's empowerment as depression, panic, addiction, or illness give way to self-definition, authenticity, and agency.

Women Speak About Anger

When a person, or a happening,
seemed to me not in keeping with my opinion,
or even my hope or expectation,
I was terrified by a vision of abandonment and wildness
which tore my heart with a kind of sorrow.
                              —Eudora Welty

This chapter transports the reader from the smorgasbord of available research and theorizing on women's anger into schools, homes, and offices
where small groups of girls and women have something to say about the
ways they experience anger. Using a structured interview format, these
conversations involve girls' and women's perceptions about how they are
viewed when they become angry. Specifically, we inquire about how significant people feel about and behave toward them when they are angry
as well as how the same people respond to angry boys and men. Answers
to these questions reveal how women perceive their relationships to be
affected when they feel angry and perhaps shed some light on the anger
socialization process as it occurs between women and their loved ones.
Also, these disclosures convey something about the ways women encounter men's anger and its social consequences.

　　　This chapter reviews conversations with fifth- and eighth-grade girls
of African American, Latin American, and White ethnicity in mixed groups.

Combined with this look at girls is a study of similar conversations among four groups of women who converse in ethnically similar groups. This collection of discourses comes from girls and women of a variety of ethnic and cultural backgrounds. However, it is beyond the scope of this chapter to represent all areas of diversity. The authors expect that this relatively small set of group discussions will serve to promote colloquy between professionals interested in women's anger from cultural, developmental, research, and theoretical perspectives.

For both girls' and women's conversations, we review the following domains. First, we look at the anger and emotion themes in women's dialogue, with attention to how anger functions in their lives and the ways in which it motivates girls and women to take action. As we determine in Chapter 2, newer and more integrated models of emotion leave room for anger's usefulness in clarifying, strengthening, and driving much of human emotional experience. So, it makes sense to look at that adaptive force in women's day-to-day encounters. Herein we also examine women's portrayals of their cultural rules and roles for feeling or using anger. Second, we canvass the area of anger in relation, and its contribution to women's self definition as well as the social imperatives that it be silenced or diverted. This focus allows us to sift through women's own words to find out about the grain and texture of their anger-related self-loss as well as situations in which they retain their angry voices and use them for clarifying relationships and needs. Finally, we study the ways in which girls' and women's anger becomes diverted and how it thus develops into symptomatology. Listening to the voices of these people as they story their experience of anger-related pain furnishes a window into their overall phenomenological process with complex emotion.

The dialogue among young girls in their urban, southwestern U.S. public schools takes place in focus-group interviews, for the most part, as well as an interview with a single eighth grader; all of the participants chose pseudonyms for the occasion. Most of the narrative entries are marked with an abbreviation of this chosen name. Each conversation involves the same structured format as follows:

What do boys think about girls who are angry?

What do other girls think about girls who are angry?

What do moms think about girls who are angry?

What do dads think about girls who are angry?

What do teachers think about girls who are angry?

What do girls think about boys who are angry?

What do other boys think about boys who are angry?

What do moms think about boys who are angry?

What do dads think about boys who are angry?

What do teachers think about boys who are angry?

Women also either choose pseudonyms (here primarily abbreviated) for their interviews or are assigned pseudonyms by the investigators. Dialogue between women takes the following structured interview format, most being directed by the participants themselves.

What do men think of women who are angry?

What do other women think of women who are angry?

What do partners or significant others think of women who are angry?

What do other family members think of women who are angry?

What do people at work think of women who are angry?

What do members of your minority group think about women who are angry within your own minority group?

How do you think members of the majority culture view women who are angry in your minority group?

When considering these questions, what do people think about angry men (versus angry women)?

One group is made up of young Muslim women from age 19 through 32 years, all friends (and some family members) who gather at one of their homes on a weekday afternoon. Another group consists of four Latin American women who work in various interrelated capacities in a suburban southwestern school district, meeting in an office at work. All in their 30s and 40s , one is originally from Puerto Rico, another from Guatemala, another identifies as Texan and the fourth is from Cuba. A third group consists of African American women in their late 30s through early 50s, well acquainted as friends, who meet in the home of one of the group members. Finally, a group of Jewish women in their late 60s and early 70s convenes in the kitchen of one of their homes and talks about their responses to these questions. Each group takes a slightly different approach to the issues, and each group is sampled here with regard to their perspectives on the domains. Girls' and women's responses to these questions are presented here for respectful observation. (Initials or psuedonyms are used in all interviews. The interviewer may be designated as "I" or "DC.") At the end of the chapter, we attempt to draw some conclusions from their words. However, interpretations are offered tentatively, with an invitation extended for continued discourse on women's experience and judgment about anger in their relationships.

☐ Themes

Anger and Emotion Themes

Girls across their four structured interviews give the following as reasons for getting angry: being humiliated in front of peers, being betrayed by friends with regard to confidences told, death in the family, illness in the family, being teased or ridiculed, being in trouble with their parents, and being ignored by their female friends who are angry. For women, the following things trigger anger:

1. Being ignored

2. Not being taken seriously

3. Being asked to do a lot of work at the last minute (on the job)

4. Being asked to do other people's work

5. Being restricted by parents from certain activities (for younger Muslim women living with parents)

6. People insulting their families or ethnicities

7. Receiving poor or incomplete service (e.g., at the auto mechanic)

8. Being misunderstood by parents

9. Receiving an angry response from one's partner (when one expects sympathy)

10. Experiencing an imbalance in household responsibilities

11. Having one's partner walk away when one is discussing anger

12. Being sexually harassed in the workplace

13. Feeling stifled in expressing one's views at work

14. Having one's family refuse to eat food one has prepared

15. Having customers/patrons at work behave inappropriately

16. People trespassing on property

17. Being patronized by people outside their cultural group

18. Spouse/partner forgetting things the woman has told them

    Both within and across the four girls' interviews, they all seem to hold negative overall definitions of anger, associating it most often with violence and other destructive ideas. Most of the girls appear able to conceptualize anger as a feeling, apart from overt behavior, although quite a few of them seem to confuse anger *toward* others with anger *from* others, directed at themselves. Especially with regard to parents, girls have more difficulty conceptualizing their own anger towards caregivers, versus being the target of caregivers' anger. Women express mixed feelings about anger but understand that others see it in pessimistic ways. There are times when women recognize the justness of anger and its protective function, but they also feel constrained by others' negative perceptions of anger.

    Anger within the girls' families is portrayed in a variety of ways. Several households are reported to be scenes of violence when family members become angry. Several instances of corporal punishment are recalled, some in response to girls' expressions of anger. Girls often express the notion of anger as being punished by parents, especially younger girls, and most significantly in relation to their mothers. In contrast, one eighth grader remarks about a persistent pattern of overall avoidance between herself and her parents, relating that she is "always angry" when she is at home.

    Second, without exception, each girl associates the idea of anger with violence in some way. Morgan, a White eighth grader, defines anger with primarily negative attributes, calling it "a violent state of mind; a volatile state of being that is more, that can be very negative." Most of the girls associate this violence with boys' anger, but Angel and Angelica, two fifth graders (white and Latin American, respectively) associate the violence with both genders.

DC: How do you two define anger, what's your definition? What's your best dictionary definition of anger? You can make something up.

AL: I feel like throwing something.

AA: When you beat somebody.

AL: Feel like throwing something across the room.

DC: A violent feeling?

AL
and AA: Yeah!

DC: Like an urge to do something . . .

AL: Bad, exactly.

DC: Do you think of bad things when you think of anger?

AA: Uh-huh.

DC: Do you ever think of good things when you think of anger?

AL: No, no, yes, well, think of beating that person up.

DC: How do you feel about boys who are angry?

CA: I do the thing she does, I run away.

M: Well, I think, me when I see guys that are angry, I feel like it
           could scare me cause boys are, can get very violent when they're
           mad and so generally I try to stay away.

These last two excerpts come from Cassandra, an African American
fifth grader and Morgan, a White eighth grader.

Women also link anger with aggression by referring to terrorism,
rape, domestic abuse and murder. However, for women, there is less tendency to fuse the two. The young Muslim women see Westerners as stereotyping their anger in violent terms, a picture that they negate. Consider the following statement by a 21-year-old Muslim woman.

S1:   The minute anything goes wrong, it's, "Oh they're going to do
           some terrorist act, because that's just the way it is, that's the
           way they deal with anger because they're so suppressed by
           their culture, their religion, they don't know what to do so they
           just turn into psychos that bomb people."

Two Latin American women, one a teacher and the other a counselor, validate the young girls' experience in testifying to the courtship vio-

lence they see in the student relationships around them. They acknowledge that increased awareness has brought some, but not enough, change.

G: And it's true that it's changing. But still, when I talk to kids
here, boys, Hispanic boys, you probably know, you know, some
of that is still there.

Everyone: Yeah, it is! It's there.

A: My son, my son.

G: And I'm like, so we're talking about things changing, but here
we have these kids . . .

A: And they say "We are going to be like our parents."

G: The anger is like that, and that's the way they think about the
girlfriend. How many girls do we know, they're abused, abusive situations? Its Hispanic boys . . .

For girls and women alike, it appears that the emotional experience
of anger cannot help but be linked with the frightening and dangerous
aggression that can result from it, a connection that is taken for granted in
some instances and wrestled with in others.

Adaptive Functions of Anger: Anger as Motivator for Approach Behavior

In several instances, girls share their impulses to *do* something when they
feel anger. For almost every query, fifth graders Angel and Angelica consistently apply action-based illustrations to talk about their perceptions.
For example, Angelica offers this description of how she knows when she's
angry:

DC: And so when you get really mad, what happens to you? How
do you know you're mad?

AL: [laughs nervously, shrugging]

AA: I know when I get mad, I crumble up paper.

DC: You crumble up paper?

AA: That helps me get rid of it.

Across both age groups girls talk about having an urge to express their anger verbally to their mothers. Although they at times refuse maternal support, their impulses may reflect continued desire to relate emotionally with their mothers despite the threat of punitive consequences. Girls seem more apt to talk about anger with or around mothers than fathers, even though they often anticipate a disapproving reaction. Fifth graders Clementine and Deborah (both African American) and Cassandra (Latin American) share the following.

CL: Like if we talking about, under our breath, and our mama over there, whooo!

DE: We better run! She come after you with a belt.

DC: That's how you deal with it when you're mad at your mom, you talk under your breath and then she gets even more mad?

DE: Uh-huh.

CA: Sometimes you just gotta tell her.

The most poignant individual themes for Whitney, an African American eighth grader, involve her descriptions of violent behavior in her immediate family, as she is both witness and direct recipient. When she speaks of her own anger toward family members, it is primarily her disdain for how her stepfather abuses her mother. Whitney tries to protect her mother from both her stepfather and her brothers.

W: My brothers, like, they get their way and stuff and they just be mad at my mom if they can't do what they want to, so my mom whip them and they try to hit her back and I jump in . . .

DC: How does he [dad] make you mad?

W: Cause he messes my mom up. And anything. And if he wants us to move, or change the channel or something, to what he wants to watch.

DC: Sometimes you give in.

W: Sometimes I don't, but sometimes he's like quiet like he wants to watch something else. He doesn't say anything. I can be mad and I can ignore him. He want to watch the news. I say, "I don't care." He don't say nothin. My mom can change the channel. He tells her to change the channel when I don't. If my mom tells me to change the channel, I do.

This final excerpt illustrates a phenomenon that apparently takes place with relative frequency in Whitney's family. Her mother becomes a mediator between Whitney and her stepfather, a position that may foster resentments between the two parents. Whitney's disdain for her stepfather has to do with his mistreatment of her mother and becomes apparent in her passive refusal to acknowledge his wishes. Each of the players in this family situation expresses anger indirectly or violently, perhaps lacking the skills or safety to deal directly and nonviolently with strong emotion. However, although Whitney must passively convey her sentiments toward her stepfather, she does find a way to express her displeasure for his abusive behavior toward her mother.

Continuing with the theme of anger's adaptive function, these young Muslim women relate some sense of gravity in expressing and dealing with anger and recognize benefits of anger expression:

S1:   When you're angry, it doesn't help to just sleep it off. You know that old saying "You can't go to bed when you're angry." People, even between other females, you can't just let it . . . leave it alone, it won't work, you have to confront it head on and deal with it right at that time.

A1:   When it's my husband, and us in this generation, he has to deal with it. He has to know, you know, why I'm angry and we have to come up with a solution together. He wouldn't dare laugh it off. He's not about to laugh it off.

Further, a Latin American woman recognizes something she wishes for herself in other women's manner of expressing anger:

I: Do they think [anger is] kind of a natural part of women's experience?

B: I think it's ok. Maybe in my situation, was because I kept it to myself. But when I see someone angry standing up for herself against another person, I go, good! That other person had it coming, good.

The older Jewish women push past a deeply embedded directive to put others before self to reach a hidden truth—that far from making us say what we do not really mean, anger exposes thoughts and feelings we do not otherwise allow ourselves to reveal.

E: Maybe it's better to get angry than to keep it all bottled up inside.

B: Well, I'm sure it is.

E: That's what they want you to believe.

R: Well, I don't know, because when you are angry you say some things that you shouldn't say, and maybe don't even mean.

S: Or things that have been bottled up for a long time, which you do mean. [Laughter]

These pieces seem to suggest that on some level women know that anger exists for a purpose, and that conveying it to its target serves some individual and relationship good.

Cultural Rules and Roles: Gender, Ethnicity, and Class

With regard to boys' anger, several themes emerge across interviews. First, common to all four interviews, girls of both grades either directly report or indirectly imply feeling fear, or responding in a fearful manner, to boys' anger. Most commonly, girls feel some kind of apprehension or anxiety in the face of an angry boy, and this usually has to do with his externalizing behaviors.

AA: Well, you know girls that, like, try to walk up to you and start something and get in your face and boys will be trying to start problems.

DC: Girls will be . . .

AL: Girls will be trying to get in your face and act—but boys will just start fighting.

AL: And there's also a boy in my class named . . . Jeff, yeah, Jeff [laughs about her disguise of the boy's name]. And you say, like, "Be quiet Jeff" [laughs] and he'll say, "Whatcha gonna do about it, I'll break every jaw in your body."

AA: I'll break every jaw in your body?

DC: That's what Jeff says?

AB: Uh-huh.

DC: What do you say?

AL: I say, "Yeah, whatever" [laughs] and I'll say, "I only have one
jaw."

Regarding the concept of gender roles, the fifth-grade girls participating in this first interview portray contrasting pictures of boys and girls
who are angry. Their immediate thoughts of angry boys have violence
attached to them. When thinking of angry girls, their first impressions
involve a withdrawal of some kind.

DC: What do boys think of other boys when they're angry?

DE: The same thing.

CL: They think of their fists.

DC: They think of their fists?

DE: They be like, "What's up man," and they be running into each
other and . . .

CL: When Deborah gets angry, she gets all mopey and she won't
talk to nobody and stuff like that.

Most commonly, girls respond to angry boys by distancing, with some
kind of ridicule also used at times in reaction to boys' anger. All behaviors
mentioned for girls in response to angry boys involve either negative acknowledgment or refusal to acknowledge boys' anger. Often, girls mention thinking of an angry boy as stupid, but it is unclear as to whether this
designation applies to boys' anger or their hostile acting out. Boys' anger
(or rather their hostility) is further perceived to be coached by fathers.
Girls of both grade groupings believe that dads encourage their sons to
aggress against peers with whom they are angry.

AA: They, they, they say, "Did you beat him up?" My dad would.
My dad and my little brother. He'll go, "So did you slug him like
I told you to?"

AL: My brother, they'll get in little boy fights and you know they'll
go, "Kick you where it hurts," and he'll go out there and punch
him in the nose.

These fifth-grade girls vilify the aggressive behavior of other angry girls. They also show disdain for their female peers who engage in gender-atypical behavior, especially when it involves an overconfidence in their ability to use violence or other displays of grandiosity.

AL: She walks around, like, all that. She goes around putting her hands in people's faces, just acts weird.

CL: She thinks she can fight everybody.

DC: Oh?

DE: She thinks she's going to win too.

DC: And do you think she's going to win or . . .

CL, CA,
and DE: No! [laugh]

Whitney and Bud, two eighth graders (African American and White, respectively), both express gender stereotyped expectations for male and female behavior. These expectations appear to spread across behavior of angry persons and of those perceiving the anger. To illustrate both points, Bud (while pretending to be a boy—an issue to be addressed later) answers the general question, "How do dads feel about angry girls?"

B: Well, see, if I was a dad and, uh, I had a daughter that was angry, I'd just kinda stay out of it. But if I had a son that was angry, like with another person you know, like a guy or something, I'd probably encourage them to like go and fight them or something. If it was a daughter, then I don't know.

DC: Would you handle it differently somehow?

B: Yeah, probably, I don't know, it depends.

DC: On what?

B: On if I was married, or if my wife lived with us.

DC: Now how would that change things for you, if you were a dad and your daughter was angry? How would that change things for you if you had a wife around?

B: Then I'd let her handle it.

This excerpt reveals a premise that although boys may handle their anger aggressively, girls should not. Reflecting the notion of boys' hostility as desirable, Bud also suggests that a father might coach his son on how to aggressively handle a peer. Further, the passage shows Bud's version of gendered parents' roles in dealing with a girl's anger. She sees Dad as ideally removed from his daughter's feeling, while relegating any parental duties around her anger to his spouse.

Another example of gender difference in the handling of strong emotion involves ethnicity as well. Whitney answers a question about possible racial differences as she watches closely for Bud's reaction. Bud does not share Whitney's perception about Black and White girls' assertiveness.

DC: Let me back up a little bit, going back to the first question, you know I asked you, "How do boys feel about angry girls?" Is it different for White girls and Black girls and Hispanic girls? Do they feel differently? What do you think Whitney, you look like you're thinking something.

W: Oh gosh [laughing and then pausing for quite a while]. If a Black girl is mad at a Black boy, it's probably 50-50 with the boys won't back down and the girls won't back down. They'll just go back and forth. And if they're mad at me, that's their problem.

DC: Okay, so what about White girls and White boys?

W: Oh my goodness [looking at Bud for reaction and laughing].

DC: Bud can you answer that?

B: All rightey. If a White girl was mad at me [Bud obviously still pretending to be a boy], I'd say well you know, she can handle it. But I think if I was mad at a White girl, I would think that she would think the same thing.

DC: So you're saying it's the same as with Black people that you wouldn't back down? That you'd both kinda be tough about it?

B: Depends on the person.

W: Like, if White girls are mad at White boys or White boys are mad at White girls, the girls seem like to give in, like to me.

DC: What do you mean?

W: Like they start to get scared of the boy or whatever, like.

DC: So the girls give in if they're White?

W: Yeah.

DC: Did you say they give in if they're Black, too?

W: No [laughing and looking at Bud].

DC: Are you afraid Bud's gonna be offended?

W: Yeah [both girls laugh].

As noted previously, Bud takes the role of a boy in answering interview questions. When the two girls are asked to use pseudonyms for the taping, Bud informs us that she is "not a girl." It is unclear what her conscious motivation is at the time for this striking performance, but it deserves mention that she attempts to take a boy's viewpoint on the majority of the questions discussed, casting aside her daughter status in favor of a dad's and boy's perspective.

DC: What do boys think about angry girls?

B: [laughing] Since I'm the guy do I have to answer that?

DC: Are you representing the boys?

B: Yep.

DC: What do boys think of angry girls?

B: It depends on who they're angry at. I mean if they're angry at you, you don't like them, but if not, I don't think it really matters.

DC: What do girls think or feel about other girls who are angry? Bud?

B: [laughing] I'm not a girl.

DC: What about your friends that are angry with anybody? Maybe your girl friends that are angry with a teacher or maybe they're angry with their parents or whatever. What do you think of them?

B: I associate more with guys.

DC: Yeah?

B: People of my own sex [laughs].

DC: What about you Bud? What do moms feel about angry girls?

B: Well, if they can't do anything to help it, they probably feel hurt. Maybe. I don't know. I'm not a mom, I'm not a daughter.

Another gender-related twist in the interview with Angel and Angelica involves their portrait of girls as more at-risk than boys for getting into troublesome situations. This portrayal also suggests a misunderstanding of one of the interview questions but nonetheless proves an interesting window into their thoughts about girls' identities.

DC: Do you think moms get scared of boys or girls more than the other when they're angry?

AL: Probably girls.

DC: Do you think they're scared of girls more?

AA: Should I say it, yeah.

AL: Can I say something?

DC: Sure.

AA: You're not gonna get mad [laughs]?

DC: I doubt it.

AL: Girls can turn out to be, they can grow up and have babies and girls can go out and get drunk and boys can, like, take them to the [AA: To the hotel.] yeah, and they'll get really scared that they're gonna get beat up and shot and get pregnant on accident.

DC: Oh, okay, so moms get scareder for their girls than they do for their boys.

AA: Yeah, cause boys can't run out and get pregnant.

Here, Angelica portrays her gender as being more vulnerable to adversity inflicted by boys, namely unwanted pregnancy and violence, and she sees mothers as more fearful for girls' well-being because of these vincibilities. Sexual, physical, and political power belong to boys in this portrayal, a notion which may relate to Bud's decision to *be* a boy throughout her interview.

Angelica also expresses the belief that girls become angry more often than boys, basing her opinion on the events described in the previous passage. However, later in the interview Angel asserts that boys, not girls, are expected to suppress their anger most of the time.

DC: What about moms and angry boys? How do they feel about angry boys?

AL: Probably the same way but a little bit worse, cause I heard that boys were supposed to hold their temper.

DC: Really, what do you mean?

AL: Like they're not supposed to lose their temper.

AA: You know how girls hold it for awhile and . . . go off and start saying stuff but boys are supposed to hold it in.

The two fifth graders suggest here that for girls, holding anger back gives rise to some kind of labile anger expression. If "go off" implies a kind of volatility, they could be describing the externalizing that can result from a period of suppression. In their view, such a release is unacceptable for boys, an idea that seems inconsistent with many of their actual descriptions of them. The girls may, however, be distinguishing between angry scenarios in which they perceive a boy to have license to immediately display his feeling, and the phenomenon of suppression to a point of inevitable release, which they associate more with girls.

Finally, with regard to girls and gendered anger, Morgan expresses surprise at hearing her own descriptions of gender bias. She reflects upon the answers she has given during the course of the interview and makes the following comment:

M: Well, as I'm listening to what I'm saying, it seems kind of, ancient. These are ideas that are making themselves known but it seems very real. But when I look at it as a second person, it's not, it sounds really antiquated, you know. It's just ideas and thoughts that we thought had gone out the door, but you know, when I'm there saying these things, it makes perfect sense. But if I'm looking at me looking at it, it's very unusual.

Moving into women's descriptions of gender intertwined with anger, this young Muslim woman expresses her distaste for seeing women display their anger outwardly:

S2:   I think it's more that, when I see a woman who is angry, "She's
           crazy, what is she thinking. She's stupid." You know it's just
           different. When I see a guy, you know, "Yeah, he has a right to
           be mad."

Are we entitled to an angry voice? The Muslim women also share
their confusion about gendered rules for feeling and expression but articulate the dilemma more clearly than do the young girls. This 21-year-old
resolves the issue for herself by pointing out change she sees in the larger
sociocultural expectations for women's and men's behavior:

S1:   I think the traditional view is that women are more passive and
           more compassionate, they have a tendency more to compro-
           mise and to come to some sort of middle ground. Whereas with
           a male, when someone is angry, usually it means that someone
           gives in one way or the other . . . with a female . . . when you
           see someone who is angry . . . you think that she's out of line,
           so to speak. Just because women are supposed to have more
           composure, are supposed to be more elegant, and not display
           anger in front of people. And I think anymore, society's chang-
           ing, that's changing. The attitude, women can display more
           anger, can display their feelings just as much as men I think.

The African American women voice clear recognition of both the
process and the result of pressures to conform to separate, gendered rules
in handling their anger.

C: If you're socialized to be gentle then you're suppose to come off
           gentle. That's the female socialization.

B: So we're suppose to be gentle, right?

C: Yeah. So women in their expression of anger to each other,
           you're suppose to be gentle. Think about it . . .

They later describe the impact of choosing genuineness over gentleness, but in these conversations, ethnicity plays a key role in the confusion
over how anger and identity relate.

D: At one time I had six other team members and they were all
           white and I was the chairperson of the department and they all

said that they were afraid of me and that I was angry all the time and I'm just talking, you know, I'm just being myself . . .

C: I just come straight at them because that's the way they have always asked me to do, come straight at them and so sometimes when I come straight at women, as women in similar situations . . .

B: It's not normal.

C: Yeah, they go, "What are you angry about?"

I: You're forceful.

C: And I'm going, "I'm not angry, I'm just . . . You need to do this . . ."

They go on to discuss a very different view of African American men's anger, adding gender to the mix of social forces in play:

C: I know that there is a tendency as it is for us as women, with Black men's anger to be not dismissed, to be re-categorized almost, in a permanent behavior.

A: Oh yes! Rage.

C: Yes, yes.

A: Rage, and I saw also that they're using it as a defense, that men have Black rage. As if this is a psychological problem that we can't help because of our color.

The topic of gentleness as a trait developed in women as a filter, or even a substitute, for their anger, surfaces again in these comments by Latin American women. The process they describe sounds something like segmentation of the angry self.

A: They [men] are not as tolerant about women to be angry. For them, it is machismo and in our culture this is really OK, but for us, no. We have to be sweet and gentle.

C: It's OK if they express their anger to us in front of other people, that's fine, you see. But for us to express anger in front of other people, that's a big no-no.

When these Jewish women ponder gender differences in anger socialization they include their subjective experiences, commenting on how
these compare with cultural evaluations and expectations.

E: I wonder if a woman is as likely to get angry or to express it as
anger, as a man.

G: There's a good thought.

B: We're more accepting.

E: Well, maybe more—I don't know if "afraid" is the word, but—
timid, about it.

R: I don't like to admit that, but that's probably true.

R: Well, anger doesn't necessarily mean screaming and yelling.

S: Well that's what I'm thinking of.

G: It can mean whatever we think.

R: It's much more acceptable from a man.

B: To be angry?

E: We don't think it should be.

R: Men can be more violent when they're angry.

All: Yes.

S: Even if they're not violent, I think they can be more
expressive.

R: They're voices are deeper. It comes across stronger. That's why
they get what they want . . .

B: I think angry men are more acceptable than angry women.

Again, the specter of men's violence haunts these women's exchanges
about how anger is a part of their experience as women, reflecting, perhaps, an omnipresent power differential within gender socialization across
cultures.

Others' Reactions to Anger and Socialization to Suppress

Girls and women both comment frequently on the specific ways others react to their expressions of anger. Although they are sometimes met with a supportive response, the majority of interactions they describe involve rejection of either the anger, the girl or woman, or both. This takes the form of either direct attack through criticism or defensive response, or more passive rejection such as withdrawal and minimization of the girl's or woman's concerns and feelings.

Girls tend to see themselves as treated fairly badly when they are angry, giving less-than-affirming examples of behavior on the parts of those perceiving both angry boys and girls. Other girls, boys, moms, dads, and teachers are depicted as giving some kind of negative acknowledgment, whether judging, pathologizing, punishing, aggressing, verbally aggressing, stifling, or controlling. Some behavioral reactions involve a refusal to acknowledge the person's anger, with an accompanying negative gesture (ridiculing, diminishing, distancing, or ignoring). Similarly, girls describe several different opinions others might have of angry boys and girls, all of which implicate the angry person with some undesirable quality. Described opinions include viewing the angry person as a coward, as self-aggrandizing, as crazy, as stupid, as petty, as mean, and as overdramatic.

W: When I'm mad at boys . . . they think I'm mean.

M: Well, a lot of the guys I see, whenever they see a girl's angry, they . . . like I said make fun of them, tease them . . .

DC: Okay, so what did the boys think of you for being mad?

DE: They thought we were wimpy and stuff.

CA: They just ignored us and stuff.

In noteworthy contrast, many of the *feelings* girls perceive on the parts of those witnessing their anger indicate affiliation. Girls of both grade groups express the belief that girls do support each other when one is angry.

M: Generally, the girls will understand and support you and work it out. Or if you're just beyond that and if you just want to be left alone kind of thing, then they'll respect that and they'll back off.

These girls express their desire to talk to each other when one of their group is angry. Clementine said "I get mad . . . I hate it when she [Carla] ignores me." Cassandra offered: "Well, I try to talk to her but the same with Clementine. She ignores everybody." Her statement also appears consistent with the girls' overall expressed means of handling anger, that is, neutralization or suppression accompanied by withdrawal (or perhaps accomplished through withdrawal).

In contrast, the girls mention several instances of what appears to be gender-atypical behavior on the part of other girls in their social network. These descriptions mock the other girls' behavior, whether or not anger is involved. For example, in response to the question, "What do girls think of other girls who are angry?" Clementine tells about another girl who acts out her anger aggressively, and Deborah helps to clarify the general opinion the group shares of this girl.

CL: Sometimes they fight [laughs]. Tara upstairs, her name's Tara and she loves to fight [others chime in with, "oh yeah"]. Always fighting, she fights everybody.

DC: What do you think of her when she's angry?

CL: I think she's all bad [laughter from all three girls].

DC: Now does that mean bad like you're scared of her or does that mean like she's kind of . . .

DE: She thinks she's all that.

CL: She thinks she can fight everybody.

In the following example, all three girls describe another girl's thwarted efforts to solicit the affection of a certain boy. They make sense of the matter by pointing to her gender-atypical behavior, casting dispersions on it. At the end of this description of generally "boyish" behavior on the part of the girl, Cassandra contributes a statement about the girl's aggression towards boys. So, not only are this person's less-than-girlish behaviors regarded negatively, her angry acting out toward male peers becomes associated in some way with her overall gender-atypicality. Her apparent confidence seems to be denigrated along with her aggressiveness.

CL: That's the boy she likes. But he don't like her because he says she act too much like a boy.

DC: Oh really?

CL: Like a tomboy.

DE: She is.

CL: She always thinks, like once she asked Chris to go with her. And she just laughed and she kept on asking and he kept on saying no.

CL: She's always acting like a boy.

DC: What is this acting like a boy stuff?

DE: Yeah, what is this . . . ?

CL: She does boy stuff.

CA: She wears boy clothes.

CL: She's always out playing with the boys. She never likes to play with the girls.

CA: She picks fights with the boys.

With regard to the same gender-atypical peer (Tara), this group depicts less parental pressure for her to excel academically. Clementine, Deborah, and Cassandra contrast this set of circumstances with their own experience of parental pressure to perform well in school. Higher expectations for girls also extends to appearance as shown in the following excerpt. Although the girls see both sexes as unattractive when angry, their interdiction for girls' anger-related unattractiveness falls more heavily. These girls' higher expectations for girls' attractiveness cause them to judge girls' appearances more harshly than that of boys.

DC: What do you look like when you're angry?

CA, CL,
and DE: Mad . . . ugly.

Girls perceive themselves to be less-than-understood by boys, dads, teachers, and sometimes mothers as well. For example, Morgan talks about her father's reaction to her anger:

M: Yeah, it frustrates me when he doesn't, he doesn't see that I'm angry. . . . He thinks I'm exaggerating but a lot of times I'm not.

Morgan consistently describes feeling diminished or not taken seriously by significant figures when she is angry, as well as a perception that girls' anger is diminished by fathers, boys and teachers. She continues to describe this phenomenon in relation to her father. When asked to think about the last time she felt really angry, Morgan recounts a story about herself and her father getting ready to leave for school in the morning. At the end of her story, she remembers being frustrated and her perception of his feeling toward her.

M: And he takes this attitude. He acts like a child, so it's really frustrating he, like, he's so, and whenever I get upset, he thinks it's funny. He thinks it's amusing. And cause I have a history of being rather dramatic, and they say, he says, "Now come on, stop being dramatic" even when I'm serious.

Similarly, in response to the question, "What about teachers and angry girls?" Morgan describes the diminishing response:

M: Um to me, it seems like teachers and angry girls, they don't take girls seriously. Sometimes they would think it's just for some silly reason, like it may be something serious but the teachers wouldn't see that, male and female teachers. It would just, it would just not even be acknowledged, "Oh they're angry, they'll get over it" kind of a thing.

The distance and diminishment Morgan describes may reflect confusion as well as feelings of helplessness or ineptitude on the part of those perceiving her. To illustrate, she gives the following continued portrayal of her father.

M: My father, he doesn't, if it's something wrong that needs to be talked about, then he'll try to talk about it with me, but generally I avoid that because he's not an easy person to talk with when I'm angry. He doesn't understand a lot of the time. A lot of times, he just doesn't get it, but if it's just anger and he doesn't understand the cause, then he'll just stay away.

DC: What do boys think of girls when girls are angry?

DE: They think you're kind of crazy when you get mad at them and stuff, and then, "I'm just playing" and then you be taking it serious and stuff.

DC: What about dads? How do dads feel about girls who are angry?

CL: My daddy pity me [laughs].

DE: If I get in trouble at school, he says, "That's okay, she ain't gonna do it no more right?" I say, "Yeah." And like if I'm fixin to get a whippin, he'll say, "Don't whip that girl, she ain't done nothin that bad." I'll be like, "Thank you daddy" [laughs].

DC: So he takes up for you?

DE, CL: Uh-huh.

DE: And then my mom starts getting mad—that she can't whip me [laughs].

Although the response appears to answer the question about how dads regard angry girls, the excerpt illustrates a confusion between experiencing personal anger and being the recipient or target of someone else's anger. Most often, connecting "anger," with "moms" or "dads" the girls give accounts of being in trouble with their parents. Both younger groups perceive anger as an admonishable offense (most often punished by mothers), whether or not aggression is its means of disclosure. The previous excerpt also highlights a dynamic in Deborah's home, wherein her father appears to support her during angry scenarios but in so doing undercuts her mother's attempts at (albeit punitive) action. This synopsis reveals a possible tendency for the sabotage of Deborah's mother's instrumentality by her father's "supportive" gestures. When one closely examines the situation, however, Deborah's father may be minimizing *both* his daughter and his spouse with this maneuver, cutting short the angry interaction between mother and daughter. Consider again the girls' angry behavior in relation to their mothers.

DC: What do moms think of girls who are angry?

CL, DE: Whoa, man, lord . . . !

DE: They say, "What's wrong with you?" and they'll go in there and get the belt and run all around the house.

M: Well, my mother generally is—when she sees me upset or angry, she wants to talk to me about it . . . she tries to help. But sometimes if I'm angry with myself or too angry, then she picks up on that and gets mad too . . .

CL: But she say stuff like, "I guess you got a boyfriend" and stuff
           like that, and I like, "No" like that and I roll my eyes and she
           get like kinda mad . . .

Mothers perform a substantial role in the socialization of girls' emotional expressivity. Girls generally have the idea that their mothers scruti-
nize or disapprove of their anger and sometimes punish it. They also seem
exquisitely sensitive to what their mothers need or want regarding emotional display. Morgan demonstrates this complex understanding of herself and her own anger in relation to others, specifically her mother. This
insight includes awareness of the range of emotion that is acceptable to
express in her household, and likely consequences of overshooting that
range.

M: Well, generally, I have to be, when someone in the house is
           emotionally unstable or has some concentration of emotion,
           you have to be careful what you say or what you do, and with
           me, if I was angry I might mention something that would strike
           a nerve with my mom so, I get too angry to realize that I'm
           saying it so when I realize I'm getting that angry, I just won't
           say anything to her. So, cause I don't want, if I get angry, some-
           times you don't see and realize what you're doing, so I have to
           be careful, cause if I don't, I might say something wrong. And
           my anger will make her angry.

Morgan not only understands the limits to the acceptability of her
expression, she also believes that when she is angry, she becomes more
likely to offend others. Taken a bit further, she experiences her anger as a
catalyst for her mother's anger. In a similar vein, Morgan protects her
mother from her (Morgan's) own anger by refusing support when she's
the most furious. To illustrate, Morgan responds to further questioning
about the acceptable range of anger expression.

DC: OK and how much do you, where's the line on what you'll
           express to her? How do you know how much is too much?
           How do you know when you've reached that line where she's
           not going to accept your anger anymore?

M: Um, well, it's hard to judge in terms of her accepting my anger.
           'Cause sometimes, she tries to be understanding and sometimes
           I'm just not receptive to that. If there's something I want, like if

> I'm getting, like if it's really too much and it's really consum-
> ing, then I don't want to, I don't want her to have to deal with
> that. So I'll block it off myself.

Morgan seems to be saying that at times, she refuses support because she sees her anger as distasteful to her mother or "too big" for her mother to handle. As her anger becomes more intense, she becomes more likely to refuse support. Her reference to "blocking it off" indicates a disavowal or diversion of affect.

Finally, Bud describes a pattern of withdrawal and avoidance that she uses in her family to deal with anger. This pattern appears to be a mutual avoidance of intense feeling and something of an everyday occur-rence. In a sense, Bud and her parents have called a truce in their struggles to love and be separate but now avoid talking with each other about much of anything.

> B: I don't know, I'm always angry when I'm home so they don't
> really do anything, so I mean, they've learned not to ask and I
> won't tell them anything. They've learned to avoid me and I
> avoid them and everything works out.

Moving to women's thoughts on how their anger is perceived, we hear consistent responses, sometimes punctuated with an ironic but hearty humor, that create a clearly negative picture, first illustrated by the Mus-lim women.

> A1:   What do they think when I'm angry? It's terrible! [general
> laughter].

The Latin American women describe others' perceptions of them when they are angry.

> C1:   That you have a problem or something, you have a personality
> problem.
> C2:   PMS [laughter].

This is an often-heard interpretation of women's anger. In a related vein, African American women talk about how they are perceived.

I: These questions are about anger.

B: Oh, Lord [laughter].

I: We all have plenty of that. What do men think of women who are angry?

B: They think we're a bitch.

A: We're overreacting. You couldn't possibly have an emotion. You're not permitted to have an emotion. That everything is not as bad as it seems.

C: You're dismissed when you're angry.

I: In what way?

C: In a sense that, if you say, "I'm angry" or you disclose that feeling, they just ignore you.

I: Why?

A: You're not allowed to have that feeling. Because they think whatever issue or whatever caused you to be angry is not as much as it seems. It's trivial, it's small.

C: We're not suppose to get angry . . . move on, real quick like.

Likewise, the Jewish women have this to say.

B: They don't like them.

G: What do you mean?

B: I think most men are put off when they encounter an angry woman . . .

These comments, in response to questions about how men view women's anger, are matched by those describing women's, family members', and majority/minority cultural response to women expressing their anger. Although some positive experiences are related (described more fully subsequently), the majority of reactions discussed are not supportive. These comments from an African American woman are representative.

D: They don't think highly of [women who are angry], they think they are just bitches.

I: So anger is not accepted?

D: No . . . either they are afraid of [her] . . . or they just think that she is crazy . . .

A Latin American woman speaks of a similar perception.

A: My family, they don't approve, my family.

G: Of other women getting angry?

A: Uh-huh, my family, they don't like it, they try to avoid it. At home, no . . .

This Muslim woman speaks of the painful minimization of her anger she experiences in her family whenever she verbalizes it. Others in her group quickly identify with her words, which echo Morgan's description of her father's reaction to her anger expression.

A2:   Otherwise they just laugh it off, "Oh you look so cute, you're mad! You look so cute when you're mad!"

S1:   It's happened to me, too.

A2:   It's happened to you?

S1:   Yeah, I mean. I'll get mad and they just start laughing. Like with my brothers, they never take me seriously. I mean . . . and it just makes you so mad, but they never take you seriously.

In the midst of a discussion about how others react, a Jewish woman is moved to describe her own discomfort in tolerating another woman's anger:

E: I think it can sometimes be embarrassing. If you are with someone who gets angry even with real provocation, even with real provocation, I think you can think, "Did she have to be so angry?"

How do women feel about others' stifling reactions to their anger? These Jewish women describe an example of how anger is engendered in women when social proscriptions for suppression are enforced:

R: In one of my jobs, I was what now would be considered harassed by a man and I first tried to nicely tell him that I didn't want his attentions and then I got angry and showed him I was angry. It didn't make any difference. Nothing I did made any difference and when I talk to my boss about it, he said, "Well you know he has a high position and I'm sure he's not going to lose his position. You either have to handle it or . . ."

S: Ignore it.

R: I would have had to leave.

G: Yeah. And that's why we have angry women.

Power Difference and Degree of Affiliation/Mutuality

In many of the women's responses, a distinction emerges between expressing anger with peers and expressing anger with those felt to be superior in some way. Take economic power for an example in this excerpt from an Egyptian Muslim woman, 21 years of age. Her friend, a 29-year-old Pakistani woman responds with her sense of how money helps women move away from their one-down positions in marriage.

S1:   Traditionally, the guy has always been in control of the situation, he's always been the head of the household, so when a woman's angry, you know, like, "Who cares." You can bitch all you want, but nothing . . . you know? I mean, you can say whatever you want, but hey, he's the one who makes the money, so, 'They're my children,' all of a sudden everything is his possession. . . Like if she's angry, she just becomes something that's unattractive that he doesn't want to deal with, so he walks away . . .

A1:   I think that's true in the traditional set-up, but nowadays, a lot of women are the bread-earners and earning more than their husbands and in those cases, I think the husband cannot ignore a woman's anger . . . I'll throw in a personal example here. My sister is a pharmacist, and my brother-in-law was out of work for a long time, and I saw the change in their relationship when he was earning well and she was at home and not working.

A young Latin American woman's comments illustrate the difference her employment has made.

A: No, he told me when we got in a fight . . . I always fight for my
            rights. I work too, to help him. So I said, "Well, I'm working,
            you need to help me in the house too." So that was my anger.

These Jewish women remember how power differential once fac-
tored into anger expression for them at work.

B: Well, it depends whether it's your boss or your coworker.

R: In the era when we worked, you played it real low key.

G: That's right.

R: Women in business were not respected if they were angry,
            aggressive.

G: Exactly.

An African American woman talks about affiliation and anger.

A: They can only identify if they're in the same category or group
            with you. I mean, I, in my job, am angry about certain things
            but then my job description, if someone say, in another profes-
            sion can't identify why I'm upset about it . . .

What she seems to be saying is that being angry at work has uniqueness for her, based upon her particular position, and that only those who
are in her shoes really stand to empathize with that anger. Another African American woman describes what she has experienced as a result of
expressing anger in relationships of unequal power. This excerpt also hints
of affiliation issues, in that people outside her immediate experience cannot fully appreciate her anger.

A: I think that would be what I would see a lot of, patronizing.
            Where they were just sort of, "Now Anna, you don't want to be
            that upset." Because I have gotten angry at work.

She later speaks about how this patronization extends to issues of
race and ethnicity, and the gratification she feels when her reality, the
events behind her anger, are made visible to others.

A: I always like it when I put my sisters, my White sisters, on the
            spot. They don't know I'm doing it and I don't do it intentional,
            it just happens and when I say this is the way this happened
            they would say, "Oh no Anna, it doesn't happen this way."
            Then something happens and they're there and they see it, I
            turn to them and say, "Now you understand." Because a lot of
            times, everybody else do not understand what you already feel
            all the time. You're already hypersensitive.

    Here, Anna insinuates that often her anger experience is an isolated
one, which may further fuel her frustration. Part of her anger involves
being the only one to see or feel the effects of something, and tremendous
relief comes at knowing others have had to look at those effects themselves.

Anger as Relational

As reflected in the types of situations that girls and women find anger-
arousing, opposition seems to happen *with* someone. Each instance of anger depicted involves a relationship of some kind, even if only that between a woman and her car dealer. Things most likely to evoke anger
have to do with being "hurt," betrayed, or taken for granted by someone
else. Referring back to the list of anger elicitors, most involve a sense of
displacement, of nonmutuality, a feeling that one is not appreciated for
one's own self or that one is being disparaged. Consider the following exchange with eighth grader Whitney.

W: And I guess it's that that made me mad cause she had said . . .
            and . . . So I told my grandma that she can pick us up and I told
            my grandma to come talk to Ms. Smith and it got really heated
            up because my grandma like started picking on me and stuff,
            right in front of Ms. Smith and Ms. Smith's like, the cause of it.

DC: What were you maddest about?

W: Um, like she embarrassed me in front of everybody . . .

    As clearly evident in the scenarios, anger is a social issue for these
girls. Refusal to talk in some form is the most commonly presented behavior of girls when angry, followed by some kind of withdrawal, *both very*

socially oriented behaviors. Refusing dinner affects girls' parents (who may be coaxing and cajoling), and withdrawal takes them away from direct contact with peers or family.

Again, nearly every episode of anger between boys and girls recalled involves some element of violence or threat thereof. Often, stories of peer interactions include an apparent squaring off or threatening or posturing ritual that seems equally likely for males and females. Paradoxically, these fifth grade girls seem to intuit a layer of fear beneath this particular boy's aggression.

DC: Have you seen him ["Jeff"] when you get angry?

AB: Uh-huh.

DC: How does he change? Do you think he's afraid of you or do you think he laughs at you or . . .

AL: He's probably afraid but he acts like he's not afraid because he's afraid, uh, Henry [laughs] and, uh, Lee [laughs again at disguised names] will, they're in fifth grade, and he tries to cover it up so they won't think he's a wimp [laughs]. And that's what he really, that's what he does.

DC: He's afraid but he doesn't want the boys to know it.

AA: He wants the boys to think that he's tough and stuff.

DC: Well that's interesting. So how does he actually act?

AL: He'll say, "What you gonna do about it?" and he'll hit us and . . .

AA: And then we'll run at him and he runs away . . .

Women portray their experiences of anger in relationship as frequently painful and unsatisfying, particularly if they find themselves caught in patterns that include rejection of their anger or escalation of conflict. However, some also describe relationships in which anger expression offers an opportunity to connect with another at a deeper level, enhancing their bond through mutual identification with the emotional experience of anger. Stories and dialogue about ways in which husbands and partners react to a woman's expressed anger are shared in all the groups. Here, the group of Jewish women compares notes:

R: He absolutely hates it when I get angry. When I start screaming he's very angry.

G: Does he walk out of the room?

R: Oh yes, big time.

B: I think D is used to it.

G: I think that M tunes it out.

B: Yeah, I think that's what D does too.

R: So what happens, if you're the kind of person who gets angry fairly often?

S: I guess I do get angry sometimes, but I'm trying to think . . . he doesn't walk out, but he responds with anger.

B: Most people do.

S: He'll stiffen up . . . get defensive.

R: If I'm angry over a long period, he would tune out and just get quiet. But if I get angry about something . . .

S: Important?

R: Then he gets angry.

Consider the young Muslim women's contributions on this issue.

F: My husband thinks I'm crazy!

A1:   OK, so like in my case, he doesn't talk at all, he just tries to run away from me and doesn't talk at all. And I talk to him by myself, so, and he thinks it is my fault and I shouldn't be angry. Most of the time. So I don't know.

These African American women debate the various responses they have experienced.

A: I think it depends on the partner. We like to generalize about men, but some are very concerned and want to sort of rectify the problem, some think that you are overreacting, that there is really not a problem, that you are blowing things out of proportion.

B: Others ask you to chill [laughter]. They don't want to hear it.

C: I think that's mostly what I've seen. They don't want to hear it, they just don't want to deal with it . . .

A: I think some significant others, they want to protect you and they want to take care of all these things that would upset you.

C: Or they say that's what they want to do.

A: I started to say that, too [laughter].

Other stories about supportive acceptance of anger depict women expressing the feeling to other women, as is the case in this comment from a 32-year-old Muslim woman:

F: Well, I think if it's peers, friends, I think there's a lot of compassion. It's almost like a support group. You know, women are in it together. And they understand it together.

Likewise, two middle-aged African American women describe how it feels to have their anger heard by friends:

A: Sometimes they're identical. You can identify what you're going through about, or frustrated about.

C: That's one of the things about Molly and I because we're in similar situations and so when I get on the phone, she knows I'm angry about something. She can always . . . she understands, it's only affecting you.

However, two Hispanic women describe how this kind of interaction has been problematic for and sometimes unavailable to them and women they know.

G: And even getting together with another woman to express their anger, now is different, but for some women it's hard to get together with another woman because the husbands usually say no. You don't do that, you don't go out and talk to another woman.

A: And they make you feel like you're less mature and all that.

G: Yes, and you're talking about our secrets, problems, so that was not a good idea. So you have to stay home and deal with the anger yourself because you are not allowed to go out and talk, too.

In spite of occasional positive outcomes, the overwhelming majority of angry interactions described by women include being the recipient of rejecting, minimizing, and even angry responses from others. Ironically, these women illustrate their desire and efforts to stay in relation when angry, despite the invalidating gestures of others. This African American woman's succinct comment underlines the isolation women often feel when they do choose to express their anger to others:

D: When you get angry you're usually alone.

Anger and Self Definition

To get at the idea of women's anger as self-defining, these examples provide a window into their personal agendas in the moment. For the girls, less emphasis falls to ownership of emotion and much more is placed on immediate behavior, which is often diversionary in some way, so it is more difficult to decipher their immediate self-definition. For women, however, anger often clearly operates to create a boundary between self and others. For some, the presence of anger is acknowledged and accepted as part of who they perceive themselves to be, as this Guatemalan woman reveals:

A: It's in our blood or somewhere, that when we feel something inside, the anger, we just want to hurt the other person with words [continues in Spanish which is then translated by another group member]. Because it's been so repressed, that when it comes out, then it's just, you want just to jump [her hands form into claws that shoot forward]. Even unconscious.

G: So it was not a feeling that you were able to show anger, like I was saying, "If you don't like it, too bad."

A: Exactly, that's the way it is. If I wanted to go visit with my friends, they [her parents] never let me go anywhere, that's the reason that I get married at 18 years old.

Here, a Latin American woman links her stifled relationship with anger to her early marriage, marking out some coupling between being denied a voice and attempting to find one through this traditional token of adulthood. In the context of anger socialization, she recalls not being able to explore things she wanted to see as a young girl, which reminds her of leaving home, taking matters into her own hands at age 18 years. Thus, her early experiences requiring anger suppression contribute to her decision to leave home and marry at a young age, an important formative event in the development of her identity. Later discussion reveals, however, that marriage failed to provide the liberation she needed in her young adult development.

Other women describe how anger expression highlights the discrepancies between how they see themselves and others' perceptions of who they are. One middle-aged African American woman tells about using her anger with a coworker as an opportunity to clarify who she is in their relationship. Ironically, her anger comes in response to complaints made by others (to her boss) who perceive her to be "too" angry.

D: He called me and said, "Well, she says that you're intimidating" and so that just really made me angry because I wasn't doing anything to her. So when I went back I said, "You know, you need to quit—if I intimidate you, you need to quit being so scared." I said, "Now, what you're experiencing is just a real Black woman."

This last sentence illustrates how anger can contribute to a sense of authenticity when it is acknowledged and owned as part of a woman's identity. Inherent in this example is the strong agency that can form a part of African American girls' and women's self concept, sometimes in sharp contrast to women of other ethnicities. Another example is found in a conversation between two older Jewish women discussing the relationship between anger and passion:

R: Don't you have to be angry to be passionate about anything? Angry because the environment is being treated badly, you're angry because people are standing outside abortion clinics and they're killing people in the name of life.

S: Exactly! So you're angry and then you become an activist, so I think you require some kind of anger to be passionate.

R: However, there are instances when anger would be appropriate for those people.

S: Maybe it is what gets them interested in what they are doing . . . then you have to start learning to prevent things in a tactful way.

Age and Generation

Women from all groups also recognize significant changes that have taken place over the past several years that impact the way women in their cultures have experienced the socialization of their anger. Most often, these developments manifest through generational differences the women readily describe. The Muslim women speak of how differently their mothers and grandmothers were angry, and how their "newer" way of expressing anger interacts with the older generation's different expectations. For example:

A1:   Yeah, I think women of the previous generation may be a little more passive, or were expected to be. But this generation is not that way.

A2:   And I understand, like, our anger, because I talk back to my father, because I'm very outspoken, I'm very blunt, and I mean, I talk back to him all the time and he's shocked, because he would never, never have talked back to his parents.

S2:   I do think age plays a lot into it, because you would never see an angry woman who was, like, 60 years old. You would never call her a name or anything, you be like, "Oh, I apologize." You know, you take that upon yourself. I mean, that's how I see it. I don't see myself yelling at some 60-year-old woman.

The group of Latin American women tell about differences that span three generations, because their age affords them interaction with both parents and children, and a viewpoint informed by both older and younger women's experience as well as their own. They speak at length about themselves, their daughters and their mothers:

I: So you saw your mothers repressed and your grandmothers repressed, like a generational kind of thing?

C: My mother never was repressed, she was always very . . .

A: Yeah, but the anger was repressed. She couldn't show it. If you couldn't show it, she couldn't show it.

C: Yeah, because the culture is . . . uh, stays ahead of us or whatever, I don't know. I think that the Americans, the last generation, were already showing the woman's rights and the anger, while we were not. So what we're doing now, probably is what the last generation Americans did. So it's not that they are different, it's that they are accepting the difference. My daughter did, she just put up with a lot less than me.

Everyone: Mm-hmm.

C: It is a big, big deal and it's totally different.

C: No, because my daughter, I never said, "Don't say that," she expresses even in front of me, she embarrassed me, but since I'm teaching her that, I cannot say, "Why you say that in front of the people?"

G: My daughter has been raised in a different way than I was raised. My mom was a teacher so I think she was a little bit ahead of it. So it's not that we were able to express entirely, but it was better. So the way my girls are being raised is that, yeah . . . when my mom comes and visits, it's like, "Wow, your girls talk about everything" and that's what she's saying, they just say how they feel. I'm like, "Yeah!" you know, and she has fun with them because, you know . . . but it's that, that's the difference.

Such comments illustrate how these mothers are purposefully directing their daughters' emotional development to include more self-expression as a result of the consequences of their own early self-silencing. The added dimension of their own mothers' reactions to this seems of great interest to them.

African American women express very similar themes and even expand slightly beyond those expressed by the other, younger women. Although they still focus on family socialization, they tie this to how those outside the family view anger:

C: It's a generational thing, I think. Because if you display anger between . . . If I think about it, if I display anger with my mother, the first thing she wants to do is say you're not suppose to be angry. If you think about it, it's your fault. She quickly wants . . . she does what men do, she dismissed the anger.

Women in the Jewish group speak of their own experiences as part of the "older generation," and their memories of previous generations. Here they talk of differences related to family life:

C: Yeah, the men were out studying the Torah or doing their shtick, and the women ran the businesses, they ran the home, and . . .

R: Yeah, and they got angry.

E: Women of that generation, they probably were pretty angry—but they kept it to themselves.

However, the older Jewish women tended to focus more heavily on their experiences in the work force, and the expectations that influenced them to hide or disguise their anger, something they do not see as prevalent for women today:

B: Well, it depends whether it's your boss or your coworker.

R: In the era when we worked you played it real low key.

G: That's right.

R: Women in business were not respected if they were angry, aggressive.

G: Exactly.

R: I mean today it's a different thing, but not in our time.

E: Right.

R: You were expected to be a lady at all times.

G: Oh yeah. Well, you don't cross anybody . . .

Anger Diversions

Now our focus shifts again from socialization themes embedded in women's dialogue to clues about how they redirect their experiences of anger. In some cases, anger diversion stands out conspicuously as women describe the means by which they protect the status quo of their intimate relationships. However, in much of the interview exchange, traces of anger diversion must be inferred by reading between the lines, listening to what *is not said* about anger experience. The majority of descriptions given for girls' angry behavior involves either problematic internalization or suppression patterns (e.g., being sick to one's stomach, refusing to eat, holding anger inside, trying to deal with it oneself, and withdrawing or isolating) or problematic externalization (e.g., aggression and verbal assault). This trend parallels conclusions generated in Chapter 4 regarding the problems with both extremes of expression, and it illustrates the bind in which girls find themselves in relation to their anger. For these girls, when one is angry, one either attempts to shut down social flow by ignoring friends and family in various ways, or one has a fight. Neither really solves the situation nor bridges relationship gaps. Neither helps these girls to claim and articulate what they desire, as both leave out any clear revelation to self or others.

Angry behaviors ascribed to girls in their interviews that are linked with keeping anger inside, versus action taken on the environment to change something noxious, tend instead to be actions taken on or within the self, as in neutralization of anger (e.g., "I try to think about other things") and refusal to eat or passive expressions made toward others that effectively distance the angry girl from people in her immediate support system. When girls describe this kind of angry action taken on the self, it is as if they depict their own adaptation to fit demands of the social context. Recall Morgan's statement about handling anger when her mother cannot.

M: If there's something I want like if I'm getting, like if it's really too much and it's really consuming, then I don't want to, I don't want her to have to deal with that. So I'll block it off myself.

Suppression

As discussed in Chapter 4, anger suppression involves fundamentally conscious adaptation by holding back thoughts and feelings that one inwardly desires to express, verbally or otherwise. As we contain this information about ourselves, *suppression* involves prolonged bodily changes that correspond with the anger response. These visceral goings-on must be inferred from what is actually said by girls and women in these interviews. Fifth grader Angelica seems to understand suppression as she describes her response to a particular female peer.

AA: She makes me want to hit people but I just hold it inside.

Recall again Morgan's comments about her suppression in relation to her mother. She comes to expect a certain reaction to her anger and has thus learned to refrain from talking aloud about her feelings.

M: And with me, if I was angry I might mention something that
          would strike a nerve with my mom so, I get too angry to realize
          that I'm saying it so when I realize I'm getting that angry, I just
          won't say anything to her.

These statements uncover fifth- and eighth-grade girls' acknowledgment of social rules concerning their self-definition with anger and highlight their ability to hold back the flow of self information. This suppression, no doubt, helps them adapt in their family and school environments
but deserves recognition for its potential stifling influence on affective exchange and relationship enhancement with others.

The young Muslim women note a parallel necessity to smooth things
over in their marriages, a duty that requires a degree of suppression.

S2:   And the woman has to come back, even though she's mad,
          even though it's not her fault . . .

S1:   She has to come back and make sure everything is OK.

This Latin American woman describes her suppression to a point of
unintentional release. She further explains how she manages anger through
self-denial.

B: I'll keep as much as I can, but then when I have to explode, I
          have to explode and I don't like that.

C: And how did you deal with everything that you kept inside?

B: I cried to myself.

A: We just repress. They feel that we should repress the anger.

G: I wonder if that comes from the way we were raised, at home,
          as a little girl, you know, you're not suppose to be angry.

A: The face that you put on for your family, there is a face that you
          put on for your coworkers, there is a face that you put on for
          your spouse or your children and sometimes things that you're
          feeling, you don't let that show and they are thinking that you
          are one way and you know you are not.

This African American woman speaks about the multiple selves she
must present to the world in her various contexts. She admits that her

internal experience of feeling differs markedly from what she allows to show on the outside. Another woman in this group depicts her own withdrawal in certain angry situations.

C: I think when my brothers know that I'm upset, I withdraw. I don't show anger. I withdraw. I'm the one who's always sitting there quiet. If I withdraw to the point that I don't answer you then you know that I'm angry. There is something brewing there.

This excerpt illustrates a *pulling away*, which also seems to involve a degree of intention. This African American woman suggests that as she pulls away, she communicates something indirectly to her family. Again, we must speculate about the degree to which her *body* becomes involved in containing the anger she feels. However, it is reasonable to assume she prolongs her nervous system's arousal by holding back this angry tide of self information.

A further example of Black women's understanding of suppression comes in how they speak about raising their children. The following statement brings gender, ethnicity, power, and anger diversion together into one bundle that this woman must pass along to her son for his own survival's sake.

C: And it's real hard as a mother of a Black male to train that Black male because you're always telling him to hold the rage, hold the anger. I know I do. I always got to remind him who he is because the rage can end up in his life and that is a fact that nobody understands, White men do not carry that all their lives. They know that they cannot misstep or they're dead.

This commentary sheds light on the intertwining of power and anger, and the necessity of those in socially dominated positions to truncate those powerful, instrumental aspects of themselves, an act that could paradoxically render them even more vulnerable to powerful others. This mother is consciously aware of her son's anger, and of her own, but must find ways of pulling the incensed feelings back inside, stopping the impulse to convey them to their target. This skill she passes on to her son in an effort to help him remain safe.

Internalization

The line between internalization and suppression is an arbitrary one, and again we rely on conjecture about what is retained cognitively and what is prolonged physiologically or held back phenomenologically. Many of the women's stories about internalization have to do with former relationships or marriages in which they found it necessary to engage in this kind of self-restraint. This Latin American woman describes her experience in a prior marriage and how her skill at internalization continues with her:

B: See, that's the same thing with me, when I was married before, I had to keep the anger to myself. I didn't have a say at the house, you know, because it was just him, he could get angry and everything but if I was to get mad, angry I would get . . . you notice I'm real quiet, y'all, so I just keep everything to myself.

As we speculate about what cognitive elements B ingests as she keeps her anger inside, our attention turns to her continued silence in angry situations. Because internalization happens over time as women swallow their anger, we can imagine that certain kinds of reorganization become necessary for B to keep quiet. This reorganization of responsibility may reside at the heart of her continued silence in relationships that are now much safer emotionally than her previous marriage. She may now possess conscious awareness of "having a say" yet unconsciously retain vestiges of beliefs from her former union. Here is another example from the Latin American group that shows the continuance from suppression to internalization:

A: Well I understand, I keep that in my mind, I try to understand the other person's feelings because I'm completely very sensitive. But if I see M angry, I say, "M, I'm sorry, I'm sorry if I did that to you, please excuse me."

B: She really does, she tries to calm the situation.

A: That's what I did with the kids too when they are angry with their teachers. I say, "Just calm down, drink a glass of water."

G: But if M comes up to you and says, "OK, M . . . you did this."

A: I say, "Oh no M, its OK, I'm sorry, I'm sorry" [laughter].

A suggests by her expressions of regret that she should apologize when she is angry, as if to insure that she has not harmed or faulted another. Taking this issue a step further, according to the older Jewish women, *guilt*, not anger, rears its head as a source of discomfort for them. Guilt represents another transformation of anger through the diversion of internalization. Like body-hate, shame and guilt come to replace outrage in women because of their greater social acceptability. Although we must again conjecture about *how* these women come to feel guilt rather than anger, internalization is a reasonable choice.

A: Yeah, Jewish mothers for example [Talking over].

A: But that's just one stereotype there are other stereotypes. There's the stereotype of the woman that's . . . laying down for the son and letting him walk all over her.

B: Guilt is what we got.

All: Yeah.

B: Now if you say *guilt* I would agree, but anger, I'm not sure.

G: I never let my kids walk over me.

S: Good for you.

B: I think I let my kids walk over me.

E: I don't know if they take advantage of it, but I'm a target.

The process revealed in these women's dialogue looks like an outgrowth of segmentation as well. They report awareness of guilt feelings in the same context in which they speak about being taken for granted by their grown children. Where does the guilt originate? How does it emerge in this conversation about anger? One woman mentions a stereotype of Jewish mothers and then another discloses her guilt feelings. How is it she feels guilt instead of anger in relation to being "walked over?" One possible answer is that the mention of anger reminds her of scenarios in which her adult children take advantage of her, one in which she *could* feel anger but instead feels as if she is at fault or inadequate in some way.

In a slightly different way, the same Jewish woman talks about her cognitive rearrangement in relation to the auto mechanic:

B: If somebody . . . if I understand that I'm dealing with a car dealership and if I'm told that it will be ready on Monday after-

noon around four o'clock then I call to make . . . Well, because
if you deal with these things then you know that they're liable
not to be ready at four o'clock so I call first and I'm less likely to
be annoyed because it's not ready and I fully expected it not to
be ready. [Um-hum]. So I can't say that I've ever gotten really
angry at car dealers or mechanics.

Here, she must *anticipate* feeling anger at being disappointed or let
down by the mechanic, make a gesture towards this person to get information that confirms her expectation, and then tell herself something about
how, because she knew it would be this way, she is not really mad. The
internal cognitive rule seems to be, "Because I wasn't really expecting you
to come through, I cannot feel angry that you in fact did not."

Segmentation

Segmentation, more difficult to discern from women's conversations, has
at its heart a clear disavowal of angry selfhood. This disavowal may take
the form of complete abstinence from anger or, rather, an eschewing of
certain aspects or manifestations of anger. Some of the older Jewish
women's conversation involves distancing from "angry women" by talking in third person about them. These women may or may not be using
the conversational distance as a way to segment themselves from their
own anger, but the style nevertheless deserves note.

G: It has to be, to me, related to something specific [referring to
       the question]. This is a general topic. Angry women.

B: Does it mean women who are angry all the time?

E: I think there are people who are angry all the time, we just
       don't happen to be those people.

R: There are times when we interpret a person's stance as being
       always angry and they may not be. They may be very troubled
       people.

R: Certainly we don't personally have any experience with a
       woman who is angry all the time.

S: I don't know anybody who is angry all the time.

R: I don't know an angry person. Do you?

B: I think that I wouldn't particularly want to be with her because it would be disquieting.

G: What about somebody who . . . or do you feel . . . do you feel that, like in some of the women's groups today, they're standing up for good causes, do you regard these women as angry women?

R: Only if they act angry.

S: Some of them are angry.

E: Yeah.

S: I don't understand what the question is [talking over each other].

B: I don't understand what causes we're talking about.

G: Abortion rights [talking over each other].

R: Activism depends on activism.

B: Sexual harassment.

E: Sometimes, they always come across angry to me.

In this third excerpt, the women are responding to the question, "How do women feel about other women who are angry?" Again, segmentation is an inference cautiously drawn from these statements, but like the case of Myra in Chapter 4, these women seem to put semantic distance between themselves and other women whom they perceive to always be angry, or to be angry about social and political causes, by choosing stereotyped cases to discuss and by avoiding their own positions on these issues. People who are *always angry* become those people interested in extreme issues, *out there* somewhere.

Externalization

In the fourth interview with fifth graders, Angel and Angelica yield information about behaviors for girls that does not fit the overall pattern of internalization and suppression. This group of fifth-grade girls reports primarily aggression, feigned aggression, and volatile verbal expression as means for *both* boys and girls to express anger, behaviors that seem to be more externalizing in nature. In none of these situations does anger receive the direct ownership and attention that is vital to creating contextual change. However, these girls seem to know something about defending their boundaries in relation to boys in their class, even if it means resorting to aggression.

AL: Like, there's this girl in our, uh, Leeanne [laughs at disguised name]. She's a really tough girl and she's already beated up a couple of people in our classroom and Tim will say something and she'll say, "What did you say?" And it'll be like, "Oh nothing," but they really do say something.

AA: Like, Deanne, yeah, and Henry [laughs at disguised names]. Like Henry, he'll call her names and Deanne will get up in his face and he won't do nothing. He'll back off because he knows that she could beat him up. Like, he talks under his breath.

Although outright aggression seems to be the most obvious way to externalize, other forms of this diversion take place as well. The young Muslim women aptly depict their gender as externalizing to avoid coming to grips with their own anger. In this example, criticizing other women is a way to avoid ownership of anger:

S1:   It is a female trait, you find other women's flaws. And I guess women tend to be more perfectionists, so they notice things like that. But some women don't know how to deal with anger, so instead they chastise them. They go, "Can you believe she did that?" Because they themselves don't know how to . . .

S2:   They're insecure about their own anger, so they . . . talk about someone else.

For certain of the women, the suppression/explosion phenomenon also becomes clear. Consider the following statements made by Latin American women:

B: I keep everything to myself because I know that when I explode, I say things that I regret later. I just keep everything to myself.

A: Well in my case, I was married to a Hispanic, there was anger almost all the time [laughter]. I would want to hit him in the face.

I: You want to hit him?

A: Yes, but he is going to hit me back if I do that first.

The threat of retaliation keeps her from acting on her desire to aggress, but in this relationship, her power to own and articulate anger is compromised. This situation probably *invites* externalization, as A's agency to use her anger is undermined.

Symptom Clusters

Our interviews with girls and women yield only a few examples of symptomatology surrounding anger or its diversion. Nonetheless, girls in particular mention some experience of somatization and consumption problems that occur with anger. Clementine, an African American fifth grader, makes reference to times when she is angry wherein she not only refuses to eat but also experiences some kind of gastrointestinal distress. Her friends notice this pattern in her as well.

C: Like, if you have a boyfriend that like, when I go home, my grandma, OK, I wouldn't eat for like a week, I wouldn't eat at school or at home. Then she'd be like, "What's wrong with you, you'd better eat your food," like, and if I would eat it would come straight back up I know . . . But she say stuff like, "I guess you got a boyfriend" and stuff like that, and I like, "No," like that, and I roll my eyes and get like kinda mad. Stuff like that and then like next week, she'll start forcing food in my mouth.

DE: When she gets mad, she don't talk to nobody in the classroom and we be like, "Clementine why you won't eat?" and she won't eat . . .

Now reading between the lines, our work with Bud, the eighth grader who takes on a boy's identity, produces some hypotheses about long-term anger diversion and resultant depression in a very young person. Bud brings with her a reputation for getting into trouble at school, appearing sullen and angry most of the time, refusing to participate in most school activities, and running away from home. Here, she describes a pattern of withdrawal and avoidance that she uses in her family to deal with anger. This pattern appears to be a mutual retreat from intense feeling and something of an everyday occurrence.

B: I don't know, I'm always angry when I'm home so they don't really do anything so I mean they've learned not to ask and I won't tell them anything. They've learned to avoid me and I avoid them and everything works out.

Bud talks of not needing this emotional connection in her family, as she stares dejectedly at her lap and pulls individual strands of hair from her head, letting them drop to the floor. She has a history of suicidal gestures as evidenced by the half-dozen or so scars on her forearms, none severe enough to cause much bleeding, only the alarm of her teachers and counselor. Thirteen-year-old Bud experiences emotional neglect on a daily basis and could be depressed as a result of any number and combination of factors. Specifically, though, she identifies herself as angry and simultaneously as holding on to her anger because there is no one to hear it.

Although the older Jewish women mention fewer examples of sickness resulting from anger diversion, they do demonstrate a sense of that phenomenon from their experiences with other people.

G: Now you people have heard the two of us kind of pick on each other. But that's who we are. But you also know it's the kind of anger that's not real important. I mean there's anger and then there's anger.

S: It goes very quickly, it's like boom, boom, boom . . .

G: Yeah, exactly.

R: You're better off being that way than the person who keeps it in forever and gets very angry.

G: Yeah, the person who keeps it in forever and then has apoplexy. I knew someone who died that way . . . be angry, angry, angry and then he exploded.

This bit of dialogue indicates some acknowledgment on the parts of these women about the hand-in-handedness of emotional and physical health. Although it may apply only to other people, the folk wisdom apparent in this conversation admits to the connection between anger and symptomatology.

☐ Summary

To summarize interview responses, girls and women depict reactions of significant people to their anger in a number of different ways. Girls say a lot about their parents' and teachers' counteractions, characterizing fathers as concerned but condescending, often distant and bewildered by their anger. They see mothers as more closely approaching or encountering the angry feelings they experience, yet as being somewhat more reactive or punitive about them in some circumstances. Teachers react differently to boys' and girls' anger as reported by these fifth and eighth graders. The girls also seem to expect gendered behavior in themselves and in their friends, pointing to boys' proclivity toward externalization and their own tendencies for diversion or silencing of anger.

Women grapple with the difficult issue of anger by noting cultural, social, and generational differences in how their anger is treated. Many of the same issues emerge between men and women as depicted between boys and girls, such as participants' feeling minimized or rejected when they're letting out feelings of opposition. Many of them stress the support they feel from other women, but also note that their peers' anger can be difficult for them to witness, as it stirs uncomfortable feelings about their own affective demonstration. Feeling the pinch of other women's overt anger displays, and recoiling in response, may parallel girls' open condemnation of their peers' gender-bending behavior, such as their aggression or defiance.

In sum, these girls and women tell us a lot about how they conceptualize, experience, and manage anger-in-relation. Their experiences seem to vary with age, ethnicity, class, social context, and other variables, and their descriptions give life to previously reviewed clinical and theoretical construals of women's anger. In the chapter to follow, we broaden our review of this qualitative material to focus on specific anger-related themes as they bear on women's formation of identity and sense of personal power.

6

CHAPTER

Synthesis and Conclusions

Anger, if it's channeled the right way,
can become quite a motivator.
—Della Reese

The first problem for all of us, men and women,
is not to learn but to unlearn.
—Gloria Steinem

This book is a coming together—a beginning to the process of an interdisciplinary integration of empirical measurement, data gathering, and more inductive dialoguing in women's anger. It starts a journey to synthesize voices from feminism, developmental psychology, and psychotherapy with evolutionary and biological perspectives, the literatures on socialization and culture, and the voices of the girls and women who generously share their stories with us. Throughout, the contrasting processes of anger as self-definition and of anger diversion are the two most important threads woven into the tapestry of this book.

In our theoretical perspective, we take a close-up, almost microscopic view of the role of gender socialization in the process of anger diversion for women and girls. From clinical practice and qualitative research interviews, we trace the manifestations of this process through girls' and women's reports of their lived experience. In all these settings, diverted anger is revealed to us in the often subtle, interrelated processes of externalization, segmentation, internalization, and suppression. Our work does *less* to illuminate what makes women angry (although there are plenty of representative examples of this in our interviews) than *how* women and girls experience and express anger. The role of anger diversion in "high profile" women's issues such as depression and eating disorders is considered on equal footing with the pervasive "subclinical" or everyday ways in which anger diversion distorts experience, silences expression, and inhibits instrumental action.

Anger as self-definition reflects the adaptive, constructive ways in which anger can be experienced and expressed. Acknowledging anger to self and learning to accept and value the social-relational messages of anger is crucial. Our anger tells us that boudaries have been crossed, that we have been lied to, that our values have been discounted, that our intentions have been distorted, and signals any number of other of countless interpersonal injustices, large or small, as they occur. Informed choices about revealing anger to others follows once anger is known and welcomed as a part of the self. In each interaction in which a girl or woman chooses to reveal her anger, self is further defined.

The remaining goals of this chapter are three-fold. First, we summarize the broad themes that emerge from integrating previous theory, research, and practice discussions with our qualitative narratives. We organize these themes into two categories, reflecting the two dominant supports of the book's framework: feminist conceptualizations and developmental theory. This material speaks to many aspects of anger diversion and to the socialization of women's and girls' anger. Second, we integrate our work with other literatures on identity development, with a particular focus on feminist identity development. This section further reflects our focus on the role of anger in self-definition. Third, we present recommendations for theory, research, and practice, and for empowering personal and social change.

☐ Summary of Emergent Themes

The summaries provided here come largely (though not exclusively) through the various girls' and women's conversations we have collected. Although we attempted to select a diverse range of women and girls in our work, we acknowledge that many voices are not represented (e.g., Asian American women, lesbian women). We also recognize that it is inappropriate to generalize from the very small numbers of girls and women who did speak with us. For these reasons, we wish to stress that the themes here reflect only our particular participants' input. This is descriptive information that serves to illustrate trends in responses of a few dozen total respondents. We feel these qualitatively derived themes are of substantial interest and can serve as an important basis for further explorations and theory building by those who will follow us.

Feminist Themes

- Fundamental tension between adaptive function and societal inhibition.

This theme runs throughout all aspects of the book, from theories to practice to the qualitative text. We accept the premise that emotion, anger included, has a fundamental evolutionary adaptive function, with corresponding physiological markers in its most basic form. At some level, almost all of the women recognize that getting angry is "natural" or "is going to happen" or "is inevitable." Women express frustration with the myriad covert norms surrounding the expression of this anger, and a keen awareness of the consequences of anger in different contexts. The societal messages to not feel, to control, to supress, or to rechannel anger somewhere else besides at its target are well learned.

- Exquisite sensitivity to power differences and degrees of affiliation/relational context.

If you sat down with many of our participants and asked them, "What are the rules about who can get angry at whom, and who can't, and when and where and how?" we think many of them could answer in detail. Although this was not a question that we asked in our focus group discussions, the dimensions of power and affiliation are clearly linked to anger expression in women and girls. Although you may feel anger toward another who is hierarchically above you (teacher, boss, parent), you do not show this anger or are very careful about how you do so.

With peers (those at an equal level of social power), anger expression is usually supported, but here there is often an interaction with affiliation. A close friend (usually of similar ethnicity) is someone with whom it is safe to express anger, but an acquaintance, even if similar to you in terms of age, socioeconomic status, and so forth, is a more risky interactional partner. Decreased affiliation brings less trust and concerns that anger expressed to a mere acquaintance may not be well received or may not be held in confidence. Many women show a clear recognition that equality of economic power within intimate relationships leads to increased freedom to express anger.

The few mentions of women in "one-up" positions come with a mixed bag of responses. Some women assert they would never let their children manipulate them and feel free to express appropriate anger to subordinate children. Others seem to fear their children's anger and thus let their children "walk all over" them. Some women in powerful positions at work feel comfortable directly expressing their anger to those working under them; others report seeking the assistance of higher level managers to resolve disputes involving anger at a subordinate.

The rules about anger expression are also mediated by cultural heritage. For example, some Latin American women note that a certain degree of anger expression is tolerated because they are known to be "naturally hot-tempered." African American women discuss the concept of "Black rage" in African American men, as well as noting that their own assertive behavior is often mislabeled as anger by Whites. Muslim women speak of religious injunctions against anger, noting that when they become angry, they often tell themselves *"Astagh-farrallah"* or *"Sabr, "* which translates as "God forgive me for being angry" and "give me patience," respectively. The older Jewish women we interviewed clearly point out the stereotypes about their culture but also express ambivalence about the accuracy of these perceptions:

E: I agree with B, I think there is an idea that Jewish women are domineering, controlling . . .

R: And demanding.

E: But we are, aren't we? [Laughter]

G: I don't know. I don't think more than any other group . . .

Notably, these women insist that none of these constructs are the same as being angry. Although it is possible that they have compartmentalized anger away from these psychological traits, it may be just as likely that there is no anger attached to these processes for them.

Interestingly, a few women and girls express indifference to the status or affiliation of the target of their anger: When they get angry, they do not care who it is, where it is, or what is going on. Listening to their voices on tape, there often is an undertone of satisfaction in their speech, which we speculate is perhaps the success of their anger in making instrumental changes in their social surround, or their sheer pleasure in flexing their personal power.

- The implied fear of anger leading to aggression in both self and others.

Most of the girls and women who made contributions to this book link anger with aggression in some way. Girls describe angry boys (and some girls) fighting, as well as angry parents and siblings hitting each other or hitting them. Women often associate anger with abuse incidents, either their own or those of people they know. Stories of beatings and murders include a theme of long-diverted anger that suddenly explodes. Although the vast majority of these stories reflect men's violence against women, there are some exceptions. Many women and girls directly or indirectly express fear that if their anger generates reciprocal anger in men or boys, the possibility of aggressive counterattack is real. Some women in therapy, when first truly recognizing and accessing their long-suppressed anger, express a fear of losing control, becoming violent, or finding they are unable to ever stop being angry.

- Men's withdrawal from girls' and women's anger.

In describing how men react to their anger, most women describe their partners as withdrawing, "tuning out," or otherwise ignoring or diminishing their anger. This highly frustrates and often insults the women involved, who note that such behavior belittles their concerns and conveys the message that they are not important enough to be taken seriously. Girls and young adult women often describe their fathers this way, but note that fathers encourage boys to be assertive and tough.

The withdrawal of men from women's anger frequently stirs up feelings of irritation for women. We can hypothesize that because anger is an approach emotion, whose ultimate aim is to contact and affect the interpersonal environment somehow (i.e., obtain a produtive response from one's partner), if that urge is thwarted, a great deal of emotional energy is left without a focal point. One thing women and girls mention that they do with such deflected anger is talking to confidantes about their anger. Using a different approach, some women appear to reframe the situation by attributing their partners' withdrawal to fear or immaturity. The use of similar techniques in or outside of therapy is noted in Chapter 4.

A minority of the women we interviewed report that their intimate partners do not withdraw from expressions of anger but become angry in return. These women frequently comment that such angry exchanges feel quite unproductive, leading to escalating anger rather than to any sort of mutual, supportive understanding of the anger or to any sort of successful problem solving.

- Sexual harassment as a source of anger.

Again, although this is not something we asked about, women in more than one focus group spontaneously mention episodes of sexual harassment on the job or at school when discussing the question related to anger in the workplace. All the women who had been involved in such situations experience them as anger-inducing and recognize the abuse of power involved. As is often true in sexual harassment scenarios, women's responses vary greatly, and the outcomes of their actions (or lack thereof) vary as well (Fitzgerald, 1990). Some women report assertively telling their harassers to stop and having the noxious behaviors cease. Some report putting up with it silently, fearing the loss of their jobs if they expressed their anger. Some report changing jobs. Some told higher-ups about the harassment but were then cautioned not to pursue any action against the offending men. What this confirms for us about women's anger at work or school is that being objectified generates strong feelings, and that perceived personal power, as well as realistic external consequences, influence the way in which these feelings are either channeled into instrumental action or diverted.

Some women express a belief or hope that things are changing regarding sexual harassment in the workplace in current times. Others feel it is a shame that flirting on the job and office romances seem to be curtailed in the present climate, although they recognize that such behaviors are not always welcomed. One woman also noted that women can sexually harass men. However, there was no debate that being sexually harassed is an anger-producing situation.

• Anger specific to prejudice identified by all minority groups.

Although girls did not mention feeling anger in relation to their cultural identity, women in all four of the focus groups did. Whether African American, Latin American, Muslim Middle Eastern, or Jewish, virtually all these women could relate incidents (that occured to them or others) of insults, ethnic jokes, discrimination, stereotyping, and misunderstanding of their culture by persons of majority heritage. For example, the young Muslim women expressed their anger about being stereotyped as "psycho terrorists," particularly during the Gulf War or after the Oklahoma City bombing. One older Jewish woman, irritation clear in her voice says, "Why are all these ethnic jokes?" When one Latin American woman notes that Americans "feel we are more emotional," another woman responds, "They don't understand the way we are, they think that we are crazy." Reflecting her anger at being often misunderstood, one African American woman comments, "Yeah, and White women, sometimes they think that you're angry when you're not. . . Angry! This is just the way that I talk, this my personality, you know? But they are intimidated by me." Another Black woman stated, "I don't think anybody's permitted to show anger but a White male and be accepted or be taken seriously."

- Recognition of individual differences in personality and dysfunction in both men and women.

Most women, and even a few of the girls in later adolescence, recognize individual differences among people; some are unusually anger-prone and others remarkably placid. These individual personalities and styles, as well as the situational determinants of anger, seem clearly recognized as women gain life experience. This recognition of differences also manifests in younger women's exceptions to the generalizations they sometimes make, to include people they know who did not fit various stereotypes, and so forth.

In terms of defining anger, women also recognize that anger can attain dysfunctional levels in both its expressed and suppressed forms. Without having the formal clinical language to label it, women demonstrate an awareness that chronic resentment can become a personality trait, or that some people seem to be consistently compelled to "rile up" others, even if the interpersonal consequences of such behavior are negative. They speak perceptively of people who hold back their anger for weeks, months, or years, only to explode in violent outbursts later on, or to drop dead from coronary failure.

Developmental Themes

- Changes in cognitive complexity over time.

As mentioned, in moving through adult development, our participants' judgements of others typically become more sophisticated. Attributions about what causes women or men to be angry take on a multidimensional view, with culture, socialization, personality, and specific context or situation all being recognized as important factors in understanding another human being's emotional reactions. In fact, some of the oldest women in our focus groups seem loath to make any generalizations at all about anger in relation to women, men, or majority or minority cultures. "It depends" seems to be the working principle behind this position.

The girls we interviewed showed quick and comfortable ease with generalizations, often only recognizing individual differences among their closest friends or family and easily lumping all others together in big groups. Little awareness of broader socialization or contextual variables emerges in their conversations, all of which fits with what we know about cognitive development (most fifth graders, for example, are likely to be at a concrete-operational level of thinking, not yet able to stand outside their immediate circumstances and evaluate in an abstract manner). The young Muslim women, in the 19- to 21-year-old range, clearly use more abstract reasoning ability and speculate about political, economic, religious, and social influences on women's and men's anger. Although sometimes resorting to somewhat simplistic explanations, they have clearly advanced from the elementary and junior high school girls in their discrimination about anger situations. As women move into their 30s, their 40s, and beyond, the trend towards more complex and situational thinking strengthens. Thus, women's understanding of anger in this small sample becomes highly contextualized with progression through the life span.

• Changes in self-definition over time.

Another developmental tendency that becomes evident as we examine women's comments is that older women have a more clearly defined sense of self. They know who they are and define themselves unapologetically. They know what makes them angry and what does not, are familiar with their own responses to anger in others, and have made a certain degree of peace with their choices about anger expression. As women mature, they often appear able to articulate which aspects of their cultures and socialization they consciously choose to retain, and which ones they fight to change.

Girls and younger women at times contradict themselves in the interviews and focus groups, usually without an awareness of these contrasts. Descriptions of angry episodes are sometimes followed by reassurances that conflicts are not real or are not really serious. Assertions about not putting up with parental restrictions and rules later become contradicted by examples of compliance and guilt. Statements that things are changing in regard to women expressing their anger are not always followed by behavioral examples. However, these contradictions should not be taken as criticisms of these girls and young women. They appear to be wrestling with the normal developmental processes of identity development in relation to others, self-definition, and degrees of individuation from family, as well as how much, how often, how honestly, and how clearly they can vent their anger and use it instrumentally with others.

• Changes in anger conceptualization over time.

This theme is similar to the first developmental theme in some respects but focuses more on women's understanding of the *concept* of anger rather than on the actual experience of anger or of the interpersonal situations surrounding anger. Girls in pre- and early adolescence give behavioral examples of anger: yelling, hitting, crying, fighting, refusing to eat, turning up the stereo. By the time late adolescence and early adulthood arrives, anger is described and understood as an internal psychoemotional state. Women at this point talk about thoughts (opinions, attributions, appraisals), feelings, and sensations associated with anger, in addition to behavioral components. It shoud be noted here as well that earlier conceptualizations of anger do not appear to drop out, but later and more elaborate understandings build on them, adding levels of internal complexity. The oldest of our participants wrestle with the truly abstract question of how to define anger. In fact, some of these women appeared irritated that we did not define anger for them!

S: This is such a hard topic because how does one define anger? Do you perceive anger in a certain way? As being directive? Does the personality of the person seem directive? It's a very hard thing, in my opinion, to do.

R: So each one of us, if we were asked to define anger, we'd define it differently . . . When you think of anger, don't you think of loud?

S: Some people say anger is loud because you're losing control.

R: Some people's anger is white-hot, it isn't loud, it's just contained . . .

E: I think the angry person herself is best able to tell when they are angry.

G: It has to be to me, related to something specific . . .

- Changes in anger expression with the changing times.

With the exception of the girls interviewed, all the women in our focus groups, regardless of age, express the feeling that women's outward anger expression is gaining in social acceptability compared with the past. Obviously, for some women this past is further away than for others, highlighting a notable absence of generational differences. Additionally, many women who were mothers feel that the situation continues to improve for their daughters, who have more and more support for expressing their anger. In a generational twist to this theme, younger women express ambivalence about taking advantage of this new, supposed openness about anger expression, not knowing if their parents (or those in their parents' generation) would be accepting of it.

- Muslim and Latin women's evolution.

Both Muslim and Latin women express the idea that what White U.S. women were doing in the late 1960s and 1970s, women of their ethnic groups are doing today. This is usually couched as "fighting for our rights," among which appears to be the right to express anger. Thus, the struggle is additionally one to break the rules; to allow anger to be expressed and to motivate the fight for social change. They seem to implicitly acknowledge that the anger felt by White U.S. women in the first wave of feminism was now a legitimate anger for their respective groups. Although White U.S. women express anger at their oppression by gender bias, there is no component of race awareness in this struggle. In contrast, for women in the two minority cultures mentioned, anger is intimately tied to the restrictions of both gender and their culture when set against the backdrop of White America.

African American women express no such sense of being "a generation behind." This may be because most of these women, and generations of their families, have been in the United States since before the time of the feminist movement, which was also a time of continued activity for civil-rights and Black-power movements. In contrast, many of the Latin and Muslim women in our groups are relatively recent immigrants or first-generation women in this country.

- Age and increased interpersonal sensitivity in girls.

The fifth-grade girls we interviewed often showed an insensitivity to the other girls in their groups, insulting or embarrassing them, either with or without intent. This lack of awareness about what might make another girl angry or hurt in the immediate moment disappears for older girls and women. With no direct clues about why this might be, we can speculate that perhaps these fifth-grade girls had not yet completely absorbed the gender-role prescriptions dictating that they should not say bad things about others, or that their levels of cognitive complexity did not yet lend themselves to taking the perspectives of others. Another possibility is that in responding to the researcher's position of authority when asked for examples of girls' anger, they focused on that task rather than on the consequences of their behaviors.

Conclusions

The broad themes in these two sections on feminist and developmental aspects of women's anger provide both support for established ideas and some new revelations. On the feminist side, it is apparent that the issues of violence, sexual harassment, and oppression—classic concerns—remain alive and well. One of the contributions of this book lies in helping to articulate how these long-standing problems, as well as others, are interconnected with the experience and expression of anger, as well as in fleshing out further examples of cultural variation in these processes.

On the developmental side, the kinds of progressions in complexity of thinking that we note are expected based on well-known aspects of cognitive and social development. Older women's abilities to encompass uncertainty, paradox, subjectivity, and dialectical tension have been noted before (e.g., Labouvie-Vief, Orwoll, & Manion, 1995), as has their more solid sense of self. Again, a contribution of this work to the current literature lies in its tracing how the specific emotion of anger is played out through the lifespan, and in elaborating on how cultural and generational differences impact this development.

☐ Integration with Feminist Identity Development and Feminist Consciousness

When we began this project, we wondered what women and girls were thinking, feeling, and doing around anger issues, and if that territory could be reasonably placed on the map of feminist identity development. Would our younger, "modern" girls be in more advanced stages than women later in life? Would women in their 40s and 50s—who came of age during the first wave of feminism—reflect more feminist consciousness than those who came before or after? What would older women be like in relation to feminism? Further, how would ethnicity play into feminist identity development?

We keep these fundamental questions in mind as we listen to the voices of women and girls talking about that most socially stigmatized of emotions for our gender, anger. It seems to us that the domain of anger is a good one to choose given the taboos against it; change in a difficult area is perhaps a more interesting indicator of the progress (or lack thereof) of the feminist agenda than some other target. In other words, we believe that healthy attitudes and actions regarding anger represent good markers for feminist identity development.

What is Feminist Identity Development and Feminist Consciousness?

Consensus is beginning to emerge about what constitutes feminist consciousness. It is a mindset, an awareness, a lens through which we eventually may come to view our lives and the lives of other men and women around us. Brabeck and Brown (1997) speak of feminist consciousness as an understanding that women and girls are members of a subordinate group, and that as members of that group they have been oppressed and wronged. It includes a fundamental support for the premise that this condition has been socially constructed and maintained and is not the result of men's nor women's hard-wired, biological nature. It includes careful attention to issues of power and hierarchy in our socialization, as well as efforts to change that socialization. Feminist consciousness promotes liberation of women and girls through communal action and through the development of a diversity of viewpoints and voices. These perspectives represent an alternative authority to traditional, dominant patriarchal narratives. For many, the development of feminist consciousness is seen as a desirable goal for both men and women.

Feminist consciousness relates closely to the idea of feminist identity development. Originally formulated by Downing and Roush (1985), the model receives more recent empirical support (e.g., Bargad & Hyde, 1991) and finds its basis in parallel models of Black identity development (e.g., Cross, 1971). The five stages of feminist identity development are (a) passive acceptance, (b) revelation, (c) embeddedness-emanation, (d) synthesis, and (e) active commitment.

Stage one, passive acceptance, typifies the woman or girl who is "either unaware of or denies the individual, institutional, and cultural prejudice and discrimination against her" (Downing & Roush, 1985, p. 698). Women at this stage are selective in their attention to information and experiences that confirm their traditional views of self and see traditional sex roles as beneficial to them. It is accepted that men are superior to women.

In the second stage, revelation, women find that a crisis, ongoing contradictions, or some other consciousness-raising events catalyze an openness to new conceptualizations and a questioning of prior assumptions. This stage is most often characterized by anger. Movement into this stage may occur abruptly but more often results from a long, slow, accumulation of reactions to everyday occurrences. Revelation could be triggered by a separation, loss of a job, involvement in a women's-studies class, a therapy experience, an awareness of an inequity against a female relative or friend, or a combination of many factors. Women in this stage often exhibit "all or nothing" thinking, believing that women are all good and men are all wrong. Downing and Roush (1985, p. 700) consider women at this stage to have a "psuedo-identity based on negation of traditional femininity and the dominant culture . . . rather than an identity based on an affirmation of the strengths of being female."

The third stage, embeddedness-emanation, initially involves the development of close relationships with like-minded women, who provide support, connection, and a safe place for a woman to develop her emerging, alternative frame of reference. This is a difficult stage, as intimate others (partners, fathers, brothers, friends) may not be supportive in many subtle, ongoing ways. In the latter part of the third stage, a less dualistic perspective begins to develop as women begin to understand the limitations of the rigidity of stage two and to mourn the loss of their former selves.

In the synthesis stage (stage four), a positive and realistic self-concept emerges as the woman learns to value many aspects of being female. Personal values come to the fore as a basis for choices, and men are evaluated on an individual basis rather than as a group. The woman in stage four acknowledges oppression- and socialization-based explanations for events, but can temper these with attributions about other types of causes. This stage may see the woman celebrating her existence and embracing authenticity.

The fifth and final stage in the model is active commitment. At this level, a consolidated identity is translated into behavior for social change. The goals of sex-role transcendence and effective action in creating a new and different future are embraced. Bargad and Hyde (1991), in their work with validating the feminist identity stages, note that it is not necessary for a woman to label herself "feminist" at any point in this model. Bargad and Hyde question whether or not the development of feminist identity is in any way different from the acquisition of a feminist value system. This debate further raises the question of whether the emergence of feminist consciousness is not virtually the same thing as well! It seems a distinct possiblility that these three concepts tap into the same underlying phenomena.

Given this overview of feminist consciousness and identity development, we now turn to the material in our own book, particularly the qualitative focus-group interviews and clinical case studies, for evidence in women's dialogue about the emergence of this kind of consciousness, and its relationship to anger. Examples of many of these stages are evident. As might be expected, there also appears to be some concurrence between age and level of identity development. Minority identity development issues are evident as well, intricately interwoven with gender awareness.

How Women and Girls Reflect Feminist Identity Development and Consciousness

The women and girls who contributed to our work seem to fall all across the spectrum of feminist identity. Although supporting evidence can be found for most of the stages, we hesitate to classify anyone as being set in a particular stage given the often limited amount of information available from each respondent. Thus, what we present here are examples of specific thoughts, perceptions, feelings, and behaviors that reflect a range of feminist consciousness, rather than a diagnostic labeling of each girl's or woman's place in the model.

Most of the youngest participants, the fifth- and eighth-grade girls, appear to be at stage one, expressing generally negative views of girls who act in nontraditional ways as well as an implicit acceptance of boys and men being stronger, more aggressive, and sometimes to be feared. This appears consistant with what we would hypothesize to occur in stage one; that anger, or at least negative attitudes and hostility, would arise toward nontraditional women and men, and positive feelings would be associated with traditional roles. Little evidence of an identity that is gender-positive was available from the girls we interviewed. However, these girls seem to have already begun to experience and clearly recognize the differences in how girls and boys are treated and perceived, and to have a sense of unfairness or injustice about these discrepancies. Girls also demonstrate the beginnings of a devaluation of boys, mainly through ridicule.

CL: Sometimes they fight. [Names a girl] . . . and she loves to fight. Always fighting, she fights everybody.

DC: What do you think of her when she's angry?

CL: I think she's all bad.

M: Well, I think, me, when I see guys that are angry, I feel like it could scare me 'cause boys are, can get very violent when they're mad and generally I try to stay away.

DC: What do girls think of boys that are angry?

AL: They think they're just trying to act bad.

AA: Yeah, trying to act typical [laughs].

In stage two, the model clearly expects anger to come to the fore in response to a new awareness of women's oppression and the unfairness associated with discrimination against women. Few women and late adolescent girls comment in ways that reflect the revelation stage in their current lives, although a number of women recall events that stand out in their minds as catalysts for questioning traditonal gender roles and express anger about these events. For example, this 70-year-old Jewish woman recollects:

G: I remember my first job, I'm fresh out of college, young, bachelor's degree, smart-ass, and my first job was a lowly clerk in a business office or whatever, typist and all that. There were ways of doing things that I could see were much more efficient ways than what they were doing in the office and could've done it in half the time so I started to suggest to my boss, "Maybe we should do . . . " Just forget it! Just keep your mouth shut. "Do it my way or you know." It would really kill me.

Late adolescent girls and some young women appear uncertain about whether or not men should be categorized as negative, condemning them in one place and then "back-pedaling" to note exceptions to their generalizations in others. In these cases, it is unclear if participants are having trouble leaving stage one or if they are entering the more relativist thinking characteristic of stage three. Similar struggles regarding minority and majority cultures appear as well. These issues come to life in a conversation among the young Muslim women, who wrestle with the stereotypes of men in American and Middle Eastern societies, as well as distinctions they make about subgroups within Muslim culture:

A1:   It's OK to be an angry man. It's much more acceptable.

S2:   But I do think there's a stereotype out there about Muslim men, that they are very overbearing and abusive.

S1:   Abusive, yeah, but that's not true. Like my dad, he can't be that way to me. And when people say something like that to me, I say, "What? No, they're not like that . . . "

S1:   Yeah, our father would never raise a hand to us.

S2:   Yeah, and never say bad things. I mean, I know more American kids who get beat around . . .

S1:   Yeah, like they get physically beaten up, but my dad would never imagine . . .

S2:   But they really do think that about us, or I see, I don't want to get very personal, but for some reason a lot of my friends think Persian guys . . . I hear them say, "Oh, Persian guys and Muslim men, they're just psycho, you can't be with them because they are so . . . "

S1:   Possessive.

S2:   Possessive, yeah, they get jealous very easily, and they're bad and they lock you up in your house and that's it.

Hostile attitudes towards men seem likely in this stage (two) and in the beginning of stage three. As women move through the latter part of stage three, emanation, and progress into synthesis and then active commitment, it follows that anger lessens or perhaps is channeled into effective social and interpersonal change. Women at various ages speak in ways that support aspects of the embeddedness-emanation stage. In terms of embeddedness, this most often manifests as expressions of solidarity with other like-minded women, who have been through similar experiences and typically share similar backgrounds. For many minority women, parallels emerge here regarding immersion in one's cultural heritage and hostility towards Whites. Our first example comes from the African-American focus group, the second from the Muslim women:

C: That's one of the things about M and I, because we're in similar situations and so when I get on the phone, she knows I'm angry about something. She can always . . . She understands, it's only affecting you.

F: It's almost like a support group. You know, women are in it together. And they understand it together.

S3:   Especially growing up here, its a lot, I mean, I think I relate better, I talk to my Muslim friends about my problems and things more than . . . with my American friends . . . they tried to understand, but it was never the same. Say, if I told S2 or S1, they would totally understand what I was going through, because they would understand there's a clash between the cultures. And so, its yeah, they're definitely more compassionate because they know what you're going through.

As far as emanation is concerned, many women follow their critiques of men as a group (e.g., as domineering, selfish, or demeaning) with examples of specific men who behave in ways that differ from their generalizations. As noted previously, there is often no definitive way to tell if this reflects emanation or return to passive acceptance. As is typical, none of the women or girls interviewed appear to have isolated themselves completely from men or boys at any point to seek out the sole company of women. They continue in their various relationships while moving into or through this (and the other) stages.

We want to be careful to note that for many minority women, whose cultures often promote a greater separation between men and women anyway, determining if such gender grouping reflects an active feminist choice or an acceptance of traditional enculturation becomes difficult. It may also be that these two elements coexist in the same woman. Perhaps having primary daily affiliation with women even contributes to emerging feminist identity. These questions and issues emerge from our dialogues with women and beg for further clarification through continued study.

Some women, particularly those who are developmentally mature, demonstrate stage-four thinking. They seem to feel secure in themselves and their gender identity, no longer view men as "the enemy," and in fact sometimes state that women who take this oppositional stance are immature or misguided. Women at this stage share more complex conceptualizations about individual men's and women's motivations, personalities, and situational realities as regards anger. As two women in the Hispanic focus group note:

G: My husband doesn't have a problem with me expressing anger. But I know that some husbands do have a problem, even in private.

B: In our case, with my husband, he's very different than other men.

Going past broad generalizations about groups of people, the older Jewish women express the following:

B: Because we live in a society with men and women and I really object to the stance that everything a man does is wrong and everything a woman does is right.

E: I agree with you.

S: Some people say anger is loud because you are losing control.

R: Some people's anger is white-hot, and it isn't loud, it's just contained.

E: I think the angry person herself is best able to tell when they are angry. I mean you can feel anger and not visibly . . .

S: Not be expressing it, just be feeling it .

G: It has to be to me, related to something specific . . .

E: I think there are people who are angry all the time, we just don't happen to be those people.

R: There are times when we interpret a person's stance as being always angry and they may not be . . .

E: There are some people who imagine injustice.

And as one Muslim woman neatly sums up:

F: It depends on personal experiences. Everybody is different. All the men are different.

We remain hard-pressed to find examples of the fifth stage of feminist identity, active commitment. Some women mention verbal support for meaningful action or social change, and other women demonstrate specific behaviors that clearly support a feminist agenda. For some women, it appears the feminist agenda just is not where they choose to spend their energy. They have other priorities and interests, but these do not discount their ability to conceptualize and interact in ways reflective of synthetic (stage four) awareness. Although Downing and Roush (1985) point out that only a few women actually evolve to the stage of active commitment, Bargad and Hyde (1991) write that stages four and five are hard to distinguish from each other in their studies. Our findings perhaps reflect similar issues. We expect that women in stages four and five accept anger as a positive part of their gender identity, clearly seeing its benefits in interpersonal relationships as well as trusting their anger to be a reliable marker for broader social injustices. As one 71-year-old Jewish woman said, "Don't you have to be angry to be passionate about anything?"

It may be that awareness of anger, not just anger itself, functions to move a woman along in the feminist identity development process. Anger occurs throughout the lifespan but comes into sharper focus at various points in time. The ability to be aware of and to tolerate a clear experience of anger that hopefully occurs as girls and women move through the stages of feminist identity development likely reflects change but also recipro-cally fuels and motivates change. In the later stages of feminist identity development, when anger awareness is assimilated into our healthy real-ity, the focus on anger diminishes as it blends in with the rest of our iden-tity and experience.

☐ Recommendations

In this section, we note our recommendations and ideas for future theory building, research, practice, and for social change. Our compilation re-flects those elements that come most strongly to our attention through the process of writing this manuscript.

For Theory

In terms of theory, we invite continued dialogue pertinent to a multidisciplinary and integrated model of women's anger, which articu-lates the place of that anger in women's and girls' overall emotional devel-opment. In our model formulation, we begin this process, and welcome further ideas on theory building and research in this vein from all corners of the behavioral, social, physical, and medical sciences.

One way of exploring models for women's anger involves continu-ing to examine the three integrated theories of emotion presented in Chap-ter 2 to determine their usefulness in specific application to women's an-ger. The present work provides a model of anger diversion as a way to look at how women *manage* the feeling. However, given the abundance of avail-able emotion theory and its relatively new arrival to the exploration of women's anger, more integrated models are needed for an overall view of anger in women as it develops and becomes a part of the sociocultural surround.

Both Lazarus' (1991) and Averill's (1997) models offer substantial possibilities as conceptual bases for understanding women's anger. Lazarus' theory of emotion encompasses cognitive, relational, and motivational aspects. It integrates physiological information and acknowledges the learned backdrop of cognitive appraisals that arise from family, socializa-tion, and culture. However, appraisal becomes the focal point of the theory and perhaps leaves the details of socialization and cultural influences un-specified. Averill offers an even more complex model than does Lazarus, relating elements of biological and social potentials with temperament, traits, intelligence, emotional rules and roles, current situational influences, and actual emotional responses. We find Averill's concepts of emotional rules and roles to be exceptionally useful, but the overall model is somewhat cumbersome, and it is hard to distinguish between some of the levels of the theory (see discussion and Figure 2, Chapter 2).

The model that we see as the best candidate for "fleshing out" a theory of women's anger would be Markus and Kitayama's (1994) cultural model of emotion. It fits well with feminist conceptualizations that the majority of gendered behavior is acquired via socialization and culture, although it does not negate biological responses involved in emotion or the evolutionary adaptability of emotion. The elaboration of the components of anger, from core cultural beliefs to social-psychological processes and then through individual realities and habitual emotional tendencies, provides a rich and complex analysis of women's anger in context. The addition of a developmental component could strengthen the model even further and show the intricacies embedded in intrapsychic response to interpsychic emotion variables.

We further suggest that it is of theoretical interest to examine the role of anger (and perhaps other emotions as well) in all models of identity development. A great number of such models taking shape over the past 20 years reflect interest in gay and lesbian identity development (Cass, 1979), ethnic and minority identity development (Atkinson, Morten, & Sue, 1993; Casas & Pytluk, 1995; Cross, 1971, 1995; Sodowsky, Kwan, & Pannu, 1995), White identity development (Helms, 1990), and of course the feminist identity development model (Downing & Roush, 1985) detailed previously. Many, but not all, of these models are linear stage models, in which an initial stage of conformity, acceptance of the status quo, or naivete precedes a period of turmoil, with questioning of earlier assumptions, beliefs, and social structures. The process eventually resolves through integration and synthesis with a new understanding of self and the social world. In such models, we hypothesize that the diversion of anger may be characteristic of earlier stages, and that the self-definitional benefits of anger come to the fore in the middle, more conflictual stages of these models. In the later stages, anger most likely assumes its adaptive role as a constructive marker for interpersonal injustice and instrumental action but is neither silenced (as in early stages) or strident (as may appropriately occur in the middle stages). Some theorists already acknowledge anger as a key component associated with changes in the middle stages of identity development (e.g., Cross, 1995; Ivey, 1995) but anger's potential role at other stages seems to have been ignored. If these theoretical propositions are substantiated, anger then becomes a common thread in our understanding of all persons' identity development, across such categories as gender, sexual orientation, and ethnicity. It stands to reason that if anger signals injustice, need, or blocked goals, the experience of it in relationships serves to bolster the realization of one's distinct identity, worthy of protection and articulation. As we *become* who we are, we are called to mark out our boundaries and let others know what we are and are not about. This process of refinement happens only if we experience ourselves as separate—and, yes, perhaps angry.

For Research

There is *always* more research to be done in such a complex area of psychology. We recommend more developmental reseach of women's anger that explores anger in older and elderly women, as virtually nothing has been written about this specific topic. Longitudinal and cohort sequential research on girls' and women's anger holds promise for benefiting this work, as cross-sectional samples (such as ours) confound development with generational and historical influences. Likewise, more research with increasingly diverse populations of women promises to refine, expand, and test the nascent themes we encountered in our own work regarding cultural, religious, and ethnic differences and similarities in anger experience and expression.

For purposes of both research and clinical practice, anger measures need to be developed using women and girls from multiple societies and ethnicities, with attention to both gender and cultural elements in their items and norms. Current instruments need to be refined and new instruments developed that have stronger theoretical or conceptual bases so that the constructs they are measuring become clear. Also, traditional conceptualizations of anger proneness and anger expression must be broadened to include the multiple and dynamic parts of women's intricate experiences with anger. For example, we assert that those most likely to suppress, internalize, or segment their experience of anger have less awareness available to answer questions about that part of themselves and thus underrespond. To address this likelihood, tests must tap the variables that accompany diverted anger—those pieces of experience that hide between the lines in the phenomenology of such experience.

Quantitative research on anger takes us only so far. Statistical differences on anger-measure scores reflect very little of life's experienced reality, and findings of no differences tend to shut down exploration of subtle meanings that may be important in the real world. We recommend additional qualitative, inductive studies of girls' and women's anger to remedy this situation, to plumb deeply into the varied nature of their relationship with this emotion. Most quantitative measures can only capture isolated individual behaviors or reactions and cannot adequately address the complexity of the interpersonal contexts in which anger arises. Qualitative methods appear better suited for examining dynamic and complex systems, in which meaning and context are paramount to understanding the phenomena involved.

Long-term studies of the effects of anger-related therapuetic interventions also deserve undertaking. Most outcome measures ignore the effects of therapy past 3, 6, or sometimes 12 months. In particular, verbal and physical cathartic techniques for anger work have not been adequately evaluated, particularly from a longitudinal perspective. The longer-term effects of women's anger work on their intimate relationships remain conspicuously absent in recent research literature. Likewise, some of the newer therapies that explicitly incorporate an emotion focus (e.g., Arauzo, Watson, & Hulgus, 1994) or use systemic and overtly feminist orientations have not been systematically evaluated for details regarding how any of these therapies might help give voice to womens' anger. Given the proven outcome effectiveness of established therapy models such as emotion-focused therapy (Greenberg & Johnson, 1988), it follows that research into newer therapies and therapeutic techniques for anger work could extend our understanding of how anger works its way into individual, relationship, and family healing.

For Practice

Our review of the treatment literature on current models for dealing with anger leads us to a number of recommendations for practice. First of all, we reiterate that anger work is complex, and that both therapy goals and techniques need to be individually tailored to each girl and woman.

Women and girls need to feel safe before exploring suppressed anger, and that safety includes not only emotional factors but environmental considerations as well. The first step in creating this safety involves providing the right amount of structure in session. The second pertains to ensuring that the practitioner and the woman or girl have adequately prepared those with whom she is in relationship for the changes she will be making in her anger expression. (It is important to recognize if significant others are not willing to accomodate changes, so as to avoid putting the client at risk.) For girls living with their families of origin, this may involve family-systems work centering on the negotiation of a new, more helpful, set of family rules; for couples in volatile relationships, systemic couples work is needed. The goal in involving significant others is to interrupt any reactionary intensification in the family's effort to enforce anger suppression as the client addresses anger issues and subsequently makes behavioral changes. Those women and girls with explosive anger or boundary difficulties need to have highly structured and well monitored outlets for their emotion, along with training in reappraisal, ownership of anger, and validation of their feelings overall. Explosion facilitates healing and clarity, if it is claimed, articulated, and treated with respect.

It is of utmost importance to address both sides of the anger "management" issue with every client. Most anger-related therapies focus solely on controlling the emotion and related behaviors. By adding a cathartic component to treatment, the highly relevant issue of women's *over*-controlled anger is addressed. However, again, catharsis alone is not likely to adequately empower a woman for optimal functionality in anger expression. It is the use of both types of skills, catharsis *and* management—appropriate, honest, anger communication—that achieves a healthy level of anger expression.

One way of individualizing one's approach to therapy would be to consider the readiness of each client to engage in the change process as it relates to her anger. A helpful model here, designed by Prochaska and Norcross (1994), identifies five stages of change with respect to therapeutic readiness. Women in the first stage, precontemplation, tend not to be aware of a problem or may deny an anger problem. In the second stage, contemplation, the woman likely demonstrates an awareness of anger issues but may not feel ready or able to make changes noticeable to others. Women in the third stage, preparation, test the waters of behavioral change. They may try out some new ways of expressing anger or interacting differently in their relationships and make real plans to carry out further change. In the action stage, visible behavioral changes begin to appear in relation to the client's anger issues. Significant others are likely to notice these changes, as they are externally observable. A woman in the last stage, maintenance, successfully makes transformations in the desired directions in her anger work and is challenged to prevent relapses to past, less growth-oriented behaviors. However, our experience suggests that once a woman reaches this point in her self-discovery, she has often experienced such a qualitative paradigm shift that "relapse" in the sense of a complete reversion to prechange levels of functioning is virtually impossible. Although women may revisit old behaviors in a brief and temporary way, their underlying awareness and understanding of themselves has fundamentally changed. As regards anger, there is often a new and permanent sense of ownership—that the relationship between self and anger is no longer separate or antagonistic. One befriends oneself in the experience of anger, rather than deserting oneself to the elements of diversion and social control.

The key to Prochaska and Norcross's (1994) highly flexible model involves matching therapeutic interventions with the stage of readiness of the client. Interventions may come from any variety of therapeutic schools, as long as they have some empirical validity. Assessment of readiness to change takes into account culture, gender, and safety factors. Of interest, some conceptual parallels emerge between Prochaska and Norcross's model and the stages of feminist, ethnic/minority, and gay/lesbian identity-development models. All contribute to the understanding of the internal upheaval involved in making paradigmatic personal change, whether claiming lost aspects of emotional life or disowned aspects of selfhood.

Those therapies that offer contextual ways of understanding clients also appear to be good candidates for working with girls' and women's anger. Systemic, family, and metaemotion-based therapies all fall into this category. A feminist framework easily blends with other specific theories, to add sensitivity to context and social conditioning. In general, feminist writers such as Miller and Surrey (1990) advocate work that would allow anger to be transformed into a vehicle for healing in relationships as well as for the individual. These writers also reflect on our cultural tendency to view anger as incompatible with love—and suggest we elevate anger to its rightful place in our intimate connections and see its beauty in protecting them. In a related vein, Francis and Pennebaker (1992) remind us that thwarting our spontaneous process of expression of thought, feeling, or other self-symbolism relates to increased stress and illness. Conversely, if we confront oppositional or negative feeling directly, we mitigate these potential damages.

This theme of interconnection (or continuity—between seeming opposites such as anger and love) shows in newer paradigms such as ecofeminism (Capra, 1996), which address social dynamics within the context of patriarchy. Ecofeminists view women's experiential knowledge as a source for ecological insight. Emphasis on the ability to embrace apparent opposites also emerges in Jung's theory as mentioned in Chapter 4. Schools of thought such as these tend to integrate mind and body, female with male, and self with other in way that promotes appreciation of the connectedness of constructs. Emotions, symptoms, diagnoses, and social forces weave themselves into a holistic pattern that respects all sides of an issue, all aspects of the anger experience, and multiple versions of reality.

For Social Change: Personal and Political Empowerment

Although some progress has been made in the feminist agenda over the past 30 years, and the voices of women and girls have been heard more often, we still need to hear more—and listen more to—the voice of female anger. This is the voice that clearly identifies insult, injustice, and discrimination as well as resistance (Brown, 1991, 1994) and change. As it is the most prohibited of female emotions, we must still rally to fight the fight for its place in the symphony of clear, powerful voices for the dismantlement of oppression and express a desire and a need for change on a larger cultural level, and to work for societal changes that benefit all of us through a reconceptualization of anger as a positive experience, helpful to us and our relationships, and a natural part of our beings.

In their discussion of reintegrating mind and body, a process that we see as very much akin to the development of a positive relationship between society and women's anger, Labouvie-Vief et al. (1995) express the scope of the changes that are needed for such a reconnection. They state, "At the cultural level, such reconstruction involves changes in the prevailing epistomologies and cosmologies of philosophy and science, as well as mythos-related fields such as literature, art, and religion. On a more concrete and action-oriented level, reconstruction also implies that such images support changes in political, social, and familial structures" (p. 252).

One of the factors that some of the women in our focus groups explicity recognize is that if there exists gender equity in income (in an intimate relationship), there exists gender equity in anger expression. Economic, educational, political, and social initiatives that assist women in attaining the same level of financial power as men may, in the long run, have liberating effects on anger expression. No longer operating from a "one-down" position, women feel more free to appropriately express their rage, frustration, or indignity when it arises.

Yet, we wholeheartedly acknowledge the delicate balancing act between this feminist agenda and the clinician's mandate to respect each woman's or girl's culture, worldview, and values, even if they do not reflect our own. We remember that the inclusion of diverse voices and respect for multiple perspectives makes up part of the feminist agenda as well. All parts of each woman deserve respect and attention.

In writing about feminist identity development, Downing and Roush (1985) speak of women learning to focus their energy toward a productive outcome. Perhaps nowhere else is there a more challenging arena in which to accomplish this than that of anger. This book includes a chronicle of the many ways in which the energy of women's anger is thwarted, choked, and twisted back on itself, preventing any possible gain. The authors conceive of the personal development of healthy anger experience and expression as an integrated part of individual empowerment and the continued use of that powerful anger as an agent for social change.

☐ A Feminist Process

In closing, we would like to share and celebrate the birth of this book with our readers. It happens that not only does this book use feminism as a theoretical base, but in the actual creation of the manuscript, a feminist process emerged. Worell and Johnson (1997) describe feminist process as one that *distributes both leadership and responsibility,* and we have shared such roles in different sections of the book, according to each of our strengths and expertise. Feminist process also *provides a structure for diversity and values all voices.* Although recognizing that we have been unable to include contributions from all possible diversities of women and girls, we make a concerted effort to sample a range of ages, ethnicities, religious backgrounds, and class memberships in our qualitative materials. Feminist process *involves decision making through consensus,* a method that we have consistently used, as a spontaneous outgrowth of our collective vision. Gaining consensus proved to be a challenging, time-consuming, but ultimately highly rewarding part of developing this book. There were days when we seemed at an impasse with conflicting feedback and unresolved concerns, but we have grown and gained tremendously through the benefits of this kind of process. *Honoring personal experience* is another hallmark of feminist process. Although none of us go into detail about our own lives, there is no denying that our personal experiences motivated us in this work, as well as serving as a filter for our interpretations. The personal experiences of the girls and women who shared their stories and perceptions speak to us in their own words. Finally, feminist process should *promote social change.* We hope this book is a contribution in the direction of continued dismantlement of patriarchy and the empowerment of women and men of all ages, cultural backgrounds, special needs, and affiliations.

Our contact with the substance of the book—the theories, the research, the girls and women who spoke—has changed us and our relationships within all our myriad roles. Perhaps each of us understands and experiences anger in ourselves and in others a little bit differently now, bringing a deeper appreciation of the rich value of women's anger to our being-in-the-world.

REFERENCES

Ainsworth, M. D. S., Bell, S. M., & Stayton, D. J. (1971). Individual differences in strange situation behavior of one-year-olds. In H. R. Schaffer (Ed.), *The origins of human social relations*. London: Academic Press.

Allgood-Merten, B., Lewinsohn, P. M., & Hops, H. (1990). Sex differences and adolescent depression. *Journal of Abnormal Psychology, 99*, 55–63.

American Association of University Women. (1991). *Shortchanging girls, shortchanging America*. Washington, DC: AAUW Educational Foundation.

American heritage dictionary, second college edition. (1982). Boston: Houghton-Mifflin.

American Psychiatric Association. (1993). Practice guidelines for eating disorders. *American Journal of Psychiatry, 150*, 207–228.

American Psychiatric Association. (1994). *Diagnostic and statistical manual of mental disorders* (4th ed.). Washington, DC: Author.

Anderson, G., Yasenik, L., & Ross, C. A. (1993). Dissociative experiences and disorders among women who identify themselves as sexual abuse survivors. *Child Abuse and Neglect, 17*, 677–686.

Aneshensel, C. S. (1992). Social stress: Theory and research. *Annual Review of Sociology, 18*, 15–38.

Arauzo, A. C., Watson, M., & Hulgus, J. (1994). The clinical uses of video therapy in the treatment of childhood sexual trauma survivors. *Journal of Child Sexual Abuse, 3*, 37–57.

Arnow, B., Kenardy, J., & Agras, W. S. (1995). The emotion eating scale: The development of a measure to assess coping with negative affect by eating. *International Journal of Eating Disorders, 18*, 79–90.

Atkinson, D. R., Morten, G., & Sue, D. W. (Eds.). (1993). *Counseling American minorities* (4th ed.). Madison, WI: Brown & Benchmark.

Averill, J. R. (1983). Studies on anger and aggression: Implications for theories of emotion. *American Psychologist, 38*, 1145–1160.

Averill, J. R. (1984). The acquisition of emotions during adulthood. In C. Z. Malatesta & C. E. Izard (Eds.), *Emotion in adult development* (pp. 23–43). Beverly Hills, CA: Sage.

Averill, J. R. (1994). In the eyes of the beholder. In P. Ekman & R. J. Davidson (Eds.), *The nature of emotion: Fundamental questions* (pp. 7–14). Oxford: Oxford University Press.

Averill, J. R. (1997). The emotions: An integrative approach. In R. Hogan, J. Johnson, & S. Briggs (Eds.), *Handbook of personality psychology* (pp. 513–543). San Diego, CA: Academic Press.

Bageley, C. (1979). Control of the emotions, remote stress, and the emergence of breast cancer. *Indian Journal of Clinical Psychology, 6*, 213–220.

223

Barbarin, O. A. (1993). Emotional and social development of African-American children. *Journal of Black Psychology, 19,* 381–390.

Bargad, A., & Hyde, J. S. (1991). Women's studies: A study of feminist identity development in women. *Psychology of Women Quarterly, 15,* 181–201.

Bartholomew, K., & Horowitz, L. M. (1991). Attachment styles among young adults: A test of a four category model. *Journal of Personality and Social Psychology, 61,* 226–244.

Beck, A. (1972). *Depression: Causes and treatment.* Philadelphia: University of Pennsylvania Press.

Beitchman, J. H., Kruidenier, B., Inglis, A., & Clegg, M. (1989). The children's self-report questionnaire: Factor score age trends and gender differences. *Journal of the American Academy of Child and Adolescent Psychiatry, 28,* 714–722.

Begley, T. M. (1994). Expressed and suppressed anger as predictors of health complaints. *Journal of Organizational Behavior, 15,* 503–516.

Berkowitz, L. (1990). On the formation and regulation of anger and aggression: A cognitive-neoassociationistic analysis. *American Psychologist, 45,* 494–503.

Bernardez, T. (1987). Women and anger: Cultural prohibitions and the feminine ideal. *Work in Progress No. 31.* Wellesley, MA: Stone Center Working Paper Series.

Bernardez-Bonesatti, T. (1978). Women and anger: Conflicts with aggression in contemporary women. *Journal of the American Medical Women's Association, 33,* 215–219.

Beutler, L. E., Engle, D., Oro-Beutler, M. E., Daldrup, R., & Meredith, K. (1986). Inability to express intense affect: A common link between depression and pain? *Journal of Consulting and Clinical Psychology, 54,* 752–759.

Beutler, L., Machado, P., Engle, D., & Mohr, D. (1993). Differential patient x treatment maintenance among cognitive, experiential, and self-directed psychotherapies. *Journal of Psychotherapy Integration, 3,* 15–30.

Biaggio, M. K., & Godwin, W. H. (1987). Relation of depression to anger and hostility constructs. *Psychological Reports, 6,* 87–90.

Birnbaum, D. W., & Croll, W. L. (1984). The etiology of children's stereotypes about sex differences in emotionality. *Sex Roles, 10,* 677–691.

Blechman, E. A., & Culhane, S. E. (1993). Aggressive, depressive, and prosocial coping with affective challenges in early adolescence. *Journal of Early Adolescence, 13,* 361–382.

Bleiker, E. M. A., Van Der Ploeg, H. M., Mook, J., & Kleijn, W. C. (1993). Anxiety, anger, and depression in elderly women. *Psychological Reports, 72,* 567–574.

Block, J. (1973). Conceptions of sex role: Some cross-cultural and longitudinal perspectives. *American Psychologist, 28,* 512–526.

Bohart, A. (1980). Toward a cognitive theory of catharsis. *Psychotherapy: Theory, Research, and Practice, 17,* 192–201.

Bowlby, J. (1973). *Attachment and loss: Separation, anxiety and anger.* New York: Basic Books.

Bowlby, J. (1988). *A secure base: Parent-child attachment and healthy human development.* New York: Basic Books.

Brabeck, M., & Brown, L. (1997). Feminist theory and psychological practice. In J. Worell & N. G. Johnson (Eds.), *Shaping the future of feminist psychology* (pp. 15–36). Washington, DC: American Psychological Association.

Brody, L. R. (1985). Gender differences in emotional development: A review of theories and research. *Journal of Personality, 53,* 102–149.

Brody, L. R., & Hall, J. A. (1993). Gender and emotion. In M. Lewis & J. M. Haviland, (Eds.), *Handbook of emotions* (pp. 447–460). New York: Guilford Press.

Brody, L. R., Hay, D. H., & Vandewater, E. (1990). Gender, gender role identity, and children's reported feeling toward the same and opposite sex. *Sex Roles, 23,* 363–387.

Bromberger, J. T., & Matthews, K. A. (1996). A "feminine" model of vulnerability to depressive symptoms: A longitudinal investigation of middle-aged women. *Journal of Personality and Social Psychology, 70,* 591–598.

Bronstein, P., Fitzgerald, M., Briones, M., Pieniadz, J., & D'Ari, A. (1993). Family emotional expressiveness as a predictor of early adolescent social and psychological adjustment. *Journal of Early Adolescence, 13,* 448–471.

Brown, L. (1989). Narratives of relationship: The development of a care orientation in girls 7 to 16. As cited in L. Stern (1991). Disavowing the self in female adolescence. *Women and Therapy, 11,* 105–117.

Brown, L. (1991). Telling a girl's life: Self-authorization as a form of resistance. *Women and Therapy, 11,* 71–86.

Brown, L. M. (1994, November). *Educating the resistance: Encouraging girls' strong feelings and critical voices.* Paper presented at the 20th Annual Conference of the Association of Moral Education, Calgary/Banff, Canada.

Brown, L. M. (1995, August). *Adolescent girls, class, and the cultures of femininity.* Paper presented at the Annual Meeting of the American Psychological Association, New York.

Brown, L. M. (1998). *Raising their voices: The politics of girls' anger.* Cambridge, MA: Harvard University Press.

Brown, L. M., & Gilligan, C. (1992). *Meeting at the crossroads: Women's psychology and girls' development.* Cambridge, MA: Harvard University Press.

Buck, R. (1982). Spontaneous and symbolic nonverbal behavior and the ontogeny of communication. In R. S. Feldman (Ed.), *Development of nonverbal behavior in children* (pp. 29–62). New York: Springer-Verlag.

Bugenhagen, R. D. (1990). Experiential constructions in Mangap-Mbula. *Australian Journal of Linguistics, 10,* 183–216.

Burke, S. G. (1992). Chronic fatigue syndrome and women: Can therapy help? *Social Work, 37,* 35–39.

Buss, A. H., & Durkee, A. (1957). An inventory for assessing different kinds of hostility. *Journal of Consulting Psychology, 21,* 343–349.

Butler, J. (1991). Imitation and gender insubordination. In D. Fuss (Ed.), *Inside/out: Lesbian theories, gay theories.* New York: Routledge.

Cacioppo, J. T., Klein, D. J., Berntson, G. G., & Hatfield, E. (1993). The psychophysiology of emotion. In M. Lewis & J. M. Haviland (Eds.), *Handbook of emotion* (pp. 119–142). New York: Guilford Press.

Campos, J. J., Mumme, D. L., Kermoian, R., & Campos, R. G. (1994). Commentary: A functionalist perspective on the nature of emotion. In N. A. Fox (Ed.), The development of emotion regulation: Biological and behavioral considerations (pp. 284–303). *Monographs of the Society for Research in Child Development, 59* (2–3, Serial No. 240).

Camras, L. A., Malatesta, C., & Izard, C. E. (1991). The development of facial expressions in infancy. In R. S. Feldman & B. Rime (Eds.), *Fundamentals of nonverbal behavior.* Cambridge: Cambridge University Press.

Capra, F. (1996). *The web of life.* New York: Anchor.

Casas, J. M., & Pytluk, S. D. (1995). Hispanic identity development: Implications for research and practice. In J. G. Ponterotto, J. M. Casas, L. A. Suzuki, & C. M. Alexander (Eds.), *Handbook of multicultural counseling* (pp. 155–180). Thousand Oaks, CA: Sage.

Cass, V. C. (1979). Homosexual identity formation: A theoretical model. *Journal of Homosexuality, 4,* 219–235.

Cassidy, J. (1994). Emotion regulation: Influences of attachment relationships. In N. A. Fox (Ed.), The development of emotion regulation: Biological and behavioral considerations (pp. 228–249). *Monographs of the Society for Research in Child Development, 59* (2–3, Serial No. 240).

Chandler, G. M. (1993). A hypnotic intervention for anger reduction and shifting perceptual predispositions. *Journal of Mental Health Counseling, 15,* 200–205.

Chodorow, N. (1978). *The reproduction of mothering.* Berkeley: University of California Press.

Cole, P. M., Zahn-Waxler, C., & Smith, K. D. (1994). Expressive control during a disappointment: Variations related to preschoolers' behavior problems. *Developmental Psychology, 30,* 835–846.

Collier, H. V. (1982). *Counseling women: A guide for therapists.* New York: Free Press.

Cook, W. W., & Medley, D. M. (1954). Proposed hostility and pharisaic-virtue scales for the MMPI. *Journal of Applied Psychology, 38,* 414–418.

Cooper, M. L., Shaver, P. R., & Collins, N. L. (1998). Attachment styles, emotion regulation, and adjustment in adolescence. *Journal of Personality and Social Psychology, 74,* 1380–1397.

Cornelius, R. R. (1984). A rule model of adult emotional expression. In C. Z. Malatesta & C. E. Izard (Eds.), *Emotion in adult development* (p. 213–233). Beverly Hills, CA: Sage.

Cottington, E. M., Matthews, K. A., Talbott, E., & Kuller, L. H. (1986). Occupational stress, suppressed anger, and hypertension. *Psychosomatic Medicine, 48,* 249–260.

Cox, D. L. (1997). Anger suppression as a vehicle for gender socialization in girls: A developmental study. (Doctoral dissertation, Texas Woman's University, 1996). *Dissertation Abstracts International, 57* (12–13), 7756.

Crawford, J., Kippax, S., Onyx, J., Gault, U., & Benton, P. (1992). *Emotion and gender.* London: Sage.

Cross, S. E., & Madson, L. (1997). Models of the self: Self-construals and gender. *Psychological Bulletin, 122,* 5–37.

Cross, W. E., Jr. (1971). The Negro-to-Black conversion experience: Towards a psychology of Black liberation. *Black World, 20,* 13–27.

Cross, W. E., Jr. (1995). The psychology of nigrescence: Revising the Cross model. In J. G. Ponterotto, J. M. Casas, L. A. Suzuki, & C. M. Alexander (Eds.), *Handbook of multicultural counseling* (pp. 93–122). Thousand Oaks, CA: Sage.

Culbertson, F. M. (1997). Depression and gender: An international review. *American Psychologist, 52,* 25–31.

Culkin, J., & Perotto, R. S. (1985). Assertiveness factors and depression in a sample of college women. *Psychological Reports, 57,* 1015–1020.

Davidson, R. J. (1993). The neuropyschology of emotion and affective style. In M. Lewis & J. M. Haviland (Eds.), *Handbook of emotion* (pp. 143–154). New York: Guilford Press.

Dawson, G. (1994). Frontal electroencephalographic correlates of individual differences in emotion expression in infants: A brain systems perspective on emotion. In N. A. Fox (Ed.). The development of emotion regulation: Biological and behavioral considerations (pp. 135–151). *Monographs of the Society for Research in Child Development, 59* (2–3, Serial No. 240).

Debold, E., Wilson, M., & Malave, I. (1993). *Mother-daughter revolution.* New York: Addison-Wesley.

Denham, S. A., Zoller, D., & Couchoud, E. A. (1994). Socialization of preschoolers' emotion understanding. *Developmental Psychology, 30,* 928–936.

Deutsch, H. (1944). *Psychology of women* (Vol. 1). New York: Grune & Stratton.

Dick, C. L., Bland, R. C., & Newman, S. C. (1994). Panic disorder. *Acta Psychiatrica Scandanivica* (Suppl. 376), 45–53.

Dodge, K. A. (1991). Emotion and social information processing. In J. Garber & K. A. Dodge (Eds.), *The development of emotional regulation and dysregulation* (pp. 159–181). Cambridge: Cambridge University Press.

Downing, N. E., & Roush, K. L. (1985). From passive acceptance to active commitment: A model of feminist identity development for women. *The Counseling Psychologist, 13,* 695–709.

Droppelman, P. G., Thomas, S. P., & Wilt, D. (1995). Anger in women as an emerging issue in MCN. *MCN: American Journal of Maternal Child Nursing, 20,* 85–94.

Dunn, J., & Brown, J. (1994). Affect expression in the family, children's understanding of emotions, and their interactions with others. *Merrill-Palmer Quarterly, 40,* 120–137.

Durel, L. A., Carver, C. S., Spitzer, S. B., Llabre, M. M., Weintraub, J. K., Saab, P. G., & Schneiderman, N. (1989). Associations of blood pressure with self-report measures of anger and hostility among black and white men and women. *Health Psychology, 8,* 557–575.

Durkin, K. (1995). *Developmental social psychology: From infancy to old age.* Cambridge, MA: Blackwell Publishers.

Earls, F. (1987). Sex differences in psychiatric disorders: Origins and developmental influences. *Psychiatric Developments, 1,* 1–23.

Ebata, A. (1987). A longitudinal study of psychological distress during early adolescence. Unpublished doctoral dissertation, Pennsylvania State University. In L. Stern (1991). Disavowing the self in female adolescence. *Women and Therapy, 11,* 105–117.

Eibl-Eibesfeldt, I. (1980). Strategies of social interaction. In R. Plutchik & H. Kellerman (Eds.), *Emotion: Theory, research, and experience: Vol. 1. Theories of emotion* (pp. 57–80). New York: Academic Press.

Ekman, P., & Davidson, R. J. (1994). *The nature of emotion: Fundamental questions.* Oxford: Oxford University Press.

Ekman, P. (1978). Facial signs. In T. Sebeok (Ed.), *Sight, sound and sense.* Bloomington, IN: Indiana University Press.

Ekman, P. (1994). All emotions are basic. In P. Ekman & R. J. Davidson (Eds.), *The nature of emotion: Fundamental questions* (pp. 15–19). Oxford: Oxford University Press.

Ekman, P., & Oster, H. (1979). Facial expressions of emotion. *Annual Review of Psychology, 30,* 527–554.

Ellsworth, P. C. (1994). Sense, culture, and sensibility. In S. Kitayama & H. R. Markus (Eds.), *Emotion and culture: Empirical studies of mutual influence* (pp. 23–50). Washington, DC: American Psychological Association.

Emerson, R., & Messinger, S. (1977). The micro-politics of trouble. *Social Problems, 25,* 121–134.

Epstein, J. N., Saunders, B. E., Kilpatrick, D. G., & Resnick, H. S. (1998). PTSD as a mediator between childhood rape and alcohol use in adult women. *Child Abuse and Neglect, 22,* 223–234.

Erikson, E. H. (1963). *Childhood and society.* New York: Norton.

Evans, D. R., & Strangeland, M. (1971). Development of the Reaction Inventory to measure anger. *Psychological Reports, 29,* 412–414.

Faber, S., & Burns, J. (1996). Anger management style, degree of expressed anger, and gender influence on cardiovascular recovery from interpersonal harassment. *Journal of Behavioral Medicine, 19,* 31–53.

Fava, M., Rappe, S. M., West, J., & Herzog, D. B. (1995). Anger attacks in eating disorders. *Psychiatry Research, 56,* 205–212.

Field, T., & Walden, T. A. (1982). Production and discrimination of facial expressions by preschool children. *Child Development, 53,* 1299–1311.

Fischer, P. C., Smith, R. J., Leonard, E., Fuquo, D. R., Campbell, J. L., & Masters, M. A. (1993). Sex differences on affective dimensions: Continuing examination. *Journal of Counseling and Development, 71,* 440–443.

Fitness, J., & Fletcher, G. J. O. (1993). Love, hate, anger, and jealousy in close relationships: A prototype and cognitive appraisal analysis. *Journal of Personality and Social Psychology, 65,* 942–958.

Fitzgerald, L. F. (1990). Sexual harassment: The definition and measurement of a construct. In M. Paludi (Ed.), *Ivory power: Sexual harassment on campus* (pp. 21–44). Albany, NY: State University of New York Press.

Fox, N. A. (1994). Dynamic cerebral process underlying emotion regulation. In N. A. Fox (Ed.), The development of emotion regulation: Biological and behavioral considerations (pp. 152–166). *Monographs of the Society for Research in Child Development, 59* (2–3, Serial No. 240).

Francis, M., & Pennebaker, J. (1992). Putting stress into words: The impact of writing on physiological, absentee, and self-reported emotional well-being measures. *American Journal of Health Promotion, 6,* 280–287.

Frank, E. F., Carpenter, L. L., & Kupfer, D. J. (1988). Sex differences in recurrent depression: Are there any that are significant? *American Journal of Psychiatry, 145,* 41–45.

Freedman-Doan, C. R., Arbreton, A. J. A., Harold, R. D., & Eccles, J. S. (1993). Looking forward to adolescence: Mothers' and fathers' expectations for affective and behavioral change. *Journal of Early Adolescence, 13,* 472–502.

Frijda, N. H., Kuipers, P., & ter Schure, E. (1989). Relations among emotion, appraisal, and emotional action readiness. *Journal of Personality and Social Psychology, 57,* 212–228.

Frijda, N. H., & Mesquita, B. (1994). The social roles and functions of emotions. In S. Kitayama & H. R. Markus (Eds.), *Emotion and culture: Empirical studies of mutual influence* (pp. 51–88). Washington, DC: American Psychological Association.

Galati, D., Scherer, K. R., & Ricci-Bitti, P. E. (1997). Voluntary facial expression of emotion: Comparing congenitally blind with normally sighted encoders. *Journal of Personality and Social Psychology, 73,* 1363–1379.

Geen, R. G. (1990). *Human aggression.* Pacific Grove, CA: Brooks/Cole.

Georges, E. (1995). A cultural and historical perspective on confession. In J. W. Pennebaker (Ed.), *Emotion, disclosure, and health* (pp. 11–24). Washington, DC: American Psychological Association.

Gilligan, C. (1982). *In a different voice.* Cambridge, MA: Harvard University Press.

Gilligan, C. (1984). *New perspectives on female adolescent development.* Unpublished manuscript, Harvard University, Cambridge, MA.

Gilligan, C. (1990). Joining the resistance: Psychology, politics, girls and women. *Michigan Quarterly Review, 29,* 501–536.

Gilligan, C. (1991). Women's psychological development: Implications for psychotherapy. *Women and Therapy, 11,* 5–31.

Gilligan, C., Lyons, N. P., & Hammer, T. (1990). *Making connections: The relational worlds of adolescent girls at Emma Willard School.* Cambridge, MA: Harvard University Press.

Gjinde, P., Block, J., & Block, J. (1988). Depressive symptoms and personality during late adolescence: Gender differences in the externalization-internalization of symptom expression. *Journal of Abnormal Psychology, 97,* 475–486.

Goldman, L., & Haaga, D. A. F. (1995). Depression and the experience and expression of anger in marital and other relationships. *Journal of Nervous and Mental Disease, 183,* 505–509.

Goldstein, H. S., Edelberg, R., Meier, C. F., & Davis, L. (1989). Relationship of expressed anger to forearm muscle vascular resistance. *Journal of Psychosomatic Research, 33,* 497–504.

Goleman, D. (1995). *Emotional intelligence.* New York: Bantam Books.

Goodman, L. A., Dutton, M. A., & Harris, M. (1997). The relationship between violence dimensions and symptom severity among homeless, mentally ill women. *Journal of Traumatic Stress, 10,* 51–70.

Goodrich, T. J., Rampage, C., Ellman, B., & Hallstead, K. (1988). *Feminist family therapy: A casebook.* New York: Norton.

Gormally, J., Black, S., Daston, S., & Rardin, D. (1982). The assessment of binge eating severity among obese persons. *Addictive Behaviors, 7,* 47–55.

Gottman, J. M., Katz, L. F., & Hooven, C. (1996). Parental meta-emotion philosophy and the emotional life of families: Theoretical models and preliminary data. *Journal of Family Psychology, 10,* 243–268.

Gray, J. A. (1982). Precis of the neuropsychology of anxiety. *The Behavioral and Brain Sciences, 5,* 464–534.

Graziano, W. G., & Bryant, W. H. M. (1998). Self-monitoring and the self-attribution of positive emotions. *Journal of Personality and Social Psychology, 74,* 250–261.

Greenberg, L. S., & Johnson, S. M. (1988). *Emotionally focused couples therapy.* New York: Guilford.

Greenberg, L. S., & Safran, J. D. (1989). Emotion in psychotherapy. *American Psychologist, 44,* 19–29.

Greer, S., & Watson, M. (1985). Towards a psychobiological model of cancer: Psychological considerations. *Social Science and Medicine, 20,* 773–777.

Grilo, C. M., Shiffman, S., & Wing, R. R. (1989). Relapse crises and coping among dieters. *Journal of Consulting and Clinical Psychology, 57,* 488–495.

Gross, J. J. (1998). Antecedent- and response-focused emotion regulation: Divergent consequences for experience, expression, and physiology. *Journal of Personality and Social Psychology, 74,* 224–237.

Gross, J. J., & John, O. P. (1997). Revealing feelings: Facets of emotional expressivity in self-reports, peer ratings, and behavior. *Journal of Personality and Social Psychology, 72,* 435–448.

Gross, J. J., & John, O. P. (1998). Mapping the domain of expressivity: Multimethod evidence for a hierarchical model. *Journal of Personality and Social Psychology, 74,* 170–191.

Grove, W., & Herb, T. (1974). Stress and mental illness among the young. *Social Forces, 53,* 256–265.

Gueldner, S. H., Butler, S., Ray, J. K., Rickets, J. L., & Schlotzhauer, P. (1994). A profile of mood in ambulatory nursing home residents. *Archives of Psychiatric Nursing, 8,* 320–325.

Guerney, B. G. (1977). *Relationship enhancement.* San Francisco: Jossey-Bass.

Harmon-Jones, E., & Allen, J. B. (1998). Anger and frontal brain activity: EEG asymmetry consistent with approach motivation despite negative affect valence. *Journal of Personality and Social Psychology, 74,* 1310–1316.

Harris, L., Blum, R. W., & Resnick, M. (1991). Teen females in Minnesota: A portrait of quiet disturbance. *Women and Therapy, 11,* 119–135.

Harris, P. L. (1989). *Children and emotion: The development of psychological understanding.* Oxford: Blackwell Publishers.

Harvey, L., & Pease, K. (1987). The lifetime prevalence of custodial sentences. *British Journal of Criminology, 27,* 311–315.

Hathaway, S. R., & McKinley, J. C. (1943). *Minnesota Multiphasic Personality Inventory.* Minneapolis: University of Minnesota.

Hazan, C., & Shaver, P. (1987). Romantic love conceptualized as an attachment process. *Journal of Personality and Social Psychology, 25,* 511–524.

Heidensohn, F. M. (1991). Women as perpetrators and victims of crime: A sociological perspective. *British Journal of Psychiatry, 158* (Suppl. 10), 50–54.

Heidrich, S. (1994). The self, health, and depression in elderly women. *Western Journal of Nursing Research, 16,* 544–555.

Heise, D. R., & O'Brien, J. (1993). Emotion expression in groups. In M. Lewis & J. M. Haviland (Eds.), *Handbook of emotions* (pp. 489–498). New York: Guilford Press.

Helms, J. E. (1990). Toward a model of White racial identity development. In J. E. Helms (Ed.), *Black and White racial identity development: Theory, research, and practice* (pp. 49–66). Westport, CT: Greenwood.

Henry, K. A., & Cohen, C. (1983). The role of labeling processes in diagnosing borderline personality disorder. *American Journal of Psychiatry, 140*, 1527–1529.

Herzog, D. B. (1984). Are anorectics and bulimics depressed? *American Journal of Psychiatry, 141*, 1594–1597.

Hetherington, M. M., & Burnett, L. (1994). Aging and the pursuit of slimness: Dietary restraint and weight satisfaction in elderly women. *British Journal of Clinical Psychology, 33*, 391–400.

Hokanson, J. E. (1970). Psychophysiological evaluation of the catharsis hypothesis. In E. Megaree & J. E. Hokanson (Eds.), *The Dynamics of Aggression*. New York: Harper & Row.

Horney, K. (1926). The flight from womanhood. *International Journal of Psychoanalysis, 7*, 324–339.

Ivey, A. E. (1995). Psychotherapy as liberation: Toward specific skills and strategies in multicultural counseling and therapy. In J. G. Ponterotto, J. M. Casas, L. A. Suzuki, & C. M. Alexander (Eds.), *Handbook of multicultural counseling* (pp. 53–72). Thousand Oaks, CA: Sage.

Izard, C. E. (1991). Perspectives on emotions in psychotherapy. In J. D. Safran & L. S. Greenberg (Eds.), *Emotion, psychotherapy and change* (pp. 280–289). New York: Guilford.

Izard, C. E. (1993). Organizational and motivational functions of discrete emotions. In M. Lewis & J. M. Haviland (Eds.), *Handbook of emotions* (pp. 631–642). New York: Guilford.

Izard, C. E. (1994). Innate and universal facial expressions: Evidence from developmental and cross-cultural research. *Psychological Bulletin, 115*, 288–299.

Izard, C. E., & Malatesta, C. Z. (1987). Perspectives on emotional development I: Differential emotions theory of early emotional development. In J. D. Osofsky (Ed.), *Handbook of infant development*. New York: Wiley.

Jack, D. (1987). Silencing the self: The power of social imperatives in female depression. In R. Formanek & A. Gurian (Eds.), *Women and depression: A lifespan perspective* (pp. 161–181). New York: Springer.

Jack, D. C. (1991). *Silencing the self: Women and depression*. Cambridge, MA: Harvard University Press.

Jack, D. C. (in press). Silencing the self: Inner dialogues and outer realities. In T. E. Joiner & J. C. Coyne (Eds.), *Recent advances in interpersonal approaches to depression*. Washington, DC: American Psychological Association.

Jack, D. C., & Dill, D. (1992). The Silencing the Self Scale: Schemas of intimacy associated with depression in women. *Psychology of Women Quarterly, 16*, 97–106.

Jacobs, G. A., & Blumer, C. H. (1985). Development of a pediatric anger expression scale. Paper presented at the meeting of Social and Behavioral Medicine, New Orleans, LA. In J. H. Kashani, L. A. Canfield, S. M. Soltys, & J. C. Reid (1995). Psychiatric inpatient children's family perceptions and anger expression. *Journal of Emotional and Behavioral Disorders, 3*, 13–18.

James, W. (1890). *The principles of psychology*. New York: Holt.

Jansen, M. A., & Muenz, L. R. (1984). A retrospective study of personality variables associated with fibrocystic disease and breast cancer. *Journal of Psychosomatic Research, 28*, 35–42.

Jaycox, L., & Repetti, R. L. (1993). Conflict in families and the psychological adjustment of preadolescent children. *Journal of Family Psychology, 7*, 344–355.

Johnson, S. (1996). *The practice of emotionally focused marital therapy: Creating connection*. New York: Brunner/Mazel.

Johnson, S., & Talitman, E. (1997). Predictors of success in emotionally focused marital therapy. *Journal of Marital and Family Therapy, 23*, 135–152.

Johnson, S., & Williams-Keeler, L. (1998). Creating healing relationships for couples dealing with trauma: The use of emotionally focused marital therapy. *Journal of Marital and Family Therapy, 24*, 25–40.

Jones, M. B., & Peacock, M. K. (1992). Self-reported anger in adolescents. *Health Values: The Journal of Health Behavior, Education, and Promotion, 16,* 11–19.

Jones, M. B., Peacock, M. K., & Christopher, J. (1992). Self-reported anger in black high school adolescents. *Journal of Adolescent Health, 13,* 461–465.

Jordan, J. V., Kaplan, A. G., Miller, J. B., Stiver, I. P., & Surrey, J. L. (1991). *Women's growth in connection: Writings from the Stone Center.* New York: Guilford Press.

Jorgensen, R. S., & Houston, B. K. (1986). Family history of hypertension, personality patterns, and cardiovascular reactivity to stress. *Psychosomatic Medicine, 48,* 102–117.

Kandel, D., & Davies, M. (1982). Epidemiology of depressive mood in adolescents. *Archives of General Psychiatry, 39,* 1205–1212.

Keck, P. E., Pope, H. G., Hudson, J. I., McElroy, S. L., Yurgelun-Todd, D., & Hundert, E. M. (1990). A controlled study of phenomenology and family history in outpatients with bulimia nervosa. *Comprehensive Psychiatry, 31,* 257–283.

Keinan, G., Ben-Zur, H., Zilka, M., & Carel, R. (1992). Anger in or out, which is healthier? An attempt to reconcile inconsistent findings. *Psychology and Health, 7,* 83–98.

Kellerman, H. (1980). An epigenetic theory of emotions in early development. In R. Plutchik & H. Kellerman (Eds.), *Emotion: Theory, research, and experience: Vol. 2. Emotions in early development* (pp. 315–350). New York: Academic Press.

Kemp, S., & Strongman, K. T. (1995). Anger theory and management: A historical analysis. *American Journal of Psychology, 108,* 397–417.

Kenny, M. E., Moilanen, D. L., Lomax, R., & Brabeck, M. M. (1993). Contributions of parental attachments to view of self and depressive symptoms among early adolescents. *Journal of Early Adolescence, 13,* 408–430.

Kessler, R. C., McGonagle, K. A., & Zhao, S. (1994). Lifetime and 12–month prevalence of DSM-III-R psychiatric disorders in the United States: Results from the National Comorbidity Survey. *Archives of General Psychiatry, 51,* 8–19.

King, C. R. (1990). Parallels between neurasthenia and premenstrual syndrome. *Women and Health, 15,* 1–23.

King, L. A. (1998). Ambivalence over emotional expression and reading emotions in situations and faces. *Journal of Personality and Social Psychology, 74,* 753–762.

Kitayama, S., & Markus, H. R. (1994). Introduction to cultural psychology and emotion research. In S. Kitayama & H. R. Markus (Eds.), *Emotion and culture: Empirical studies of mutual influence* (pp. 1–22). Washington, DC: American Psychological Association.

Klinnert, M. D., Campos, J. J., Sorce, J. F., Emde, R. N., & Svejda, M. (1980). Emotions as behavior regulators: Social referencing in infancy. In R. Plutchik & H. Kellerman (Eds.), *Emotion: Theory, research, and experience: Vol. 2. Emotions in early development* (pp. 57–86). New York: Academic Press.

Kloosterman, P. (1990). Attributions, performance following failure, and motivation in mathematics. In E. Fennema & G. C. Leder (Eds.), *Mathematics and gender.* New York: Teachers College Press.

Knight, R. G., Ross, R. A., Collins, J. I., & Parmenter, S. A. (1985). Some norms, reliability, and preliminary validity data for an S-R inventory of anger: The Subjective Anger Scale (SAS). *Personality and Individual Differences, 6,* 331–339.

Kohut, H. (1971). *The analysis of the self.* New York: International Universities Press.

Kopper, B. A., & Epperson, D. L. (1991). Women and anger: Sex and sex-role comparisons in the expression of anger. *Psychology of Women Quarterly, 15,* 7–14.

Kring, A. M., & Gordon, A. H. (1998). Sex differences in emotion: Expression, experience, and physiology. *Journal of Personality and Social Psychology, 74,* 686–703.

Kune, G. A., Kune, S., Watson, L. F., & Bahnson, C. B. (1991). Personality as a risk factor in large bowel cancer: Data from the Melbourne colorectal cancer study. *Psychological Medicine, 21,* 29–41.

Labouvie-Vief, G., Orwoll, L., & Manion, M. (1995). Narratives of mind, gender, and the life course. *Human Development, 38,* 239–257.

Lang, P. J. (1983). Cognition in emotion: Concept and action. In C. Izard, J. Kagan, & R. Zajonc (Eds.), *Emotion, cognition and behavior* (pp. 192–226). New York: Cambridge University Press.

Lazarus, R. S. (1991). Progress on a cognitive-motivational-relational theory of emotion. *American Psychologist, 46,* 819–834.

Lazarus, R. S., Averill, J. R., & Opton, E. M., Jr. (1970). Toward a cognitive theory of emotions. In M. Arnold (Ed.), *Feelings and emotions* (pp. 207–232). San Diego, CA: Academic Press.

Lemkau, J. P., & Landau, C. (1986). The "selfless syndrome": Assessment and treatment considerations. *Psychotherapy, 23,* 227–233.

Lerman, H. (1996). *Pigeon-holing women's misery: A historical and critical analysis of the psychodiagnosis of women in the twentieth century.* New York: Basic Books.

Lerner, H. (1985). *The dance of anger.* New York: Harper & Row.

Leserman, J., Li, Z., Drossman, D. A., & Hu, Y. J. B. (1998). Selected symptoms associated with sexual and physical abuse history among female patients with gastrointestinal disorders: The impact on subsequent health care visits. *Psychological Medicine, 28,* 417–425.

Lester, D. (1989). Relationship between locus of control and depression mediated by anger toward others. *Journal of Social Psychology, 129,* 413–414.

Levenson, R. W. (1988). Emotion and the autonomic nervous system: A prospectus for research on autonomic specificity. In H. Wagner (Ed.), *Social psychophysiology and emotion: Theory and clinical applications* (pp. 17–42). London: Wiley.

Levenson, R. W. (1992). Autonomic nervous system differences among emotions. *Psychological Science, 3,* 23–27.

Lewis, H. B. (1983). *Freud and modern psychology.* New York: Plenum Press.

Lewis, M. (1993). The emergence of human emotions. In M. Lewis & J. M. Haviland (Eds.), *Handbook of emotion* (pp. 223–236). New York: Guilford Press.

Liddle, H. A. (1994). The anatomy of emotions in family therapy with adolescents. *Journal of Adolescent Research, 9,* 120–157.

Lunbeck, E. (1987). A new generation of women: Progressive psychiatrists and the hypersexual female. *Feminist Studies, 13,* 513–543.

Magai, C., Distel, N., & Liker, R. (1995). Emotion socialization, attachment, and patterns of adult emotional traits. *Cognition and Emotion, 9,* 461–481.

Main, M., & Solomon, J. (1986). Discovery of a disorganized disoriented attachment pattern. In T. B. Brazelton & M. W. Yogman (Eds.), *Affective development in infancy.* Norwood, NJ: Ablex.

Malatesta-Magai, C. (1991). Development of emotion expression during infancy: General course and patterns of individual difference. In J. Garber & K. A. Dodge (Eds.), *The development of emotional regulation and dysregulation* (pp. 49–68). Cambridge: Cambridge University Press.

Manassis, K., & Kalman, E. (1990). Anorexia resulting from fear of vomiting in four adolescent girls. *Canadian Journal of Psychiatry, 35,* 548–550.

Marion, M. (1994). Encouraging the development of responsible anger management in young children. *Early Child Development and Care, 97,* 155–163.

Markus, H. R., & Kitayama, S. (1991). Culture and the self: Implications for cognition, emotion and motivation. *Psychological Review, 98,* 224–253.

Markus, H. R., & Kitayama, S. (1994). The cultural shaping of emotion: A conceptual framework. In S. Kitayama & H. R. Markus (Eds.), *Emotion and culture: Empirical studies of mutual influence* (pp. 307–338). Washington, DC: American Psychological Association.

Martin, R., & Watson, D. (1997). Style of anger expression and its relation to daily experience. *Personality and Social Psychology Bulletin, 23,* 285–294.

Maser, J. D., & Dinges, N. (1992–1993). Comorbidity: Meaning and uses in cross-cultural clinical research. *Culture, Medicine, and Psychiatry, 16*, 409–425.

Masters, J. C. (1991). Strategies and mechanisms for the personal and social control of emotion. In J. Garber & K. A. Dodge (Eds.), *The development of emotional regulation and dysregulation* (pp. 182–207). Cambridge: Cambridge University Press.

Matheson, J. (1992). Working with adolescent girls in a residential treatment centre. *Journal of Child and Youth Care, 7*, 31–39.

Mayer, J. D., Salovey, P., Gomberg-Kaufman, S., & Blainey, K. (1991). A broader conception of mood experience. *Journal of Personality and Social Psychology, 60*, 100–111.

McClure, B. A., Miller, G. A., & Russo, T. J. (1992). Conflict within a children's group: Suggestions for facilitating its expression and resolution strategies. *School Counselor, 39*, 268–272.

McConatha, J. T., Lightner, E., & Deaner, S. L. (1994). Culture, age, and gender as variables in the expression of emotion. *Journal of Social Behavior and Personality, 9*, 481–488.

McDonough, M. L., Carlson, C., & Cooper, C. R. (1994). Individuated marital relationships and the regulation of affect in families of early adolescents. *Journal of Adolescent Research, 9*, 67–87.

McKay, M., Rogers, P., & McKay, J. (1989). *When anger hurts.* Oakland, CA: New Harbinger Publications.

Melnechuk, T. (1988). Emotions, brain, immunity, and health: A review. In M. Clynes & J. Panksepp (Eds.), *Emotions and psychopathology* (pp. 181–248). New York: Plenum Press.

Mikula, G., Scherer, K. R., & Athenstaedt, U. (1998). The role of injustice in the elicitation of differential emotional reactions. *Personality and Social Psychology Bulletin, 24*, 769–783.

Mikulincer, M. (1998). Adult attachment style and individual differences in functional versus dysfunctional experiences of anger. *Journal of Personality and Social Psychology, 74*, 513–524.

Miller, J. B. (1976). *Toward a new psychology of women.* Boston: Beacon Press.

Miller, J. B. (1991). The construction of anger in men and women. In J. V. Jordan, A. G. Kaplan, J. B. Miller, I. P. Stiver, & J. L. Surrey (Eds.), *Women's growth in connection: Writings from the Stone Center* (pp. 181–196). New York: Guilford Press.

Miller, J. B., & Surrey, J. (1990). Revisioning women's anger: The personal and the global. *Work in progress, No. 43.* Wellesley, MA: Stone Center Working Paper Series.

Mills, P. J., & Dimsdale, J. E. (1993). Anger suppression: Its relationship to b-adrenergic receptor sensitivity and stress-induced changes in blood pressure. *Psychological Medicine, 23*, 673–678.

Mirowsky, J., & Ross, C. E. (1986). Social patterns of distress. *Annual Review of Psychology, 12*, 23–45.

Mitchell, J. (1974). *Psychoanalysis and feminism.* New York: Pantheon Books.

Montemayor, R., Eberly, M., & Flannery, D. J. (1993). Effects of pubertal status and conversation topic on parent and adolescent affective expression. *Journal of Early Adolescence, 13*, 431–447.

Morand, P., Thomas, G., Bungener, C., Ferreri, M., & Jouvent, R. (1998). Fava's anger attacks questionnaire: Evaluation of the French version in depressed patients. *European Psychiatry, 13*, 41–45.

Morones, P. A., & Mikawa, J. K. (1992). The traditional Mestizo view: Implications for modern psychotherapeutic interventions. *Psychotherapy, 29*, 458–466.

Müller, M. M., Rau, H., Brody, S., Elbert, T., & Heinle, H. (1995). The relationship between habitual anger coping style and serum lipid and lipoprotein concentrations. *Biological Psychology, 41*, 69–81.

Munhall, P. (1993). Women's anger and its meanings: A phenomenological perspective. *Healthcare for Women International, 14*, 481–491.

Neuman, D. A., Houskamp, B. M., Pollock, V. E., & Briere, J. (1996). The long-term sequelae of childhood sexual abuse in women: A meta-analytic review. *Child maltreatment: Journal of the American Professional Society on the Abuse of Children, 1,* 6–16.

Nichols, M. P., & Schwartz, R. C. (1995). *Family therapy: Concepts and methods.* Needham Heights, MA: Allyn & Bacon.

Nolen-Hoeksema, S. (1987). Sex differences in unipolar depression: Evidence and theory. *Psychological Bulletin, 101,* 259–282.

Nolen-Hoeksema, S. (1990). *Sex differences in depression.* Stanford, CA: Stanford University Press.

Novaco, R. W. (1975). *Anger control.* Lexington, MA: Lexington Books.

Nyhlin, H., Ford, M. J., Eastwood, J., Smith, J. H., Nicol, E. F., Elton, R. A., & Eastwood, M. A. (1993). Non-alimentary aspects of the irritable bowel syndrome. *Journal of Pyschosomatic Research, 37,* 155–162.

Oatley, K. (1993). Social construction in emotions. In M. Lewis & J. M. Haviland (Eds.), *Handbook of emotions* (pp. 341–352). New York: Guilford Press.

O'Hanlon, W. (1996, October). *Brief solution-oriented approaches with couples.* Seminar presented at the New England Educational Institute, Santa Fe, NM.

Orenstein, P. (1994). *School girls: Young women, self-esteem, and the confidence gap.* New York: Anchor Books, Doubleday.

Oster, H., Hegley, D., & Nagel, L. (1992). Adult judgments and fine-grained analysis of infant facial expressions: Testing the validity of a priori coding formulas. *Developmental Psychology, 28,* 1115–1131.

Pang, K. Y. (1990). Hwabyung: The construction of a Korean popular illness among Korean elderly immigrant women in the United States. *Culture, Medicine, and Psychiatry, 14,* 495–512.

Panksepp, J. (1994). The basics of basic emotion. In P. Ekman & R. J. Davidson (Eds.), *The nature of emotion: Fundamental questions* (pp. 20–24). Oxford: Oxford University Press.

Papero, D. V. (1990). *Bowen family systems theory.* Needham Heights, MA: Allyn & Bacon.

Pederson, P. B., & Ivey, A. (1993). *Culture-centered counseling and interviewing skills: A practical guide.* Westport, CT: Praeger.

Pennebaker, J. W. (1989). Confession, inhibition, and disease. In L. Berkowitz (Ed.), *Advances in experimental social psychology* (Vol. 22, pp. 211–244). New York: Academic Press.

Pennebaker, J. W., & Roberts, T. A. (1992). Toward a his and hers theory of emotion: Gender differences in visceral perception. *Journal of Social and Clinical Psychology, 11,* 199–212.

Pennebaker, J. W., & Susman, J. (1988). Disclosure of trauma and psychosomatic processes. *Social Science Medicine, 26,* 327–332.

Perls, F. (1969). *Gestalt therapy verbatim.* Lafayette, CA: Real People Press.

Perrin, S., Van Hasselt, V. B., & Hersen, M. (1997). Validation of the Keane MMPI-PTSD scale against DSM-III-R criteria in a sample of battered women. *Violence and Victims, 12,* 99–104.

Petersen, A. (1988). Adolescent development. *Annual Review of Psychology, 39,* 583–607.

Phelps, L., & Bajorek, E. (1991). Eating disorders of the adolescent: Current issues in etiology, assessment, and treatment. *School Psychology Review, 20,* 9–22.

Plutchik, R. (1980). Emotions in early development: A psychoevolutionary approach. In R. Plutchik & H. Kellerman (Eds.), *Emotion: Theory, research, and experience: Vol. 2. Emotions in early development* (pp. 221–258). New York: Academic Press.

Plutchik, R. (1997). The circumplex as a general model of the structure of emotions and personality. In R. Plutchik & H. R. Conte (Eds.), *Circumplex models of personality and emotions* (pp. 17–46). Washington, DC: American Psychological Association.

Ponterotto, J. G. (1998). Charting a course for research in multicultural counselor training. *The Counseling Psychologist, 26,* 43–68.

Ponterotto, J. G., Casas, J. M., Suzuki, L. A., & Alexander, C. M. (Eds.). (1995). *Handbook of multicultural counseling.* Thousand Oaks, CA: Sage.

Porges, S. W., Doussard-Roosevelt, J. A., & Maiti, A. K. (1994). Vagal tone and the physiological regulation of emotion. In N. A. Fox (Ed.), The development of emotion regulation: Biological and behavioral considerations (pp. 167–188). *Monographs of the Society for Research in Child Development, 59* (2–3, Serial No. 240).

Pribram, K. H. (1980). The biology of emotions and other feelings. In R. Plutchik & H. Kellerman (Eds.), *Emotion: Theory, research, and experience: Vol. 1. Theories of emotion* (pp. 245–270). New York: Academic Press.

Prochaska, J. O., & Norcross, J. C. (1994). *Systems of psychotherapy.* Pacific Grove, CA: Brooks/Cole.

Pugliesi, K. (1987). Deviation in emotion and the labeling of mental illness. *Deviant Behavior, 8,* 79–102.

Pugliesi, K. (1992). Premenstrual syndrome: The medicalization of emotion related to conflict and chronic role strain. *Humboldt Journal of Social Relations, 18,* 131–165.

Rachman, S. (1978). *Fear and courage.* San Francisco: Freeman.

Rebert, W. M., Stanton, A. L., & Schwartz, R. M. (1991). Influence of personality attributes and daily moods on bulimic eating patterns. *Addictive Behavior, 16,* 497–505.

Rhodewalt, F., & Morf, C. (1998). On self-aggrandizement and anger: A temporal analysis of narcissism and affective reactions to success and failure. *Journal of Personality and Social Psychology, 74,* 672–685.

Riley, W. T., Treiber, F. A., & Woods, M. G. (1989). Anger and hostility in depression. *Journal of Nervous and Mental Disease, 177,* 668–674.

Robins, P.M., & Sesan, R. (1991). Münchausen syndrome by proxy: Another women's disorder? *Professional Psychology: Research and Practice, 22,* 285–290.

Rogers, C. R. (1959). A theory of therapy, personality, and interpersonal relationships, as developed in the client-centered framework. In S. Koch (Ed.), *Psychology: A study of a science* (Vol. 3, pp. 184–256). New York: McGraw-Hill.

Rosaldo, M. Z. (1984). Toward an anthropology of self and feeling. In R. A. Shweder & R. A. LeVine (Eds.), *Culture theory: Essays on mind, self, and emotion* (pp. 137–157). Cambridge: Cambridge University Press.

Rubenstein, C. S., Altemus, M., Pigott, T. A., Hess, A., & Murphy, D. L. (1995). Symptom overlap between OCD and bulimia nervosa. *Journal of Anxiety Disorders, 9,* 1–9.

Russell, J. A. (1997). How shall an emotion be called? In R. Plutchik & H. R. Conte (Eds.), *Circumplex models of personality and emotions* (pp. 205–220). Washington, DC: American Psychological Association.

Rusting, C. L., & Nolen-Hoeksema, A. (1998). Regulating responses to anger: Effects of rumination and distraction on angry mood. *Journal of Personality and Social Psychology, 74,* 790–803.

Rutter, M. (1986). The developmental psychopathology of depression: Issues and perspectives. In M. Rutter, C. Izard, & P. Read (Eds.), *Depression in young people: Development and clinical perspectives* (pp. 3–30). New York: Guilford.

Saarni, C. (1989). Children's understanding of strategic control of emotional expression in social transactions. In C. Saarni & P. L. Harris (Eds.), *Children's understanding of emotion.* Cambridge: Cambridge University Press.

Saarni, C. (1993). Socialization of emotion. In M. Lewis & J. M. Haviland (Eds.), *Handbook of emotions* (pp. 435–446). New York: Guilford Press.

Sabini, J., & Schulkin, J. (1994). Biological realism and social constructivism. *Journal for the Theory of Social Behaviour, 24,* 207–217.

Sadker, M., & Sadker, D. (1994). *Failing at fairness: How America's schools cheat girls.* New York: Charles Scribner's Sons.

Sayfer, A. W., & Hauser, S. T. (1994). A microanalytic method for exploring adolescent emotional expression. *Journal of Adolescent Research, 9,* 50–66.

Schacter, S., & Singer, J. E. (1962). Cognitive, social and physiological determinants of emotional state. *Psychological Review, 69,* 379–399.

Scherer, K. (1984). Emotion as a multicomponent process: A model and some cross-cultural data. In P. Shaver (Ed.), *Review of personality and social psychology, 5,* 37–63.

Scherer, K. R. (1994). Toward a concept of "modal emotions." In P. Ekman & R. J. Davidson (Eds.), *The nature of emotion: Fundamental questions* (pp. 25–31). Oxford: Oxford University Press.

Schimmack, U., & Diener, E. (1997). Affect intensity: Separating intensity and frequency in repeatedly measured affect. *Journal of Personality and Social Psychology, 73,* 1313–1329.

Schimmack, U., & Hartmann, K. (1997). Individual differences in the memory representation of emotional episodes: Exploring the cognitive processes in repression. *Journal of Personality and Social Psychology, 37,* 1064–1079.

Schimmel, S. (1979). Anger and its control in Graeco-Roman and modern psychology. *Psychiatry, 42,* 320–337.

Schulz, R., & Heckhausen, J. (1996). A life span model of successful aging. *American Psychologist, 51,* 702–714.

Schweder, R. A. (1993). The cultural psychology of the emotions. In M. Lewis & J. M. Haviland (Eds.), *Handbook of emotions* (pp. 417–434). New York: Guilford Press.

Schweder, R. A. (1994). "You're not sick, you're just in love": Emotion as an interpretive system. In P. Ekman & R. J. Davidson (Eds.), *The nature of emotion: Fundamental questions* (pp. 32–44). Oxford: Oxford University Press.

Seabrook, E. G. (1993). Women's anger and substance abuse. In S. P. Thomas (Ed.), *Women and anger.* New York: Springer.

Seiden, A. (1989). Psychological issues affecting women throughout the life cycle. *Psychiatric Clinics of North America, 12,* 1–24.

Seidlitz, L., & Diener, E. (1998). Sex differences in the recall of affective experiences. *Journal of Personality and Social Psychology, 74,* 262–271.

Sharkin, B. S. (1993). Anger and gender: Theory, research, and implications. *Journal of Counseling and Development, 71,* 386–389.

Sharkin, B. S., & Gelso, C. J. (1991). The Anger Discomfort Scale: Beginning reliability and validity data. *Measurement and Evaluation in Counseling and Development, 24,* 61–68.

Shedler, J., Mayman, M., & Manis, M. (1993). The illusion of mental health. *American Psychologist, 48,* 1117–1131.

Showalter, E. (1985). *The female malady: Women, madness and English culture, 1830–1980.* New York: Penguin.

Siegel, J. M. (1986). The multidimensional anger inventory. *Journal of Personality and Social Psychology, 51,* 191–200.

Skinner, B. F. (1953). *Science and human behavior.* New York: Macmillan.

Smith, C. A., Haynes, K. N., Lazarus, R. S., & Pope, L. K. (1993). In search of "hot" cognitions: Attributions, appraisals, and their relation to emotion. *Journal of Personality and Social Psychology, 65,* 916–929.

Smith, C. A., & Lazarus, R. S. (1990). Emotion and adaptation. In L. A. Pervin (Ed.), *Handbook of personality: Theory and research* (pp. 609–637). New York: Guilford.

Smith, T. W., & Allred, K. D. (1989). Blood pressure reactivity during social interaction in high and low cynical hostile men. *Journal of Behavioral Medicine, 11,* 135–143.

Smith, T. W., & Frohm, K. D. (1985). What's so unhealthy about hostility? Construct validity and psychosocial correlates of the Cook and Medley Ho Scale. *Health Psychology, 4,* 503–520.

Snaith, R. P., & Taylor, C. M. (1985). Irritability: Definition, assessment and associated factors. *British Journal of Psychiatry, 147,* 127–136.

Snell, W. E., Jr., Gum, S., Shuck, R. L., Mosley, J. A., & Hite, T. L. (1995). The Clinical Anger Scale: Preliminary reliability and validity. *Journal of Clinical Psychology, 51*, 215–226.

Sodowsky, G. R., Kwan, K. K., & Pannu, R. (1995). Ethnic identity of Asians in the United States. In J. G. Ponterotto, J. M. Casas, L. A. Suzuki, & C. M. Alexander (Eds.), *Handbook of multicultural counseling* (pp. 123–154). Thousand Oaks, CA: Sage.

Solomon, R. C. (1976). *The passions*. Garden City, NJ: Anchor Press/Doubleday.

Sommers, S. (1984). Adults evaluating their emotions: A cross-cultural perspective. In C. Z. Malatesta & C. E. Izard (Eds.), *Emotion in adult development* (pp. 319–338). Beverly Hills, CA: Sage.

Spence, J., & Helmreich, R. (1979). *Masculinity and femininity: Their psychological dimensions, correlates and antecedents*. Austin: University of Texas Press.

Sperberg, E. (1992). *The effects of anger suppression and sex role orientation on depression in women college students*. Unpublished manuscript, Texas Woman's University, Denton.

Sperberg, E. D., & Stabb, S. D. (1998). Depression in women as related to anger and mutuality in relationships. *Psychology of Women Quarterly, 22*, 223–238.

Spicer, J., Jackson, R., & Scragg, R. (1993). The effects of anger management and social contact on risk of myocardial infarction in type As and type Bs. *Psychology and Health, 8*, 243–255.

Spielberger, C. D. (1988). *State-trait anger expression inventory*. Odessa, FL: Psychological Assessment Resources.

Spielberger, C. D., Jacobs, G. A., Russell, S., & Crane, R. J. (1983). Assessment of anger: The state-trait anger scale. In J. N. Butcher & C. D. Spielberger (Eds.), *Advances in personality assessment* (Vol. 2, pp. 161–189). Hillsdale, NJ: Erlbaum.

Spielberger, C. D., Johnson, E. H., Russell, S. F., Crane, R. J., Jacobs, G. A., & Worden, T. I. (1985). The experience and expression of anger: Construction and validation of an anger expression scale. In M. A. Chesney & R. H. Rosenman (Eds.), *Anger and hostility in cardiovascular and behavioral disorders*. New York: Hemisphere/McGraw-Hill.

Stansbury, K., & Gunnar, M. R. (1994). Adrenocortical activity and emotion regulation. In N. A. Fox (Ed.), The development of emotion regulation: Biological and behavioral considerations (pp. 108–134). *Monographs of the Society for Research in Child Development, 59* (2–3, Serial No. 240).

Stapely, J. C., & Haviland, J. M. (1989). Beyond depression: Gender differences in normal adolescents' emotional experiences. *Sex Roles, 20*, 295–308.

Stearns, C. Z., & Stearns, P. (1986). *Anger: The struggle for control in America's history*. Chicago: University of Chicago Press.

Stein, N. L., Trabasso, T., & Liwag, M. (1993). The representation and organization of emotional experience: Unfolding the emotion episode. In M. Lewis & J. M. Haviland (Eds.), *Handbook of emotions* (pp. 279–300). New York: Guilford Press.

Steiner, M. (1997). Premenstrual syndrome. *Annual Review of Medicine, 48*, 447–455.

Steiner-Adair, C. (1986). The body politic: Normal female adolescent development and the development of eating disorders. *Journal of the American Academy of Psychoanalysis, 14*, 95–114.

Steinhausen, H. C., & Vollrath, M. (1993). The self image of adolescent patients with eating disorders. *International Journal of Eating Disorders, 13*, 221–227.

Stern, L. (1991). Disavowing the self in female adolescence. *Women and Therapy, 11*, 105–117.

Stevens-Long, J. (1990). Adult development: Theories past and future. In R. A. Nemiroff & C. A. Colarusso (Eds.), *New dimensions in adult development* (pp. 125–169). New York: Basic Books.

Street, S., & Kromrey, J. D. (1994). Differences in adjustment issues for male and female adolescents. *Special Services in the Schools, 8*, 143–154.

Suarez, E. C., & Williams, R. B. (1990). The relationship between dimensions of hostility and cardiovascular reactivity as a function of task characteristics. *Psychosomatic Medicine, 52,* 558–570.

Sue, D. W., & Sue, D. (1990). *Counseling the culturally different: Theory and practice* (2nd ed.). New York: John Wiley.

Suh, E., Diener, E., Oishi, S., & Triandis, H. C. (1998). The shifting basis for life satisfaction judgments across cultures: Emotions versus norms. *Journal of Personality and Social Psychology, 74,* 482–493.

Sullivan, H. S. (1953). *The interpersonal theory of psychiatry.* New York: W. W. Norton.

Tangney, J. P., Wagner, P., Fletcher, C., & Gramzow, R. (1992). Shamed into anger? The relation of shame and guilt to anger and self-reported aggression. *Journal of Personality and Social Psychology, 62,* 669–675.

Tavris, C. (1989). *Anger: The misunderstood emotion* (rev. ed.). New York: Simon & Schuster.

Tennant, C. C., & Langeluddecke, P. M. (1985). Psychological correlates of coronary heart disease. *Psychological Medicine, 15,* 581–588.

Thoits, P. A. (1985). Self-labeling processes in mental illness: The role of emotional deviance. *American Journal of Sociology, 92,* 221–249.

Thomas, S. P. (1989). Gender differences in anger expression: Health implications. *Research in Nursing and Health, 12,* 389–398.

Thomas, S. P. (1993). *Women and anger.* New York: Springer.

Thomas, S. P., & Atakan, S. (1993). Trait anger, anger expression, stress, and health status of American and Turkish midlife women. *Health Care for Women International, 14,* 129–143.

Thompson, C. (1942). Cultural pressures in the psychology of women. *Psychiatry, 5,* 331–339.

Thompson, J. M., & Hart, B. I. (1996, August). *Attachment dimensions and patterns associated with silencing the self.* Paper presented at the 104th Annual Convention of the American Psychological Association, Toronto, Ontario.

Thompson, R. A. (1991). Emotional regulation and emotional development. *Educational Psychology Review, 3,* 269–307.

Thompson, R. A., & Lamb, M. E. (1980). Individual differences in dimensions of socioemotional development in infancy. In R. Plutchik & H. Kellerman (Eds.), *Emotion: Theory, research, and experience: Vol. 2. Emotions in early development* (pp. 87–114). New York: Academic Press.

Tiller, J., Schmidt, U., Ali, S., & Treasure, J. (1995). Patterns of punitiveness in women with eating disorders. *International Journal of Eating Disorders, 17,* 365–371.

Tomkins, S. S. (1962). *Affect, imagery, consciousness* (Vol. 1). New York: Springer.

Tomkins, S. S. (1963). *Affect, imagery, consciousness* (Vol. 2). New York: Springer.

Toner, B. B., Garfinkel, P. E., & Garner, D. M. (1986). Long-term follow-up of anorexia nervosa. *Psychosomatic Medicine, 48,* 520–529.

Toner, B. B., Garfinkel, P. E., & Garner, D. M. (1988). Affective and anxiety disorders in the long-term follow-up of anorexia nervosa. *International Journal of Psychiatry in Medicine, 18,* 357–364.

Triandis, H. C. (1994). Major cultural syndromes and emotion. In S. Kitayama & H. R. Markus (Eds.), *Emotion and culture: Empirical studies of mutual influence* (pp. 285–306). Washington, DC: American Psychological Association.

Tschannen, T. A., Duckro, P. N., Margolis, R. B., & Tomazic, T. J. (1992). The relationship of anger, depression, and perceived disability among headache patients. *Headache, 32,* 501–503.

Underwood, M. K., Coie, J. D., & Herbsman, C. R. (1992). Display rules for anger and aggression in school-age children. *Child Development, 63,* 366–380.

Van Goozen, S., Frijda, N., & Van de Poll, N. (1994). Anger and aggression in women: Influence of sports choice and testosterone administration. *Aggressive Behavior, 20,* 213–222.

Von Franz, M. L. (1993). *Psychotherapy*. Boston: Shambhala.

Walden, T. A. (1991). Infant social referencing. In J. Garber & K. A. Dodge (Eds.), *The development of emotional regulation and dysregulation* (pp.69–78). Cambridge: Cambridge University Press.

Wallen, J. (1992). A comparison of male and female clients in substance abuse treatment. *Journal of Substance Abuse Treatment, 9*, 243–248.

Way, N. (1995). "Can't you see the courage, the strength that I have?" Listening to urban adolescent girls speak about their relationships. *Psychology of Women Quarterly, 19*, 107–128.

Weiner, B., & Graham, S. (1989). Understanding the motivational role of affect: Lifespan research from an attributional perspective. *Cognition and Emotion, 3*, 401–419.

Weinrich, J. D. (1980). Toward a sociobiological theory of the emotions. In R. Plutchik & H. Kellerman (Eds.), *Emotion: Theory, research, and experience: Vol. 1. Theories of emotion* (pp. 113–140). New York: Academic Press.

Weissman, M. M., & Klerman, G. L. (1987). Gender and depression. In R. Formanek & A. Gurian (Eds.), *Women and depression: A lifespan perspective* (pp. 3–26). New York: Springer.

Wetzel, J. W. (1994). Depression: Women at risk. *Social Work–Health Care, 19*, 85–108.

Whiffen, V. E., & Clark, S. E. (1997). Does victimization account for sex differences in depressive symptoms? *British Journal of Clinical Psychology, 36*, 185–193.

Wierzbicka, A. (1994). Emotion, language, and cultural scripts. In S. Kitayama & H. R. Markus (Eds.), *Emotion and culture: Empirical studies of mutual influence* (pp. 133–196). Washington, DC: American Psychological Association.

Williams, R. B., & Barefoot, J. C. (1988). Coronary-prone behavior: The emerging role of the hostility complex. In B. K. Houston & C. R. Snyder (Eds.), *Type A behavior pattern: Research, theory, and intervention* (pp. 189–211). New York: Wiley.

Wood, W., Christensen, P. N., Hebl, M. R., & Rothgerber, H. (1997). *Journal of Personality and Social Psychology, 73*, 523–535.

Woodhouse, L. D. (1990). An exploratory study of the use of life history methods to determine treatment needs for female substance abusers. *Response to the Victimization of Women and Children, 13*, 12–15.

Woods, N. F., Lentz, M. J., Mitchell, E. S., Shaver, J., & Heitkemper, M. (1998). Luteal phase ovarian steroids, stress arousal, premenses perceived stress, and premenstrual symptoms. *Research in Nursing and Health, 21*, 129–142.

Worell, J., & Johnson, N. G. (1997). Introduction: Creating the future: Process and promise in feminist practice. In J. Worell & N. G. Johnson (Eds.), *Shaping the future of feminist psychology* (pp. 1–14). Washington, DC: American Psychological Association.

Yager, J., Rorty, M., & Rossotto, E. (1995). Coping styles differ between recovered and nonrecovered women with bulimia nervosa, but not between recovered women and non-eating-disordered control subjects. *The Journal of Nervous and Mental Disease, 183*, 86–94.

Yonkers, K. A. (1997). Antidepressants in the treatment of premenstrual dysphoric disorder. *Journal of Clinical Psychiatry, 58* (Suppl. 14), 4–10.

Young, T. J. (1991). Locus of control, depression, and anger among native Americans. *The Journal of Social Psychology, 131*, 583–584.

Zahn-Waxler, C., Cole, P., Richardson, D., Friedman, R., et al. (1994). Social problem solving in disruptive preschool children: Reactions to hypothetical situations of conflict and distress. *Merrill Palmer Quarterly, 40*, 98–119.

Zahn-Waxler, C., Cole, P., Welsh, J. D., & Fox, N. A. (1995). Psychophysiological correlates of empathy and prosocial behaviors in preschool children with behavior problems. *Development and Psychopathology, 7*, 27–48.

Zelin, M. L., Adler, B., & Myerson, P. G. (1972). Anger self-report: An objective questionnaire for the measurement of aggression. *Journal of Clinical and Consulting Psychology, 39*, 340.

Zuckerman, M. (1977). Development of a situation-specific trait-state test for the prediction and measurement of affective responses. *Journal of Consulting and Clinical Psychology, 45,* 513–523.

Zuckerman, M., & Mellstrom, M. (1977). The contributions of persons, situations, modes of response and their interactions in self-reported responses to hypothetical and real anxiety-inducing situations. In D. Magnusson & N. S. Endler (Eds.), *Personality at the crossroads: Current issues in interactional psychology.* Hillsdale, NJ: Erlbaum.

INDEX